MIGRATION IN THE MAKING OF THE GULF SPACE

Edited by Noel B. Salazar, University of Leuven, in collaboration with ANTHROMOB, the EASA Anthropology and Mobility Network.

WORLDS IN MOTION

This transdisciplinary series features empirically grounded studies from around the world that disentangle how people, objects, and ideas move across the planet. With a special focus on advancing theory as well as methodology, the series considers movement as both an object and a method of study.

Recent volumes:

Volume 11
MIGRATION IN THE MAKING OF THE GULF STATE
Social, Political, and Cultual Dimensions
Edited by Antía Mato Bouzas and Lorenzo Casini

Volume 10
WE ARE ALL AFRICANS HERE
Critical Engagements
Kristín Loftsdóttir

Volume 9
LIMINAL MOVES
Traveling Along Places, Meanings, and Times
Flavia Cangià

Volume 8
PACING MOBILITIES
Timing, Intensity, Tempo and Duration of Human Movements
Edited by Vered Amit and Noel B. Salazar

Volume 7
FINDING WAYS THROUGH EUROSPACE
West African Movers Re-viewing Europe from the Inside
Joris Schapendonk

Volume 6
BOURDIEU AND SOCIAL SPACE
Mobilities, Trajectories, Emplacements
Deborah Reed-Danahay

Volume 5
HEALTHCARE IN MOTION
Immobilities in Health Service Delivery and Access
Edited by Cecilia Vindrola-Padros, Ginger A. Johnson, and Anne E. Pfister

Volume 4
MOMENTOUS MOBILITIES
Anthropological Musings on the Meanings of Travel
Noel B. Salazar

Volume 3
INTIMATE MOBILITIES
Sexual Economies, Marriage and Migration in a Disparate World
Edited by Christian Groes and Nadine T. Fernandez

Volume 2
METHODOLOGIES OF MOBILITY
Ethnography and Experiment
Edited by Alice Elliot, Roger Norum, and Noel B. Salazar

For a full volume listing, please see the series page on our website:
https://www.berghahnbooks.com/series/worlds-in-motion

Migration in the Making of the Gulf Space

Social, Political, and Cultural Dimensions

Edited by
Antía Mato Bouzas and Lorenzo Casini

berghahn
NEW YORK • OXFORD
www.berghahnbooks.com

First published in 2022 by
Berghahn Books
www.berghahnbooks.com

© 2022, 2025 Antía Mato Bouzas and Lorenzo Casini
First paperback edition published in 2025

All rights reserved. Except for the quotation of short passages
for the purposes of criticism and review, no part of this book
may be reproduced in any form or by any means, electronic or
mechanical, including photocopying, recording, or any information
storage and retrieval system now known or to be invented,
without written permission of the publisher.

Library of Congress Cataloging-in-Publication Data

A C.I.P. cataloging record is available from the Library of Congress
Library of Congress Cataloging in Publication Control Number: 2021056850

British Library Cataloguing in Publication Data

A catalogue record for this book is available from the British Library

ISBN 978-1-80073-350-3 hardback
ISBN 978-1-80539-751-9 paperback
ISBN 978-1-80539-927-8 epub
ISBN 978-1-80073-351-0 web pdf

https://doi.org/10.3167/9781800733503

Contents

List of Figures — vii

Acknowledgments — viii

Introduction — 1
    Antía Mato Bouzas

    Part I. Cosmopolitanism, Belonging, and National Imaginaries

    Chapter 1 Exhibiting Tolerance: Citizenship, Contingency, and Contemporary Art in the UAE Pavilion, 2009–2017 — 21
    Elizabeth Derderian

    Chapter 2 The Gulf as an Unhomely Home: Reconfiguring Citizenship and Belonging in Diasporic Narratives on Second-Generation Migrants — 43
    Nadeen Dakkak

    Chapter 3 Navigating the Cosmopolitan City: Emirati Women and Ambivalent Forms of Belonging in Dubai — 67
    Rana AlMutawa

    Part II. Aspirational Gulf

    Chapter 4 Dubai as Heterotopia? The Aspirational Politics of Everyday Cosmopolitanism in Gulf Space — 89
    Jaafar Alloul

    Chapter 5. A Strangeness One Can Occupy: Clothes and Their Codes in the Photographs of Gulf Migrants from Kerala — 115
    Mohamed Shafeeq Karinkurayil

Conclusion The Gulf Space in Words: In Dialogue with
Author Deepak Unnikrishnan 135
Lorenzo Casini and Deepak Unnikrishnan

Index 154

Figures

1.1	Installation of "1980–Today: Exhibitions in the UAE," Sharjah, UAE, 2016. © Elizabeth Derderian.	29
1.2	Catalogs for the 2009, 2011, 2015, and 2017 UAE Pavilions at the Venice Biennale. © Elizabeth Derderian.	34
5.1	Abdul Gafoor and his brother, Abu Dhabi, 1981. Reproduced with permission.	122
5.2	On top of the world, Kerala, 1980. Reproduced with permission.	123
5.3	With friends, Abu Dhabi, 1979. Reproduced with permission.	127

Acknowledgments

This book is the outcome of an intense scholarly exchange that began at Leibniz-Zentrum Moderner Orient (ZMO), Berlin, in December 2019 as part of a project conducted by Antía Mato Bouzas and funded by the Deutsche Forschungsgemeinschaft (DFG). We would like to express our gratitude to the DFG and the ZMO that gave us the opportunity to start envisioning this work. At ZMO we would like to thank in particular Ulrike Freitag, Heike Liebau, Claudia Ghrawi, Sarah Jurkiewicz, Dietrich Reetz, Reyazul Haque, and Diana Gluck.

We would also like to express our gratitude to the Centre Français de Recherche de la Péninsule Arabique (CEFREPA—formerly known as Centre Français d'Archéologie et Sciences Sociales CEFAS) in Kuwait and very specially to its director Abbés Zouache. CEFREPA was our host institution in Kuwait, and it is an excellent example of a European institution promoting research and academic exchange in the Gulf. We have no words to express the sense of hospitality provided by Abbés Zouache and his approach to promote the work of European as well as Kuwaiti academics, both established and young scholars. We are indebted to Dima Assad for facilitating our work but also for discussing with us the "plurality" of Gulf spaces. She is a great thinker and has become a good friend.

Finally, we cannot forget Tom Bonnington and Anthony Mason, editors at Berghahn Books, for their trust in us and for supporting this publication throughout this difficult period. We also express our deep gratitude to London Metropolitan University for providing a grant to edit this volume.

Introduction

Antía Mato Bouzas

Migration is a constituent feature of Gulf societies. It is framed in temporary terms, as if migrants remained for the period of their contracts and then left, presumably without a trace. Yet, migration has been a constant phenomenon for many decades, which in some cases has involved various generations of the same family and from the same communities. This volume examines the social reality of the permanent transient resident who is an active part of the process of placemaking and of the transmission of knowledge in the region. The contributions, which are from various disciplinary fields, draw on two main assumptions: first, that migration is regarded as integral to Gulf societies; and second, that the Gulf continues to exert an influence on other regions by way of migration diplomacy and on the construction of transnational spaces that involve citizens and noncitizens living in the Gulf. The chapters underscore how nonnationals of different categories try to appropriate this space as their own in what amounts to claims of membership. The volume also includes the often-underrepresented perspective of those who belong to the nation—that is, the ways in which citizens, in this case women from privileged classes, distinguish between "Gulf" and "non-Gulf" spaces in their condition as a minority group. Most of the contributions focus on the United Arab Emirates (UAE), yet the issues addressed in the chapters are representative of the rest of the Arab states in the Gulf. By being and living in the Gulf, migrants engage in a dialogical relationship with these ever-present others. However, this presence also affects the ways citizens and government actors negotiate their "own" Gulf spaces.

The aim of this book is to analyze how, by constructing new spaces, migration is shaping the Gulf Arab states. The volume emphasizes in particular the interactions of political, economic, social, and cultural fields. In this volume the notion of Gulf space bears a transnational dimension; what happens in the Gulf impacts the regions that send migrants there. Chapter 6 illustrates this in relation to the impact of Gulf migration on sartorial practices in the Indian state of Kerala. Therefore, the focus of this volume is not only on the Gulf states, but also on the regions that send migrants there. This approach reveals an "enlarged" Gulf space whose influence in other regions is enduring. Other contributions, such as those written by authors brought up in the Arab Peninsula, underscore the tensions that exist between the lived space of constant segregation and the representational space of the Gulf as a cosmopolitan place. How does this "enlargement" in terms of the Gulf's influence in other regions relate to its "shrinkage," given that the Gulf is the result of what remains after constituting a wide range of outsiders?

Migration and the Gulf

Migration is central to the configuration of the contemporary Gulf. Although previous mobilities to the Gulf region existed, notably linked to the slave trade and labor movement and trade under the British and Ottoman empires (Freitag 2020), state formation and nation building processes have worked, to a great extent, to erase part of that past. The movement of people to this region, which has been almost exclusively for labor purposes, shares characteristics with other migrant movements elsewhere, but it is framed and organized in substantially different terms. Migration to the Gulf responds to the logic of modernization. However, the constant and continued dependency of the mainly smaller Gulf states on resources (natural resources such as water and land, and human resources such as labor), along with their inability to produce added-value goods (except for the development of services), casts serious doubts about the success of this modernization process. The rentier model of the state does not so much foster industrialization processes as it does dominate the manner of improving the population's standard of life and stimulate further service investments once the oil reserves have run out (Massey et al. 1998: 134-35). This "rentier logic" can also be found in other spheres of socioeconomic life, such as in the sponsorship system for developing businesses in which foreign entrepreneurs need national partners to develop any type of economic activity. In many cases, national partners limit themselves to providing their names and receiving potential benefits without playing a role (Gardner 2008: 72-73). The transformative process of modernization is further hampered by the perpetuation of a model of dependency that relies on high levels of temporary foreign populations to keep the economy running while denying them legal and political rights; it also has difficulties in developing a native labor force in key sectors.

Like other movements of migrants to developed countries, migration to the Gulf is organized along the logic of the "guest worker" or the *Gastarbei-*

ter, although it differs from these movements on the issue of the possibility of sociopolitical inclusion in the receiving society. Migrants in the Gulf, for example, cannot attain citizenship and other permanent benefits, such as health care or a pension after retirement. Except for very exceptional cases, their stay in the Gulf is bound by a date of departure and by their belonging elsewhere. There is a strong hierarchy to this migrant system in which Europeans and Americans occupy top positions, and a racial component, which reproduces orientalist views that correlate types of workers with specific jobs (Gardner and Nagy 2008; Walsh 2012; Ahmad 2017). This segmentation is reflected in a language that classifies a variety of self-definitions and the identifications of others as ranging from "expatriates" and "migrants" to "temporary workers" (Mato Bouzas 2018; Horinuki 2020: 36).

The distinction between citizen and noncitizen is equally crucial to understanding the specifics of Gulf migration and to the construction of a racialized Arab Gulf identity, as already shown in the classical ethnographic work on Kuwait authored by Anh Longva (1997). This distinction functions similarly to other segregated societies, such as in the case of the legally sanctioned apartheid system that existed in South Africa, or in the structural differentiation between Palestinians and Jews that exists within Israel. In the Gulf, however, the central issue of discrimination has to do with the foreign nationality of migrants and the particularities of the *kafala* labor system that almost reduces migrants to a commodity (Mato Bouzas 2018: 5). Even though the migrant foreigner is erased from what could be defined in the Lefebvrian sense as the abstract space of economic management (see Lefebvre 1991: 306–18), he or she cannot go unnoticed in the streets and in the urban landscapes of Gulf cities. Migrants appropriate and shape those places, and in so doing, they fully inhabit Gulf space.

Although Gulf migration has been a topic of interest (in macroeconomic terms) for economists and demographers for decades, it was in the 1990s that the broader dimensions of this phenomenon began to attract specific attention. Addleton explored migration to the Gulf from Pakistan by focusing his study on the conditions of both the sending and the receiving societies, and he pointed out the importance of remittances for the development of the Pakistani economy (Addleton 1992). The social dimension of migration has been addressed by Longva in her pioneering ethnographic study on Kuwait, *Walls Built on Sand* (1997), in which she demonstrates how migration plays an essential role in politics and nation building processes in the Gulf. However, it was not until very recently that issues such as the diversity of these migrant populations, the ways they cope with the *kafala* sponsorship system, and their mobility strategies began to receive more systematic attention (Gardner and Nagy 2008; Shah 2004; Shah and Fargues 2011). This literature has a strong focus on South Asians because they are among the largest migrant groups in the Gulf (Jain and Oommen 2016). However, over the years, academic scholarship has increasingly addressed the case of long-stablished communities such as Arab communities (Babar 2017), and the lesser-explored African and Asian groups such as Eritreans and Filipino groups (Thiollet 2007; Malik 2017; Hosoda 2020). In addition to the interest in migrant communities in the Gulf states, research on Gulf migration addresses the impact of migrant activity in Gulf societies and in the sending areas, and issues of gender, entrepreneurship, and the historical aspects of regional integration (Gamburd 2002; Osella and Osella 2007; Thiollet 2007; Hosoda 2020). Many of these works focus on the lives of migrant communities in Gulf societies and on how the Gulf experience influences their lives after their return—and in so doing they contribute to the understanding of Gulf space (Gardner and Nagy 2008; Babar 2017; Ishi et al. 2020; Ahmad 2017). The transnational dimension of the Gulf is an underlying element in many of these works (Walsh 2012). In this respect, the present volume connects with already existing literature on the topic but centers its attention on how Gulf space is being produced.

This volume focuses on the space inhabited by migrants and former migrants in the Gulf cities, the abstract space they help produce and model through their work (and from which they are excluded), their use of public space, and their social interactions and memory. By relating migrants' experiences to the general context of the Gulf, this volume attempts to make sense of how Gulf governments attempt to portray the Gulf as an "open" and "cosmopolitan" space while at the same time maintaining segregation and exclusion at the societal level. On the one hand, the definition of Gulf migration as "temporal" appears problematic because this allegedly temporary system has reproduced permanent states of precarity over time. On the other hand, the long existing sediments left by generations of migrants in Gulf societies—composed of their transfer of knowledge, their lives in specific city areas, their memories, their appropriation of places—that are characteristic of social diversity in the Gulf are removed in the framing of a contemporary Gulf cosmopolitanism. The latter, as Craig Calhoun would argue, is defined in liberal terms because Gulf cosmopolitanism is articulated in terms of being free from social belonging rather than recognizing a special sort of belonging (Calhoun 2003: 532).

Research in the Gulf states is difficult and expensive. The topic of migration is sensitive because it intertwines with other equally delicate sociopolitical questions about the authoritarian regimes present in the Gulf region (Matsuo 2020: 55–56). However, the social contexts of each of these countries are different and, following the developments of the Arab Spring uprisings and protests, they have been made less accessible to researchers. In addition, major transformations are taking place in the region due to the policies of replacing foreign workforces with national ones; in each of the respective countries, these policies are known as Saudianization, Kuwaitization, Omanization, and so on. Moreover, the yet-to-be-studied forceful expulsion of migrants due to the pandemic in 2020 poses additional challenges to the continued building of a consistent corpus of research.

Former research on the melting pot that is Bahrein (Gardner 2008; Louër 2008; Nagy 2008) has proven difficult in recent years owing to the dramatic developments after the uprising in 2011 (Khalifa 2011; Louër 2013). The case of Oman is substantially different because, alongside the policies of Omanization and the deployment of Arabness as a key marker of national identity, the country is also tacitly recognizing the historical importance of its society's composite culture. This understanding can be seen when visiting the National Museum of Oman in Muscat, or through its not-exempt-from-criticism display in award-winning literary works such as *Celestial Bodies* by Jokha Alharthi (2019). Except for religiously related questions, research on migration to Saudi Arabia focuses mostly on the sending areas and is connected to the migrants' working experiences in these societies (Sons 2020). An open discussion about belonging and membership is still lacking in Saudi Arabia, although the literary analysis provided by Nadeen Dakkak in this volume shows an emerging concern with these questions. Both Oman and Saudi Arabia, unlike the other smaller Gulf states, are geographically large and have a majority national population, both of which significantly affect their approach to the management of migration.

Most of the research that has been produced on migration to the Gulf in recent years, however, focuses on the smaller states, especially on the UAE, and focuses prominently on the city of Dubai as a paradigm of "Gulf cosmopolitanism," on Kuwait, and, to a lesser extent, on Qatar. The book by Neha Vora on Indian middle-class groups in Dubai made a significant contribution to this subfield by highlighting the production of a neoliberal form of belonging because, "they [middle-class Indian migrants] are integral to the operation of governance, to national identity and citizenship, and to the functioning of Dubai's liberalized and globalized market forms" (Vora 2013: 3). Rather than stressing the impossibility of membership and the ways in which this can be achieved, other studies of long-term rooted communities such as Pakistanis and Iranians emphasize the role of Gulf cities simply for what they are (Errichiello 2018; Moghadam 2013). This latter approach is adopted by most of the contributors to this volume, as exemplified by Dakkak in her literary analysis of the novel *Samrawit*, in which the main character reflects on the long presence of Eritreans and other groups in the city of Jeddah. However, the question of citizenship can be a determining factor for nonnational artists while representing the nation internationally at cultural events, which Derderian aptly raises as a question with regard to the ambivalence of the state on the issue of membership. Academic scholarship on the topic of migration to Kuwait highlights how the Gulf experience has an underlying interactional component that can deeply affect the trajectories of migrants on matters of faith (Ahmad 2017), which is also addressed by Alloul and Karinkurayil in this volume. However, the Kuwaiti case is also relevant because, although this country recognizes a "composite" culture as part of the nation-building process in the sense that the most prominent families in Kuwait acknowledge a foreign Iranian, Iraqi, or Saudi origin (which is compatible with Kuwaitness), it bars bottom-tier groups in the society such as the *bidun* from nationalization (Beaugrand 2019). Finally, research on Qatar has also addressed how, as part of its cultural diplomacy, the government has promoted cosmopolitan ideals through the building of museums (Koch 2019), an issue that is closely linked to issues of labor (Donini 2019). Other publications that focus on this state address the social diversity of its communities with regard to the question of citizenship (Babar 2017; Malik 2017).

This rather sketchy landscape of research on migration to the Arab states in the Gulf shows that, despite the homogenous labor system of sponsorship implemented in all of them, the domestic contexts of each of these states are different. Yet the question of membership and the social and labor rights of communities of migrant origin (including stateless people such as the *bidun*) permeates much of this research. In this sense, the contributions to this volume reflect the state-of-the-art contemporary research on Gulf migration. Most of the chapters, however, directly or indirectly focus on the UAE, and, more concretely, on the cities of Dubai and Abu Dhabi. Although in terms of representation this can be seen as a limit to our claim of examining "Gulf space," the topics proposed in each chapter center on the different dimensions of this space. They consider the experiences of those raised in the region, as Dakkak does in her chapter, and as discussed in Casini's interview with the acclaimed author Deepak Unnikrishnan in the Conclusion. They also envisage the migrant trajectories in the Gulf and the enduring influence of this experience on their lives, as shown in the works of Alloul and Karinkurayil. Related to this is the migrants' constant negotiation of spaces, whether as nationals or as "contingent citizens" who are entitled to membership through national and cosmopolitan paradigms, which is analyzed by AlMutawa and Derderian.

As an epistemological tool, the notion of Gulf space in this volume allows the contributors to overcome the dichotomies of citizen/noncitizen and receiving/sending migrant regions and shifts the focus of inquiry to the existing social realities created by these very separations. These realities are exemplified by the case of the youth of migrant origin who are brought up in the Gulf cities, and who, once they reach the age of majority and can no longer remain under their parents' visas, will often need to leave for a third country to study and work so that they can later return to what they feel is their home. The meaning of home as a place of safety becomes, in the Gulf context, redefined as a struggle for a home. Similarly, some of the works in this volume explore the meanings of Gulf-branded cosmopolitanism in terms of embracing selective inclusion, or "contingent citizenship," and in terms of incorporating the class aspirations of Europeans of Maghrebi migrant origin. Two challenges emerge in our dealing with the notion of Gulf space: that of conceptually grasping the transience associated with this space, which is constituted by precariousness, and that of the still-unacknowledged enduring element (or influence) of this space that has resulted from the multiple interactions of the trajectories of migrant lives and the engagement of individuals and groups from the Gulf with others in different regions. Drawing on Henri Lefebvre's argument that space is produced by specific actors for certain purposes (Lefebvre 1991: 84–85), this volume examines the disentanglement of what the Gulf means for different groups of people whose life trajectories are connected to the region in order to critically reflect on the intersection of mobility with citizenship, modernity, and cosmopolitanism.

Mobility, Modernity, and Citizenship

During my second fieldtrip to Kuwait in January–February 2019, which was part of a project funded by the German Research Foundation (DFG-Deutsche Forschungsgemeinschaft) in which I studied a migrant and development network between Kuwait and northeastern Pakistan (Mato Bouzas 2018), I by chance met Muhammad, a taxi driver whom I later interviewed several times, often while traveling in the city. I initially approached him in Urdu, or the creole Hindostani often employed in the Gulf, and then we slowly switched to English, a language he spoke fluently. Muhammad was born in Kuwait, although his family hailed from the city of Sialkot, in Punjab, Pakistan. His father and other relatives were carpenters and were recruited to work in the oil fields of preindependent Kuwait because at that time there was a significant amount of available work in carpentry. The whole family lived in Kuwait for several decades, with some interruptions of up to two years, until the oil crisis of 1973 when they returned to Pakistan. Muhammad went back to Kuwait and has been moving between Kuwait and Pakistan since then. He narrated the story of his early childhood and recalled that the family was living in the desert.

"Kuwait at the time was only desert, nothing else. One day, a government official came to the oil field and asked my father if he would like to register us as Kuwaiti nationals, but he refused."

"Why?"

"Because at the time [early 1960s], Pakistan was a young nation and there were many expectations. Kuwait was not modern, and there was only desert, and no cities—nothing of what you can see all around now [he gestures with his head to the city landscape marked by high buildings]. The British had just granted independence, but there was nothing here except for oil. My father thought that Pakistan had a bigger future, and it was better for us to remain Pakistani nationals."

"But if you now had Kuwaiti nationality, and not Pakistani, you would be receiving many benefits from the state."

"Yes, you are right. My father made a mistake. . . . Mine is a wasted life."

The conversation with Muhammad and the meaning of a "wasted life" is revealing when examining his whole trajectory, which is beyond the scope of this introduction. Muhammad spoke Arabic fluently with a Kuwaiti accent, something he said allowed him some privileged access to Kuwaiti society in terms of relations and friendship. Yet, in the end, he was living with his brother in an apartment, and his life was not that different from the segregated nature of other migrants' lives in the city.

The excerpt above reveals the often-neglected aspects of the way we approach the study of migration to the contemporary Gulf. Migration to the Gulf can be described in terms of South-South mobility in the sense that the Gulf states, despite being able to achieve high standards of living for their citizens, share a history of colonization or indirect rule similar to those of the sending regions. This "shared past" is present in the ways migrants deploy their relationship to this region. This relationship unfolds the complexity of Southern geographies of belonging and different understandings of modernity. For Muhammad's father, Kuwait was not modern at the time, especially as compared with the promising future of Pakistan during the "Decade of Development" (1958–1968). The issue of nationality, however, became important for Muhammad, whose wife and three children returned to Sialkot in the 1990s because his earnings were not enough to keep them with him. Moreover, after working and living most of his life in Kuwait, it was difficult for him to settle back in Pakistan.

Citizenship is often linked, in migrants' narrations, to modernization projects in which the attainment of naturalization or some form of membership is important for those who have established stable ties in the region, such as is the case of second generations or long-term residents. Throughout the research I conducted among unskilled and semiskilled migrant workers from northeastern Pakistan (the administrative division of Baltistan) in Kuwait, however, the question of citizenship did not appear to be relevant. This was because, in their condition as poor migrants at the bottom of the social ladder, these workers could not even consider it, and also because this migration channel was formed almost exclusively of married men with responsibilities back home, and because the community exercised tight social control among its members. None of them mentioned the idea of staying in the Gulf, except for two men who had better jobs and whose children were born and raised in Kuwait. Citizenship, as understood by migrants, is connected to the economic and social benefits attached to this form of membership, but also, and mainly for generations raised in the Gulf, it is a matter of security, namely, of having one's own place and thus preventing further displacement.

Although some youth born and/or raised in the Gulf are able to stay there and continue to work, a common path for them is having to decide when they reach the age of majority whether to move back to their parents' countries (as they hold their parents' nationalities) or try for, via higher education, the possibility of being naturalized elsewhere in Europe, the United States, Canada, or Australia. Citizenship, in this latter sense, is about the possibility of having a home, a home of a certain kind (in the general Anglo-speaking developed world), a home that can prevent further compulsory mobility because it offers security in many aspects of life.

Apart from the need for citizenship based on the need for legal, social, and economic rights, there is the question of the real emotional and affective attachment to the Gulf developed by many long-term residents and by those brought up in these societies. This volume addresses this issue in narrative and artistic fields, although the political dimension of citizenship with regard to the Gulf still remains largely unexplored. What kind of challenges does the question of citizenship pose regarding the Gulf? Is the issue only about a love for the place and the wish/right to belong to that place? Is it about access to benefits? Or does it also have to do with the possibility of participation in and/or accepting the nonparticipatory processes of these mainly authoritarian monarchies? In rather informal conversations about the events surrounding the Kuwaiti Arab Spring that I had with Kuwaiti intellectuals who were sympathetic to the idea of providing some rights for migrants, I observed the fact that the question of citizenship intersects with the political balances in these states. The granting of citizenship rights to migrants, which was under debate in late 2020 in the UAE (Naar 2020), opens the question of the sharing of state resources that is the basis of the welfare system. It also affects political balances because, as other scholars have observed, migrants are perceived as being protected by these monarchies (Matsuo 2020: 54–56).

As with the case above of Muhammad, many blue-collar migrants in the Gulf are trapped within a continual circle of mobility that deprives them of stable affective and social relations. Although many envisage migration as a period in their lives when they can save up for the future, probably for no small number this period comprises decades that span most of their adult lives. This can be the sense in which the expression a "wasted life" is used—that is, a life that is devised to provide for others (the family and relatives) without the physical presence of, and support from, these others, but also a life without a place of one's own. In this view, the relationship of mobility and citizenship underscores the role of the Gulf as a "producer" of various categories of outsiders, whether as stateless people, contingent citizens, or, by default, as "nominal" citizens of third states (i.e., those children who automatically become citizens of their parent's countries). The existence of a significant number of noncitizens—the majority of whom are in the UAE, Qatar, Kuwait, and Bahrein—creates tensions with those who are entitled to citizenship in terms of access to a generous welfare state system, the literal occupation of spaces, and the rights of majority/minority groups. In this context, citizenship for noncitizens appears to be a marker of class, gender, and race; it is a consumerist item that sometimes can be purchased or recognized if one possesses enough economic resources. Also, in some Gulf states the granting and revoking of citizenship rights adheres to a policy of eliminating dissent. The state's production of a range of outsiders implies that these "outsiders" must be prepared for mobility because a constant sense of insecurity permeates their lives.

Gulf Space: Some Considerations about Transnationalism and Cosmopolitanism

The Gulf continues to exert an important influence in other regions, whether in the neighboring territories of the Indian Ocean, such as Kerala or Balochistan (Jamali 2020) and various regions in East Africa, or in more remote places in eastern Asia. This contemporary influence is due not only to the location of the Gulf's ports along major sea trading routes, but also to the fact that the Gulf is the birthplace of the tradition of Islam and it exercises a moral role for all Muslims. Moreover, an element of historical continuity also can be seen in the high density of the Gulf region's relations with territories such as the Indian state of Kerala, which is exemplified by the fact that around 5.5 percent of Kerala's population has migrated to different Gulf countries (Rajan 2020).

Migration is central to the building of Gulf transnationalism in that the activities and ties of locals (citizens) and noncitizens are characterized by relatively stable connections across borders, which configure transnational spaces. Migration triggers a number of engagements beyond the field of migration. Through the knowledge that they gain about sending societies, actors from the Gulf become involved in other regions, such as in the case of Gulf charities and NGOs. Philanthropic activities abroad by wealthy Gulf merchant classes can sometimes be considered to be an external action on behalf of the state's foreign policy; and also, these activities amount to a form of governance in other regions (Mato Bouzas 2018). Equally, migration relates to the security-military survival of the state, as exemplified in the arrangement made between Bahrain's monarchy and Pakistan for Pakistani military to provide personnel for Bahrain's armed forces (Louër 2013). Those "mercenaries" lead transnational lives through their relatively privileged condition in Bahrain and back in Pakistan.

Yet, when we refer to the Gulf, the temporal character of transnational migrant activity raises questions about the very concept of transnationalism because, as it has been already noted, most of the migrants lead lives orientated to their home areas, and once their contracts in the Gulf end, they will be replaced by new labor. On the other hand, generations of families have been migrating to the Gulf for decades or even centuries now; they have been living there for most of their adult working lives and have raised their children in these societies. They certainly are diasporic in character (Unnikrishnan 2020). Moreover, the effects of transnational activity in the case of the Gulf can be better examined through places, which, unlike migrants, remain and become testimonies of this Gulf transnationalism (see Dakkak in Chapter 2). Thus, transnationalism in the global South differs substantially from that of the North in the sense that the impossibility of inclusion at one end (in this case the Gulf) creates permanent vulnerable lives for migrant workers. However, for those who are able to access certain privileges in the Gulf, such as naturalization, housing, and substantial economic benefits, they can indeed be considered, to some extent, transnational subjects in the general sense of the term. The role of the postcolonial state in shaping this transnationalism is, therefore, determinative.

The bulk of foreign workers in the Gulf constitute, as defined by Andrew Gardner, a transnational proletariat because although migrants develop ties between nations, their whole lives are oriented toward their home areas (Gardner 2008: 56). Their lives differ substantially from those identified by Gardner as the diasporic elite who are able to deploy a strategic transnationalism (Gardner 2008: 58). This differentiation is based on social and geographical mobility and is strongly connected to the dominance of the urban character of the Gulf cities. However, this mobility, whether social or geographical, tends to be generally understood as a progressive force marked by the decreasing importance of the national frameworks (Sheller and Urry 2006; Mezzadra and Neilson 2013). Yet for those in the lower ranks of the social ladder, the national frame of their home societies, which are in developing countries that are unable to provide basic security to their population, is decisive. For this group, mobility to the Gulf is limited to the movement back and forth between two ends (although places of destination can vary) and in no way has a positive connotation.

Migrant groups from middle- and upper-middle-class backgrounds, however, are able to mobilize their resources and passports, and the Gulf experience provides them with access to multiple working and living locations. Despite the impossibility of attaining citizenship, they can certainly deploy a strategic transnationalism, a sort of "flexible citizenship" (Ong 1999, 112-13), through various forms of perceived inclusion in the Gulf. European migrants of Maghrebi origin in the Gulf, as Alloul shows in this volume, are able to mobilize the value of their European passports and education together with their condition of being Muslim Arab speakers. For them, the Gulf represents a place to fulfill their aspirations of social mobility. Moreover, they share the perception of being culturally included in a society in which, unlike many Arab-Muslim majority states, the Arab-Muslim tradition exercises a hegemonic role through the economic power and the distribution of wealth in these states. Equally, the Gulf merchant classes with their philanthropic work abroad and the white-collar professionals of migrant background with their privileged condition who are under the purview of inter-state special agreements are examples of groups that fit the classical definition of transnationalism in terms of their capacity to influence local conditions in other states or territories. Religious groups, however, are a different matter.

Transnationalism is central to the building of Gulf societies because the presence of large migrant populations, who, as opposed to the group of citizens, are in some cases the majority group, is a constitutive feature that directly impacts the nation building processes in those societies. In her anthropological study of the relations between migrants and local populations in Kuwait, Longva acknowledges the importance of the transnationalism of foreign populations in the building of an ethnocratic society that is based on segregation (Longva 1997). Similarly, in this volume AlMutawa also reflects on the impact of these foreign populations on Emirati women's negotiation of their access to city spaces in Dubai that are considered "non-Emirati" and cosmopolitan, and the preservation by these women of a cultural-religious identity. Transnationalism in the case of the Gulf exposes the vulnerabilities of the nation building process because although migrants (of all social backgrounds) contribute to the identity formation of those societies, they are strategically selected by these governments to provide an image of openness. In general terms, "blue-collar transnationalism" in the Gulf is completely absent in the shaping of a national identity, while the acknowledgment of a "white-collar transnationalism," even when these subjects are never fully included as part of the nation, functions to portray Gulf space as cosmopolitan. This is nowhere more evident than in the UAE, Qatar, and probably Bahrain, where the deployment of an elitist cosmopolitanism is part of the state's cultural diplomacy.

Although Gulf societies have been historically diverse and hosted individuals and groups from other regions, after their independence they followed exclusivist "racial" nation building projects. How does this reconcile with claims to cosmopolitanism? This question has been raised by political geographers such as Koch through an analysis of the iconic dimension of the building of museums in the UAE and Qatar (Koch 2019). Koch argues that the narrative of cosmopolitanism arises in terms of the idea of the commodification of cosmopolitanism. The latter requires that those participating noncitizens and corporate allies convey the message that this cosmopolitanism is being realized (Koch 2019: 354). Derderian, in this volume, examines the ambivalent inclusion faced by artists who are long-term residents of the Emirates and whose works are selected to represent national cosmopolitan projects. She argues that these artists "are selected to represent the nation because they can never be a part of it—so long as they remain foreigners, that is, contingent citizens, they can perform receiving the state's generosity at allowing them to reside there." They function to "hide" the social diversity that already exists in society and highlight a cosmopolitanism from above (Calhoun 2002).

Gulf cosmopolitanism is essentially framed in terms of "access" and as the product of (individual) "aspirations" rather than in terms of universal moral obligations and as a discussion over the recognition of equal and just rights. Examples of the former are provided in the chapters by AlMutawa and Alloul. AlMutawa explores the use of exclusive spaces of leisure and consumption through Emirati women in the city of Dubai where they perceive both embracing and exclusionary feelings of belonging. Also, Alloul provides a more complex account by which Dubai "forms a deeply affectionate counter-space to Europe" in his already mentioned study of Europeans of Maghrebi origin who fulfill their upward mobility by navigating in the racialized Gulf space, which privileges and facilitates inclusiveness for Arab-speaking Muslims with "whitened" European passports. Instead, cosmopolitanism in terms of moral obligations and inclusion emerges in the literature written by non-Gulf-citizen authors examined by Dakkak, who argues that these works narrate lived experiences of diasporic subjects and, in so doing, make these subjects' presence integral to the Gulf societies.

Presentation of the Book

This book is organized along two main thematic areas: Gulf cosmopolitanism, belonging, and national imaginaries; and the Gulf as an aspirational place. Both themes are related to each other because the deployment of Gulf cosmopolitanism intersects with the portrayal of the Gulf as a place to fulfill life and attain life expectations. The contributions in the first section, however, share a reflection on how national representations and sentiments of belonging create various forms of exclusion. The chapters critically examine cosmopolitanism with regard to its ideal of inclusion, because Gulf cosmopolitanism, as deployed by some of these states, undermines claims of belonging and citizenship (Derderian) and reduces the "cosmopolitan space" to that of consumption (AlMutawa). Between these two poles lies a real claim of a cosmopolitan space as lived by generations of migrants who made the Gulf their homes (Dakkak).

In Chapter 1, Derderian explores the use of noncitizen artists in the UAE Pavilion at the Venice Biennale, between 2009 and 2017. Despite the fact that these artists are barred from becoming part of the polis, their participation in national events shows Emirate reliance on noncitizen artists as a way of displaying its tolerance and cosmopolitanism and shifts the attention of migration to a specific relation of the state and culture. Dakkak in Chapter 2 reflects on the possibilities of citizenship that come out of claiming belonging in the two novels *Samrawit*, by Haji Jaber (2012), and *Temporary People*, by Deepak Unnikrishnan (2017), which are set in the cities of Jeddah and Abu Dhabi, respectively. Dakkak claims that the lived experiences narrated in these works are diasporic and can be read as claims to recognition that differ from other migrant groups; but these stories also highlight the diasporic character as a constitutive element of the Gulf space. AlMutawa in Chapter 3 offers the other dimension, that of the citizens, through an ethnographic study of the experiences of Emirati women from the upper-middle classes of the city of Dubai. AlMutawa examines how women negotiate the use of "cosmopolitan" spaces (of consumption and leisure) in the city against their own cultural traditions, citizenship rights, and belonging. Both Derderian and AlMutawa discuss Gulf cosmopolitanism as a tool of governance from above, while Dakkak addresses the recognition of the transient character of the migratory experience from below.

The contributions in section two focus on the impact of the migrant experience in the Gulf at the level of society or at the level of personal trajectories. The two chapters in this section highlight the character of the Gulf as an aspirational place that continues to hold attraction for all kinds of migrants. In Chapter 4, Alloul analyses how Dubai becomes a heterotopian space where the feelings of exclusion and inferiority experienced in Europe by educated Europeans of Maghrebi background become thoroughly reversed. As Alloul highlights in his contribution, the apparently frictionless homecoming in the Gulf of privileged laborers can take place despite the racial features enmeshed in EU citizenship. In Chapter 5, Karinkurayil examines a much larger and better-known social group in the Gulf: migrants from the Indian southern state of Kerala. He focuses on the role of pictures and looks specifically at the sartorial choices of the people portrayed in these pictures, and how these choices create a specific imaginary of the Gulf as an aspirational space. The author's analysis emphasizes the transnational nature of this process and the impact of these imaginable narratives in the region of Kerala.

In the Conclusion, Casini dialogues with author Unnikrishnan on the major themes touched on in his novel *Temporary People*, which largely coincide with those of this book. Unnikrishnan became actively involved in the discussion surrounding this publication project. He is therefore in a privileged position to comment on the main themes discussed by the other contributors and relate them to his own life experience as a writer from the Gulf.

Antía Mato Bouzas is senior lecturer in Politics and International Relations at London Metropolitan University and associate researcher at Leibniz-Zentrum Moderner Orient (ZMO), Berlin. She is the author of *Kashmir as a Borderland: The Politics of Space and Belonging across the Line of Control* (Amsterdam University Press, 2019). Her current research project, funded by the DFG (Deutsche Forschungsgemeinschaft, the German Research Foundation), examines migration from northeastern Pakistan to the Gulf.

REFERENCES

Addleton, Jonathan S. 1992. *Undermining the Centre: Gulf Migration to Pakistan*. Karachi: Oxford University Press.
Ahmad, Attiya. 2017. *Everyday Conversions: Islam, Domestic Work, and South Asian Migrant Women in Kuwait*. Durham: Duke University Press.
Alharthi, Jokha. 2019. *Celestial Bodies*. Inverness, Scotland: Sandstone Press.
Babar, Zahra, ed. 2017. *Arab Migrant Communities in the GCC*. London: Hurst.
Beaugrand, Claire. 2019. *Stateless in the Gulf: Migration, Nationality and Society in Kuwait*. London: I. B. Tauris.
Calhoun, Craig. 2002. "The Class Consciousness of Frequent Travelers: Toward a Critique of Actually Existing Cosmopolitanism." *The South Atlantic Quarterly* 101, no. 4: 869-97.
———. 2003. "'Belonging' in the Cosmopolitan Imaginary." *Ethnicities* 3, no. 4: 531-68.

Donini, Antonio. 2019. "Social Suffering and Structural Violence: Nepali Workers in Qatar." In *The ILO @ 100*. International Development Policy Series, volume 11, edited by Christophe Gironde and Gilles Carbonnier, 178-99. Geneva: Graduate Institute Publications, Brill-Nijhoff.

Errichiello, Genaro. 2018. *"Dubai Is a Transit Lounge:" Migration, Belonging and National Identity in Pakistani Professionals in the UAE*. PhD thesis. Loughborough: Loughborough University Press.

Freitag, Ulrike. 2020. *A History of Jeddah: The Gate to Mecca in the Nineteenth and Twentieth Centuries*. Cambridge, UK: Cambridge University Press.

Gamburd, Michele R. 2002. *Transnationalism and Sri Lanka's Migrant Housemaids: The Kitchen Spoon's Handle*. New Delhi: Vistaar.

Gardner, Andrew. 2008. "Strategic Transnationalism: The Indian Diasporic Migration in Bahrein." *City & Society* 20, no. 1: 54-78.

Gardner, Andrew, and Sharon Nagy. 2008. "Introduction: New Ethnographic Fieldwork Among Migrants, Residents and Citizens in the Arab States of the Gulf." *City & Society* 20, no. 1: 1-4.

Horinuki, Koji. 2020. "International Labor Migration and the Arab Gulf States: Trends, Institutions, and Relations." In *Asian Migrant Workers in the Arab Gulf States*, edited by Ishii, Hosoda, Matsuo, and Horinuki, 23-52. Leiden: Brill.

Hosoda, Naomi. 2020. "A Case of Filipino Workers in the UAE." In *Asian Migrant Workers in the Arab Gulf States*, edited by Ishii, Hosoda, Matsuo, and Horinuki, 172-93. Leiden: Brill.

Ishii, Masako, Naomi Hosoda, Masaki Matsuo, and Koji Horinuki, eds. 2020. *Asian Migrant Workers in the Arab Gulf States* (The Intimate and the Public in Asian and Global Perspectives 10). Leiden: Brill.

Jain, Prakash C., and Ginu Zacharia Oommen, eds. 2016. *South Asian Migration to Gulf Countries: History, Policies and Development*. Delhi: Routledge.

Jamali, Hafeez A. 2020. "Shorelines of Memory and Ports of Desire: Geography, Identity, and the Memory of Oceanic Trade in Mekran (Balochistan)." In *Reimagining Indian Ocean Worlds*, edited by Smriti Srinivas, Bettina Ng'weno, and Neelima Jeychandran, 165-79. London: Routledge.

Khalifa, Reem. 2011. "Pearl Democracy." *The European* (11 November). Accessed 10October2020. https://www.theeuropean.de/en/reem-khalifa—2/6174-the-arab-spring-in-bahrain.

Koch, Natalie. 2019. "Capitalizing on Cosmopolitanism in the Gulf." *Current History* 118, no. 812 (Dec.): 349-54.

Lefebvre, Henri 1991. *The Production of Space*. Translated by Donald Nicholson-Smith. Oxford: Blackwell.

Longva, Anh N. 1997. *Walls Built on Sand: Migration, Exclusion and Society in Kuwait*. Boulder, CO: Westview Press.

Louër, Laurence. 2008. "The Political Impact of Labor Migration in Bahrain." *City & Society* 20, no. 1: 32-53.

———. 2013. "Sectarianism and Coup-Proofing Strategies in Bahrain." *Journal of Strategic Studies* 36, no. 2: 245-60.

Malik, Saadia I. 2017. "Identity, Citizenship and 'Home' through the Transnational Perspective(s) of Second Generation Sudanese Migrants in Qatar." *Diaspora Studies* 10, no. 2: 175–92.
Massey, Douglas S., Joaquín Arango, Graeme Hugo, Ali Kouaouci, Adela Pellegrino, and J. E. Taylor, eds. 1998. *Worlds in Motion: Understanding International Migration at the End of the Millennium*. Oxford: Oxford University Press.
Mato Bouzas, Antía. 2018. "From the Karakoram Mountains to the Arabian Sea: Migration, Development and Religion in the Making of Transnational Spaces." *ZMO Working Papers* 21. http://www.zmo.de/publikationen/WorkingPapers/mato_bouzas_2018.pdf.
Matsuo, Masaki. 2020. "Political Economy of the Labor Market in the Arab Gulf States." In *Asian Migrant Workers in the Arab Gulf States*, edited by Ishii, Hosoda, Matsuo, and Horinuki, 53–72. 2020. Leiden: Brill.
Mezzadra, Sandro, and Brett Neilson. 2013. *Border as Method, or The Multiplication of Labor*. Durham: Duke University Press.
Moghadam, Amin. 2013. "De l'Iran imaginé aux nouveurs foyears de l'Iran: pratiques et espaces transnationaux des Iraniens à Dubaï." *Arabian Humanities* 2 (online edition).
Naar, Ismaeel. 2020. "UAE Set to Amend Law Granting Citizenship to Expats with Certain, Criteria: Report." *Al Arabiya*. 30 September. Accessed 8 October 2020. https://english.alarabiya.net/en/News/gulf/2020/09/30/UAE-set-to-amend-law-granting-citizenship-to-expats-with-certain-criteria-Report.
Nagy, Sharon. 2008. "The Search for Miss Philippines Bahrain—Possibilities for Representation in Expatriate Communities." *City & Society* 30, no. 1: 79–104.
Ong, Aihwa. 1999. *Flexible Citizenship: The Cultural Logics of Transnationalism*. Durham: Duke University Press.
Osella, Filippo, and Caroline Osella. 2007. "Muslim Entrepreneurs Between India & the Gulf." *ISIM Review* 19 (Spring): 8–9.
Rajan, Irudaya S. 2020. "An Expert Explains: What Is the Future of Migration from Kerala?" *The Indian Express*. 27 April. Accessed 8 October 2020. https://indianexpress.com/article/explained/what-is-the-future-of-migration-from-kerala-coronavirus-6380548/.
Shah, Nasra. 2004. "Gender and Labour Migration to the Gulf Countries." *Feminist Review* 77, no. 1: 183–85.
Shah, Nasra, and Philippe Fargues. 2011. "Introduction." *Asian and Pacific Migration Journal on Migration in the Gulf States: Issues and Prospects*. 20, no. 3–4: 267–72.
Sheller, Mimi, and John Urry, eds. 2006. *Mobile Technologies of the City*. London: Routledge.
Sons, Sebastian. 2020. *Arbeitsmigration nach Saudi-Arabien und ihre Wahrnehmung in Pakistan: Akteur*innen und Strategien der öffentlichen Sichtbarmachung*. Heidelberg: CrossAsia-eBooks (Media and Cultural Studies, Band 1). http://crossasia-books.ub.uni-heidelberg.de/xasia.
Thiollet, Hélène. 2007. "Refugees and Migrants from Eritrea to the Arab World: The Cases of Sudan, Yemen and Saudi Arabia 1991–2007." *Migration and Movements in the Middle East and North Africa series*. Forced Migration & Refugee Studies Program.

The American University in Cairo. Accessed 8 October 2020. American University in Cairo: http://schools.aucegypt.edu/GAPP/cmrs/Documents/HeleneThiollet.pdf.

———. 2011. "Migration as Diplomacy: Labor Migrants, Refugees, and Arab Regional Politics in the Oil-Rich Countries." *International Labor and Working Class History* 79 (Spring): 103–21.

Unnikrishnan, Deepak. 2020. "The Hidden Cost of Migrant Labor: What It Means to Be a Temporary Person in the Gulf." *Foreign Affairs*. 7 February. Accessed 6 October 2020. https://www.foreignaffairs.com/articles/india/2020-02-07/hidden-cost-migrant-labor.

Vora, Neha. 2013. *Impossible Citizens: India's Dubai Diaspora*. Durham: Duke University Press.

Walsh, Katie. 2012. "Emotion and Migration: British Transnationals in Dubai." *Environment and Planning D: Society and Space* 30: 43–59.

PART I

Cosmopolitanism, Belonging, and National Imaginaries

CHAPTER 1

Exhibiting Tolerance
Citizenship, Contingency, and Contemporary Art in the UAE Pavilion, 2009–2017

Elizabeth Derderian

"We stood out a lot in Europe. It was me and three other Emirati girls," Eman remarked of her travel to the Venice Biennale as part of a delegation representing the United Arab Emirates (UAE) several years prior. The Venice Biennale, founded in 1895, is one of—if not the—most elite contemporary art events in the world, in which displays are organized by national pavilions. Describing her work with the UAE pavilion at the Biennale, Eman shared, "We were all staying in one house, me and three other Emirati girls; we were doing everything together. The locals would ask us where we were from. [The other girls would] say, 'We're Emirati.' I'd never get a chance to say where I'm from. I'm Palestinian." Eman continued:

> So I started asserting. My close friend at that time was like, "Why do you feel the need to continue to assert that you're Palestinian? I see you doing this." I'm not Emirati. Why should my identity be sort of sweeped [*sic*] under the carpet when it's convenient because you wanna represent the UAE? She said, "You don't identify with the UAE?" Yes, I do, but I'm not a citizen. It's hard for me to wholeheartedly just say, I'm from Dubai, I'm from the UAE, when I don't have any rights in that place. That was the first time it actually dawned on me that I'm not Emirati.[1]

Eman's wording reflects her ambiguous situation as someone born and raised in the UAE, but who carries foreign citizenship documentation. The

Biennale precipitated the awkward situation of representing a nation where she was born and raised, but in which she could not claim citizenship, and caused Eman to experience her exclusion in a stark, new way. In referencing the "three other Emirati girls," she implied that they are like her, even as she marked her difference by emphasizing her Palestinian identity. Her status as a UAE-born person of Palestinian descent, carrying a Jordanian passport, complicates easy categories of citizenship and belonging, and her reflections on representing the UAE at the Venice Biennale hint at the crucial role that art, museums, and culture play in contests of national representation.

In the UAE, as in many contemporary states, museums serve as key sites for nation-making projects. State actors use museum displays as public spaces of presentation to help codify a particular national heritage and identity and define who is and is not part of that nation, often drawing on the cultural contributions of citizens to do so. Extensive literature documents this paradigm and the ways state actors deploy art and culture to inculcate citizens into the nation's heritage and to forge an imagined community (Anderson 2006; Bennett 1995; Bourdieu 1993; Coffey 2012; Duncan 1995; Foster 2002; Karp 2006; Lloyd and Thomas 1998; Macdonald 2006; Myers 2002; Pieprzak 2010; Prior 2002; Watenpaugh 2004; Winegar 2006). Dating back to the 1792 founding of the Louvre as a royal collection converted into a public museum in post-Revolutionary France, museums and culture are also often used both to brand the state internationally and to model the nation for a domestic audience (Exell 2016; Levitt 2015; McClellan 1994). Yet increasing transnational migration for work (as well as museum franchising) in recent years has complicated the extant culture–state paradigm, challenging the ways that art and museums can be deployed in nation-building projects. Broadly speaking, how do states use museums and art to represent the nation when the nation is substantially populated by noncitizen migrants, as in many of the Arab Gulf states? How do state actors working in the cultural realm frame the role of those noncitizens, and how do they draw on the cultural contributions of both citizens and noncitizens?

At the intersection of studies on migration, the state and representation, and contemporary art, this chapter explores how migrants are integral to spaces and projects of national representation in the UAE, precisely because they are not citizens. State actors use them to showcase the Emirati state as tolerant of its multicultural population. This production of multicultural tolerance requires that noncitizen artists continue to reside in the UAE yet never become citizens, because they could not then serve as proof of the state's tolerance. They must remain in the nation, but never become a part of it: after all, the nation requires the presence of "others" to be cosmopolitan and tolerant. These artists are then *contingent citizens*, as they are at times considered "Emirati enough" to represent the state and at others excluded from it.[2] Rendering these artists contingent citizens also allows the state to simultaneously acknowledge the presence of these communities while maintaining the state as ethnically homogeneous. Their contingency is a technique of governmentality, a means of managing and sanitizing difference. It is also another way in which state authorities, structures, and laws produce a sense of limbo for internal minorities and resident noncitizens (see also Lori 2019).

The Venice Biennale, given its seminal importance in the contemporary art world and its longstanding tradition of organizing contemporary art by and into national pavilions, is an excellent site to examine these questions; and the UAE, with a population comprised largely of noncitizen migrants, is an apt case study. Since the UAE's political unification in 1971, citizenship transmission has become increasingly restricted. Rough estimates approximate that 15 percent of the UAE's resident population hold Emirati citizenship, and 85 percent carry foreign papers.[3] Many Gulf states are majority-foreign, because citizenship is transmissible only through patrilineal descent; there is no naturalization process and no birthright citizenship. Moreover, women married to nonnationals cannot pass their citizenship on to their children. To be a citizen, a person must hold *both* an Emirati passport and a family card proving their lineage, called a *khulasat qaid*. Alongside studies of the ambiguous, messy realities of legal or extralegal migration and naturalization (Coutin 2007; Gomberg-Munoz 2017), or those that bring into focus the "gap between legal citizenship and social citizenship" (Grewal 2014: 4), the UAE case is noteworthy in that government agents have found ways to codify placing certain populations in near-permanent limbo (Lori 2019).

In addition, the UAE enforces employment quotas, known as workforce nationalization or Emiratization, in many sectors, and has an established pattern of national representation in hiring that heightens the stakes of selecting artists and curators for biennials. Cynics might cite the small number of Emirati citizens overall and argue that the UAE simply ran out of citizen artists by the 2017 pavilion, thus explaining the inclusion of noncitizen artists. There is, however, no shortage of citizen artists, and it is more likely that such a move was driven by a desire to brand the Emirati art world as cosmopolitan.

This use of noncitizen artists as a means of demonstrating the state's tolerance and cosmopolitanism is predicated on a set of beliefs and assumptions that Jessica Winegar has termed "the humanity game." Writing about the surge of exhibitions of Arab and Muslim artists in the US in a post-9/11 context, Winegar noted that many arts organizers relied on the "art as evidence of humanity" theory to showcase the humanity of Arab and Muslim peoples: "these events are structured around two related assumptions: that art is a uniquely valuable and uncompromised agent of cross-cultural understanding; and that art constitutes the supreme evidence of a people's humanity" (Winegar 2008: 652).

Organizers based in the Emirates have often uncritically adopted this twinned narrative—that art can serve as a depoliticized cross-cultural "bridge of understanding," and position the art scene as proof of the state's cosmopolitan diversity and tolerance and therein repudiate the mass media depictions of the country as an authoritarian human rights abuser.[4] In this discourse, art remains the ultimate indicator of a community's values of tolerance and cosmopolitanism. Artists in the UAE thus carry a significant representational burden: their work and existence is often used to defray criticisms of the state's rigid restrictions on freedom of expression and abysmal track record on labor abuses. In this instance, artists become embodiments of the state's cosmopolitanism and tolerance.

My analysis draws from the exhibition catalogs of the pavilions and the official UAE Pavilion web archive. Where relevant, I also weave in interviews and participant observation from ethnographic fieldwork I conducted in the UAE art scene between 2015 and 2017. First, I provide the context for the inaugural Venice Biennale pavilion and then analyze the 2009 pavilion itself. Between 2010 and 2016, international media and other forces constantly coupled the UAE's artistic development projects to discourses of labor and human rights, offering these abuses as proof of the state's intolerance and lack of humanity. By 2017, state actors had begun to draw on the cultural contributions of long-term resident, noncitizen artists to represent the state as tolerant of multiculturalism. Overall, juxtaposing the 2009 and 2017 pavilions shows that state actors reaffirm the extant culture-state paradigm, relying on citizens to create a cultural lineage for the country, and also redefine it in their use of noncitizens to showcase the state as tolerant of multiculturalism.

The UAE Pavilion at the 2009 Biennale, in Context

The UAE participated in the Venice Biennale for the first time in 2009. At the time, joining the Biennale was a logical next step, given the heady growth of the UAE's art sector in the early 2000s. Indeed, there have been "Emirati" artists since the creation of the Emirates in 1971, and the first Sharjah biennial was held in 1993, founded by Sharjah ruler Sheikh Sultan al Qasimi. However, a number of factors contributed to the developments in the early 2000s. First, the daughter of Sheikh Sultan, Shaikha Hoor al Qasimi, completed her BFA in London in 2002 and returned to the UAE, where she assumed control of the biennial and reoriented it to render it more legible to a contemporary art audience. Several commercial art galleries opened in Dubai in or around 2005, and in 2006, plans for Saadiyat Island, near the capital city Abu Dhabi, began to trickle out. By 2007, full plans had been released for Saadiyat, which was to include (among other venues) the Louvre Abu Dhabi, Guggenheim Abu Dhabi, and Zayed National Museum, all designed by star architects.[5] Significant international backlash toward the museums erupted. European and American curators and arts professionals were often vocal critics, claiming art and artists could not thrive in an authoritarian country infamous for its lack of freedom of speech and massive labor abuses. The chancellor of New York University (NYU) called Abu Dhabi a "tabula rasa," and one journalist wrote, "Abu Dhabi has relatively few artistic or literary traditions" (Krieger 2008). Undeterred by these critiques, the UAE's art scene continued to grow: the first iteration of the commercial art fair Art Dubai was held in 2007, followed closely by Abu Dhabi Art, and Sotheby's held its first auction in Dubai. In 2008, Tashkeel Art Center was established in Dubai as an art studio and the Dubai Culture Council reorganized into the Dubai Culture and Arts Authority to assert oversight of the burgeoning cultural sector; the Creek Art Fair (now Sikka) was inaugurated in Dubai's Bastakiya (now rebranded as Al Fahidi) neighborhood; and March Meeting, an annual convening of arts professionals, began in Sharjah.[6] Given this flurry of growth, and to further legitimize the growing arts scene in the country, officials looked to the Venice Biennale.

At the 2009 Biennale, the UAE was essentially represented twice. Dr. Lamees Hamdan, a medical doctor, commissioned the official pavilion, entitled *It's Not You, It's Me*, which Tirdad Zolghadr curated. The Abu Dhabi Arts and Cultural Heritage Authority (ADACH, since reorganized several times and as of this writing, operating as the Department of Culture and Tourism) presented a "project" entitled "ADACH Platform for Visual Arts in Venice," organized by prominent French curator Catherine David. Why two displays? As they looked to join a contemporary art market, UAE-based arts professionals had to restructure organizations and exhibitions to fit into the forms legible to that world: biennials and commercial art fairs replaced the annual works-in-progress shows of artist cooperatives and *majlis*-style artists' socialization (Derderian 2020). The national presentation in two distinct spaces, with two distinct curatorial visions, can be partially attributed to this broader process of reconfiguration, and the kinds of struggles that transpire in that flattening and codification. The dual representation was perhaps a manifestation of the competition between emirates: Abu Dhabi, Dubai, and Sharjah each have discrete cultural strategies and typically act individually rather than in concert as a federation.

I focus here on the pavilion, rather than the project, largely because it was the official pavilion, and its position has been reified in subsequent years as art historians and future pavilion curators referenced back to *It's Not You, It's Me* (often omitting the ADACH platform from the archive altogether). Zolghadr's vision was to make the 2009 UAE pavilion a meta-pavilion, describing it as "a pavilion on exhibition making. Reflecting on the very act of national showcasing, artistic documentation and curatorial testimony in a place like Venice, Mother of all Biennials" (Zolghadr 2009: 130). Zolghadr here acknowledged the legitimizing nature of the Biennale. He was likely aware of how international media would interpret the pavilion and its theme of national representation.

The catalog text often assumes Emirati citizenship, specifying only the status of the noncitizen and thereby rendering citizenship the unmarked norm. While featuring Lamya Gargash, the pavilion also had a "showcase" that juxtaposed the work of "UAE artists" Hassan Sharif, Ebtisam Abdulaziz, Tarek Al Ghoussein, and Huda Saeed Saif (Zolghadr 2009: 134). The catalog's "Index of Projects and Participants" does not list nationalities for Sharif, Abdulaziz, or Saif. Al Ghoussein is introduced as "UAE based" and "a Palestinian, born in Kuwait" (Zolghadr 2009: 146). The only citizenship that was flagged, then, is the noncitizen—all the other artists are implicitly understood to be Emirati citizens. At the same time, the text emphasizes Al Ghoussein's Arabness and his connection to the Gulf region.[7]

Questions of work were already deeply correlated to citizenship and representation in many other arenas in the UAE, so it could reasonably be assumed that the question of staffing the pavilion would be high profile and scrutinized (at least domestically) based on questions of citizenship. Across many sectors of the economy, the UAE has enacted workforce nationalization policies, reserving certain jobs or a percentage of roles at a company (or even within an industry) for Emirati citizens. This practice, called Emiratization, also cropped up in how curators selected artists for exhibitions. For example, just prior to the 2009 Biennale, an exhibition entitled *Emirati Expressions* was among the first of several shows that explicitly and intentionally only included Emirati citizen artists.[8] When it came to selecting which artists and curators would represent the UAE at its inaugural pavilion, citizenship status was thus paramount. Hamdan relates the search for a curator, noting that the pavilion team "asked itself some fundamental questions. Should the UAE recruit an international star curator for its debut in Venice? Should it insist on an Emirati curator?" (Hamdan 2009: 142). In the end, they chose Zolghadr, an international (noncitizen) curator familiar with the UAE, a choice that appeared to be aimed at ensuring the pavilion's legitimacy. At the time, there were a few Emirati citizens with formal training as curators, but none yet had the experience curating such internationally visible shows as the Venice Biennale, Documenta, or the like.

There was still an element of unabashed national promotion in the 2009 pavilion, as well as an attempt to scope out a national cultural lineage and history of artistic production. The UAE pavilion consisted of three major parts: Gargash's portrait series *Familial*, a series of maquettes of UAE arts infrastructures, and a section with video interviews of current figures in the Emirati art scene. In terms of programming and performances, there was also the Jackson Pollock Bar, which was a "reenactment of the first UAE Pavilion press conference" (Zolghadr 2009: 148), and a series of "conversations." Despite being a contemporary art venue, the pavilion also displayed "traditional 'national expo' elements," such as "architectural models of UAE museum infrastructure from the present Sharjah Art Museum and Sharjah Museum of Islamic Civilization to the currently planned Saadiyat Island Abu Dhabi, featuring a Louvre, a Guggenheim, and a Pavilion Park for an upcoming biennial, but also Dubai's Universal Museum" (Zolghadr 2009: 133-34).[9] Even as Gargash's portraits of empty rooms in cheap hotels celebrate a side of Dubai that is not often celebrated, the exhibition also included the glamorous and spectacular depictions of Abu Dhabi's Saadiyat Island. Zolghadr juxtaposed the maquettes of extant infrastructure and the artist showcase, with its promising future—the proof of the country's cultural history—in the maquettes of Saadiyat Island and Gargash's photo series.

Despite being mildly facetious about the use of artists to represent nations, Zolghadr still chose Gargash for such a role—noting that this practice was largely uninterrogated in the art community: "By and large, among the art professional tribe, the question of why an artist should need to be packaged as 'national export,' as opposed to a 'good artist,' is limited to sarcastic comments over Illy's espressos" (Zolghadr 2009: 132). At the time, Gargash was quite young (b. 1982, aged twenty-seven during the 2009 Venice Biennale) to receive such international exposure. Selecting Gargash offered a number of advantages: She is an Emirati citizen, thus representing the nation's young and emerging talent. Gargash works in photography, a popular medium and one strongly associated with contemporary art (more so than, for example, modern art). In the context of the pavilion Gargash represented the UAE's bright cultural future.

While the deployment of artists as national export was ostensibly unquestioned within the art community, within the UAE the link between artists and national representation was significantly more important. Thus internal concerns in the UAE, with workforce nationalization and representation, butted up against an international art world pseudodisdain for national representation, setting the two at odds. The positioning of the pavilion was, in many outlets, overtly nationalist. Then minister of culture, youth & community development Abdul Rahman Bin Mohammed Al Owais wrote in the foreword to the exhibition catalog: "Recognizing the role of art in fostering harmony among nations . . . the UAE actively supports the development of the arts in their many forms and encourages the work of its talented citizens . . . . The UAE has succeeded in presenting its artists' achievements to other nations . . . and will continue to bestow international recognition on UAE artists" (Al Owais 2009: 156). Note the "art as bridge of understanding discourse" here, and how UAE authorities were keen to assert that the country had significant artistic achievements. Thus the focus was on bolstering the artwork of citizens, establishing the UAE's legitimacy in an international art scene that often doubted its credentials. He concludes by emphasizing the legitimating role of this biennial: "By taking its place now on the international platform of the Venice Biennale, the UAE demonstrates its determination to keep pace with developments in contemporary art and to communicate with a broad audience" (Al Owais 2009: 156). If the pavilion was a performance of the UAE's legitimacy, it is worth asking who was envisioned as that performance's intended audience, especially given the pavilion's title: *It's Not You, It's Me*.

The accompanying programming was also largely oriented toward promoting a national art scene. Three of the five "conversations" that accompanied the exhibition were about national branding: one on the national anthem, one on branding Dubai through Al Quoz as a cultural district, and one on "imagining and building a nation from scratch" (Zolghadr 2009: 150). There is thus an interesting contradiction—one narrative of the UAE's storied history and rich culture; another of starting from a blank slate or "scratch," which obviously cannot both be true.

The 2009 pavilion was meant to showcase the work of Emirati citizen artists, asserting the presence of a vibrant contemporary art scene. By 2017, the UAE pavilion adopted a different tactic: asserting the cosmopolitanism and tolerance of the UAE by focusing on the cultural contributions of *non*-citizens, thereby revealing the ways transnational migration is shifting the paradigm of national cultural representation.

2010–16—Coupling Labor and Art: Playing the Humanity Game

What contributed to these tectonic shifts in representational practice? In the intervening years, the UAE art scene continued to grow at a rapid clip; in addition, critics and organizers wrestled over the right to define the burgeoning art scene, increasingly correlating developments in the UAE's art scene to important questions about the treatment of migrant laborers in the country and freedom of expression.

The UAE art scene grew quickly: commercial art fairs Abu Dhabi Art (initially Art Paris Abu Dhabi) and Art Dubai gained momentum; in 2009, Sharjah Art Foundation emerged as a permanent institution to "ensure continuity with the history of the [Sharjah] Biennial while offering a year-round programme of exhibitions and events" (Sharjah Art Foundation, n.d.). Plans for the Saadiyat Island project slowed after the 2009 global financial crash but did not derail entirely. Commissioner Lamees Hamdan appointed Vasif Kortun to curate the 2011 UAE Pavilion, *Second Time Around*. The pavilion featured Shaikha Lateefa bint Maktoum, Reem al Ghaith, and Abdullah al Saadi. The catalog describes UAE artists and organizers as part of an "evolving art scene" (Hamdan 2011: 9), whose members "work around the clock to firmly establish themselves" (Al Owais 2011: 5)—overtly referencing the scrutiny organizers felt themselves to be under.

Aware of the UAE's visibility and the Venice Biennale's role as legitimator, Kortun noted that after the UAE's 2009 Venice debut, "the UAE was everywhere in the arts media. It seemed that Venice was another station marking the transformation of the contemporary art context in the Gulf" (Kortun 2011: 13). He also wrote, "The UAE art scene's most recent series of international headlines reveals the complexities and requirements of becoming a world player" (Kortun 2011: 12). Kortun here alluded to events

Figure 1.1. Installation of "1980–Today: Exhibitions in the UAE," Sharjah, UAE, 2016. © Elizabeth Derderian.

that had unfolded just prior to the June opening of the Venice Biennale: Sharjah's biennial had opened in March, and on 6 April 2011, its director Jack Persekian was abruptly fired. By 11 April, high-profile figures in the art world had begun circulating a petition to protest his firing. Simultaneously, Gulf Labor, a coalition of artists mostly based outside the Gulf, initiated conversations with Guggenheim leadership about the treatment of construction workers on Saadiyat and released some preliminary information around the time the Venice Biennale opened. Given this maelstrom of attention to both professional and manual labor in the UAE art world, it makes sense that the 2011 UAE pavilion organizers would attempt to preemptively address these issues.

Media dispatches continued to link subsequent UAE pavilions in Venice to labor abuses and disputes. The 2013 pavilion, *Walking on Water*, featured an immersive video installation by Mohammed Kazem, curated by Reem Fadda. By this point, the NYU campus on Saadiyat, including the NYUAD Art Gallery, was open, and Louvre organizers had begun holding temporary exhibitions on Saadiyat to cultivate audiences for the future Louvre (scheduled to open in 2012, then 2013, then 2015, then 2016, which finally opened in November 2017). The Salama Foundation, based in Abu Dhabi, welcomed the first cohort of its Emerging Artists Fellowship program in partnership with faculty from RISD in 2013–2014; Art Dubai launched a nonprofit educational initiative called Campus Art Dubai. Yet news reports also highlighted strikes by ArabTec workers at the Louvre Abu Dhabi site, and violence in the ArabTec worker compounds throughout the summer attracted yet more media attention and criticisms.

In 2015, the press release for the Emirati pavilion highlighted the appointment of the first Emirati (read: citizen) for the pavilion—the daughter of Sharjah ruler and director of the Sharjah Art Foundation, Shaikha Hoor al Qasimi. The exhibition featured "15 Emirati artists" (UAE Pavilion 2015). Following the Biennale, the exhibition traveled to the Sharjah Art Foundation and remained on view for several months. This exhibition firmly established a cultural history of the Emirates and defined a canon of Emirati (citizen) artists. It also heralded the beginning of a series of five- and ten-year celebrations of arts organizations in the UAE that cascaded across the next two years. These celebrations were overshadowed by more media reports of labor and free speech violations. After the UAE denied entry to Andrew Ross, Ashok Sukumaran, and Walid Raad (all members of Gulf Labor) in early 2015, Gulf Labor members undertook several interventions in subsequent months, ranging from petitions, open letters, and the publication of a book (Ross 2015) to staging an intervention at the Venice Biennale. Media attention again coupled questions of the UAE's labor record to its art scene.

The growth and potential of the UAE's art scene has, then, long been intertwined with questions over the treatment of laborers and tussles over freedom of expression, the latter questions often seen to delegitimize or foreclose the former. While art could function to produce a national historical narrative and a cosmopolitan status, the UAE now needed to palliate these critics of its intolerance and discriminatory treatment of migrant workers. A new approach was necessary, and it took the form of proclaiming tolerance. In 2016, the UAE government created a ministry of happiness and a ministry of tolerance. UAE rulers appointed a minister of state for tolerance, passed several antidiscrimination and antiextremism laws, created two Twitter accounts devoted to promoting tolerance (@VOTolerance, voice of tolerance or *sawt al-tasamah*, and @uaetolerance), and launched the National Tolerance Programme, which includes archaeology and history, as well as humanity, among its seven key pillars.[10] The art world was, unsurprisingly, conscripted into this project as well.

Playing with Contingency and Representation in the 2017 Pavilion

After years of media attention that consistently coupled arts and cultural developments with questions of labor, the UAE pavilion opted to draw attention to the country's diverse population (rather than avoid it). This move posits diversity as a strength rather than a liability, but also co-opts it into the process of national representation—eventually reasserting the exclusion and nonbelonging of noncitizen artists. The mere presence of residents with different citizenship statuses is offered as proof of the state's civility and tolerance of a multicultural and diverse population. Under "humanity game" logics, organizers posit tolerance as contrapuntal to claims of authoritarianism.

Yet for this logic to hold, for the state to appear tolerant of others, these noncitizens must remain residents *and simultaneously* outside the nation as other, never to be incorporated. Were they to become citizens, there would be no one for the state to tolerate. That is, to perform receiving the state's generosity, noncitizens must be outside the nation—they must remain other. I term them *contingent citizens*. Ironically, organizers choose these noncitizens to represent the state precisely because they can never be a part of it. Conscripting citizens to perform the nation is not a new strategy, but conscripting noncitizens is, a practice born of accelerating transnational migration for work and the increasing practice of city and national branding projects.

How did these selective exclusions operate, and in what situations were artists deployed contingently? Arts organizers constantly highlighted the duality of residents' citizenship status to emphasize the state's generosity and that communities of different backgrounds reside harmoniously in the country. This strategy emerged as a discursive technique of governance and managing difference. One organizer claimed to "giv[e] opportunities to all emerging artists, curators and writers be it our own *Emiratis, but also foreigners*, to develop their skills, crafts and careers while at the same time advancing our own cultural landscape" (bin Sultan 2016: 11—emphasis here and following is mine). Another proclaimed that the organization "has supported emerging *Emirati artists and UAE-based artists*" (Warehouse 421 2017: 23). In another instance, a curator wrote, "Our residency programme is important for the UAE as it offers artists based here, be they *Emiratis or other nationals*, to develop their practices in new environments and take time to focus on artistic research" (MacGilp 2016: 10).

This consistent marking of coresidents' otherness also emerged in talks and public events: when describing the constituency of the Salama Foundation at Sharjah March Meeting in 2016, one staff member said: "We are investing in the future of the United Arab Emirates by investing in its people. Our definition of the people is both *UAE nationals, and the long-term residents* of the United Arab Emirates. The people living here." By repeatedly underscoring the presence of nonnational artists living and working peaceably alongside citizen artists, organizers portrayed the state as welcoming, cosmopolitan, and tolerant. In the process, however, they simultaneously and consistently reaffirmed nonnationals as outsiders by marking citizenship status.

Overall, state actors rely on art as a key indicator of tolerance—specifically on the presence of noncitizen artists to portray the state as tolerant of resident "others" and difference, and as a place where many kinds of people live together harmoniously although the majority cannot claim citizenship. Prohibiting naturalization creates the necessary conditions for performing tolerance, as it produces others who can be referenced to demonstrate the state's tolerance of their presence. The UAE government website states, "With more than 200 nationalities living peacefully and successfully in the UAE, the UAE society has been an undisputed example of being a tolerant and inclusive country" (UAE Government 2018). Note the distinction made between society and country: the society includes others, which makes the country (read: its citizens and the state) tolerant and inclusive. Multiculturalism discourses in effect served to emphasize differences amongst the UAE population in order to allow the state to appear tolerant, while glossing over frictions (which K. Anthony Appiah [1994] notes is typical of multiculturalism discourses).

The 2017 UAE pavilion occurred amid an ongoing domestic campaign to promote tolerance after years of media scrutiny criticizing the state's labor policies. By 2017, commissioning power had shifted from Dr. Hamdan to the Salama Foundation, run by the wife of the ruler of Abu Dhabi. This shift places the UAE's national pavilion directly under control of members of the royal family—it is, indisputably, an act of national representation controlled by state actors. The 2017 pavilion was entitled *Rock, Paper, Scissors: Positions in Play*. Hammad Nasar, its curator, selected artists Nujoom Alghanem, Dr. Mohamed Yousif, Sara Al Haddad, Vikram Divecha, and Lantian Xie. The catalog does not codify the presentation of artist's biodata; rather, it appears that artists were permitted to self-describe. Sara Al Haddad's bio notes that she is "an artist based in Dubai"; and Lantian Xie's, "an artist from Dubai." Meanwhile Divecha's reads, "Vikram Divecha (born 1977, Beirut) is a Mumbai-bred artist based in Dubai" (UAE Pavilion 2017a). The group is diverse in terms of citizenship status and national affiliation, gender, generation, and preferred media. Nasar wrote in the catalog: "this group of artists also represents the diverse and complex demographics of the UAE, where most of its population does not hold Emirati citizenship. Home is thus only superficially the passports we carry . . . . The potential of play to transform a place into home presents a counterpoint to the mercantile forms of cosmopolitanism that rely on the UAE's, and in particular, Dubai's role as an entrepot" (Nasar 2017a: 16). Nasar's curatorial statement highlights the limited capacity of documents like passports to forge belonging and centers instead on the agency of UAE residents in making the place their home. Nasar also openly acknowledges the population differential in the UAE—and gestures to the Gulf's long history as a crossroads of commercial trade and exchange (Bishara 2017; Bose 2006; Ho 2006).

Pavilion press releases trumpeted the diversity of the participants and promoted the concept of home as a form of affective belonging—without acknowledging that many could not make it their legal home. The press release stated that the exhibition included work "by five artists who are nationals and long-term residents who call the UAE home" (UAE Pavilion 2017c). Note the reference to the status binary as described above, again discursively reiterating a difference between citizens and noncitizens. While it may seem paradoxical for a state that goes to such lengths to prohibit legal assimilation, this nurturing of affective belonging and the feigning of equality in "calling the UAE home" are critical in formulating contingent citizenry. In this instance, state actors want artists to feel a connection to the UAE and to want to be included in it.

Entering the pavilion itself, a visitor would have read wall text that described the "idea of playfulness as an influential strand in artistic practice in the United Arab Emirates" and noted that "play is part of making a place 'home,' and then learning to navigate its rules—seemingly arbitrary, often changing, and always open to chance" (UAE Pavilion 2017b). The exhibi-

Figure 1.2. Catalogs for the 2009, 2011, 2015, and 2017 UAE Pavilions at the Venice Biennale. © Elizabeth Derderian.

tion thus presented play as a means to socialization or perhaps assimilation, even as it itself exhibited tolerant multiculturalism in its diverse array of voices. The oars of Mohamed Yousif's *Al insiyabiyya bil majadeef taht al maa* (the flow of underwater paddles, 1995–2017) hung suspended across from Sara Al Haddad's *can't you see how i feel* (2017): pink weaving colonizing and reinterpreting a column of the building itself. Both installations played with natural materials and space. Walking further into the pavilion, visitors came across Vikram Divecha and Nujoom Alghanem's pieces. A stack of reproduced journals from art circles in the UAE in the 1980s, *Silsilat al Ramad*, were reproduced and positioned in a column adjacent to Divecha's *Degenerative Disarrangement* (2017). At the end of the pavilion, Al Haddad's woven installation *don't you ever leave me alone* (2017) stretched like a screen, casting lattice-like shadows on the floor.

In addition to a taxidermied peacock, *Taxidermy Peacock*, Lantian Xie presented *Half Cup Saffron*: an installation of tea, sugar, and condensed milk in a white cup perched atop a hot plate. Nasar situates the work as follows: "Indian Ocean cosmopolitanism is also explored in *Half Cup Saffron* . . . chai was originally brought to the Gulf from South Asia, and has since seeped across class and ethnic distinctions to become one of the most popular hot drinks in the region" (Nasar 2017b: 232). Xie's work connects the Gulf to South Asia, a common linkage, and reinforces an image of the Gulf as cosmopolitan. Yet it also disrupts easy tropes by focusing on a culinary rather than labor flow—an attempt, perhaps, to reorient the conversation toward how various communities who live in the UAE make it home, to focus on their agency and take it seriously on its own terms.

Alongside the featured artists, Nasar also commissioned a wide variety of writers, curators, and artists to produce programming and texts affiliated with the pavilion, including WTD Magazine, Dr. Uzma Rizvi, Murtaza Vali, Deepak Unnikrishnan, Osman Samiuddin, and Hind Mezaina. The pavilion also commissioned work by longtime Dubai residents Ramin Haerizadeh, Rokni Haerizadeh, and Hesam Rahmanian, and programming collaborations with Sharjah Art Foundation, NYU Abu Dhabi Art Gallery, Alserkal Avenue, Tashkeel, Maraya Art Center, and Warehouse 421—nearly all the active art organizations in the UAE at the time. Nasar's roster represents the diversity of the UAE art scene that I also witnessed while conducting fieldwork and is noteworthy in the breadth of his inclusion. It is also worth adding that Nasar, as the other pavilion curators before him, would have necessarily operated under the constraints of what the commissioner would approve. Creating programming and secondary commissions could be one way to include the contributions of those who may have been prevented from representing the nation in more high-profile roles.

Yet in general, using the presence of a diverse population to claim tolerance is a flawed argument, one that relies on several underlying assumptions. First, claiming that tolerance can be demonstrated by a diverse population living together in the absence of violent uprisings ignores the coercive powers of the Emirati police and surveillance state that rarely result in public physical violence, but are violent nonetheless. Second, this formulation focuses on diversity as if it were the ends itself: it is diversity for diversity's sake, not an acknowledgment, interrogation, or dismantling of the underlying and systemic forms of racism and oppression, particularly neoliberal capitalism, that drive the migration that results in this diversity. Diversity is not equality: UAE society is severely stratified by national affiliation and class, enacted through the *kafala* system, geographic segregation (Elsheshtawy 2008; 2010), and other modes. Diversity is especially not equality when diversity categories are the basis of exclusions and lack of privilege. State actors, aware that the Gulf is often perceived as treating foreigners poorly, strategically draw on the cultural contributions of long-term residents to present the state as cosmopolitan and to benefit from the residents' talents, all while asserting they remain outside the bounds of the nation. They are selected to represent the nation because they can never be a part of it—so long as they remain foreigners, that is, contingent citizens, they can perform receiving the state's generosity at allowing them to reside there. Some accept this. Others, like Eman, eventually leave the UAE and relocate to countries that permit naturalization.

Conclusions

Questions of who can represent the nation, and when, are not limited to the Arab Gulf, of course. After Boon Jong Ho's film *Parasite* received the 2020 Academy Award for Best Picture and Ho gave his thank-you speech in his native tongue, significant Twitter and social media backlash revealed widespread public sentiments correlating national representation and cultural production. That a Korean-language film (even one that asserts the hegemony of English language within its plot!) could be ranked more highly than any English-language American film and receive Hollywood's highest honor rankled a disturbingly large segment of Americans emboldened by the Trump administration to publicize their racist and white nationalist views. Across the Atlantic, at the time of this writing, French artist Zineb Sedira has been selected to represent France in the upcoming Venice Biennale. Her selection, as a French person of Algerian descent, has stirred dissent—anti-Arab sentiment in France has a lengthy history. The controversy over Sedira also reveals how whiteness is so often embedded in projects of representation in Western contexts. In particular, critics have called out her support for Palestinians and criticism of the state of Israel as problematic, showing that for many, a state's selection of an artist can appear to be a tacit endorsement of their personal political stances. These contests reveal the affective power of representation, and how and why we should be paying attention to matters of culture to understand broader political shifts and hierarchies.

As exhibitionary practices shift in response to increasing migration and transnationalism, to navigate issues of financial stability, and to maintain audiences in the twenty-first century, it is critical to pay attention to the social ramifications of these shifts. After all, who are these shows for? Whom do they include? Whom do they exclude? Whose vision do they promulgate? How will states deploy art and culture as forms of soft power in increasingly transnational contexts? The Emirati reliance on noncitizen artists to evidence its tolerance and cosmopolitanism is one potential direction to which the state-culture paradigm can move in such an era of increasing migration, and is perhaps a harbinger of the political—and politicized—role culture can play in the state-building efforts of the future.

Acknowledgments

Thank you to Laura Goffman, Nazlí Özkan, and Antía Mato Bouzas for their invaluable feedback on earlier drafts of this chapter.

Elizabeth Derderian holds a PhD in anthropology from Northwestern University and an MA in Near Eastern and Museum Studies from New York University. Her research focuses on the politics of contemporary art worlds and states' uses of art and culture. She is an assistant professor of anthropology and museum studies at the College of Wooster.

NOTES

1. Eman is a pseudonym, per anthropological disciplinary norms to protect interlocutors from potential retribution.
2. A constituent part of the nation that can never be acknowledged as such, noncitizen resident artists in the UAE are not necessarily ethnic minorities who carry citizenship and come to represent the nation, as in the case of Aboriginal artists in Australia (Myers 2002) or Asian, African American, Latinx, or Native American artists in North American contexts (Davalos 2004; Dávila 1999; Davis Ruffins 1992; Fuller 1992; Kuo Wei Tchen 1992; Lavine 1991; Marzio 1991). Nor are these communities a postcolonial, external other against which the nation defines itself, a phenomenon several studies have analyzed (Lionnet 2004; McLeod 2004; Pieprzak 2010; Salamandra 2004).
3. Accurate statistics can be hard to come by as governments do not release this information, deeming it sensitive. For more on citizenship in the Gulf, see Alshehabi 2021; Alshehabi, Khalaf, and Hanieh 2015; Beaugé 1986; Beaugrand 2017; Diop,

Johnston, and Trung Le 2015; Gardner 2010; Kanna 2011; Le Renard 2019; Longva 1997; Lori 2019; Vora 2013, 2018.
4. This chapter is not intended to debate these charges or refute them—the UAE employs large numbers of exploited workers, mostly from South Asia, and the *kafala* sponsorship system that undergirds this process only deepens that exploitation by obfuscating accountability and thereby slowing any potential amelioration of conditions. Rather than challenging facts or acting as an apologist for the regime, I am interested in ways state actors promulgate a conditional reasoning that ties tolerance to the mere presence of bodies from diverse backgrounds, and wherein artists are an indicator of tolerance and the state's civility (more simply put, the logic runs: if there are diverse populations not in revolt, the regime must be tolerant; if there are artists working there, the regime must be civilized).

    I use the term "citizen artists" in this chapter as shorthand for "artists who currently hold Emirati passports and family cards." Because many of my interlocutors would self-describe as "Emirati," whether they presently hold citizenship or not, I try to avoid using this designation because I do not wish to reaffirm any single definition of what or who counts as Emirati. Instead, I analyze the terms used in publications and attempt to preserve artists' self-identification, in whatever terms they do so.
5. The Louvre Abu Dhabi opened in November 2017, the Guggenheim Abu Dhabi team announced they were "moving forward" again in April 2019 (as of this writing, the construction has yet to begin), and the *Khaleej Times* reported in November 2019 that the Zayed National Museum would open "in a few years." Other elements of the Saadiyat Cultural District, such as the biennial park, the maritime museum, and performing arts center, have largely vanished from public discourse since the 2008 financial crash.
6. The Bastakiya neighborhood derives its name from Bastak, a provincial capital city in Iran and that city's language. Bastaki migrants have long settled on the northern shores of the Arabian Peninsula, especially during the final years of the Qajar dynasty in the early twentieth century (for more on Iranians in Dubai, see Moghadam 2013). The Dubai government rebranded the area as "Al Fahidi," Arabizing the nomenclature, during a neighborhood restoration project beginning in the mid-2000s.
7. In this and other instances, including Eman's example, I observed that non-Emirati Arabs, rather than other demographically significant groups in the UAE population such as people from South Asia or the Philippines, were often selected to represent the nation—a practice that aligns with the Emirati state's growing ethnonationalism (also analyzed by Lori 2019, Kanna 2011, Vora 2013, and others).
8. *Emirati Expressions*, curated by Anne Baldessari, held 20 January–16 April 2009 at Emirates Palace, Abu Dhabi, UAE. Editions of *Emirati Expressions* were also held in 2011 (*Emirati Expressions II*, affiliated with Stephen Shore), 2013 (*Emirati Expressions: Realised*), and 2015 (*Emirati Expressions IV: Conventions of the Arts*).
9. According to a 2009 ARTnews article, Dubai announced plans to build eight museums, including "a universal museum, curated by three German institutions, for

which the content has not yet been defined." As of this writing in spring 2020, no such plans have been realized.
10. "Humanity" is a delightfully unspecific pillar here. In addition, the inclusion of archaeology is interesting. Archaeological excavations in the UAE have uncovered evidence of pre-Islamic civilizations, and in one instance, evidence that a queen ruled parts of what is now the emirate of Sharjah. These excavations have not been featured extensively in the (state-controlled) UAE press, likely because they disrupt the current political regime's version of the region's history.

REFERENCES

Al Owais, Abdul Rahman Bin Mohammed. 2009. "Foreword." In *It's Not Me It's You*, edited by Tirdad Zolghadr, 156. United Arab Emirates Pavilion for the 53rd Venice Biennale: Dubai.

———. 2011. "Foreword: Minister of Culture, Youth, and Community Development." In *Second Time Around: The Pavilion for the UAE at the 54th International Art Exhibition / La Biennale di Venezia*, edited by Vasif Kortun, 5–6. Published by United Arab Emirates Ministry of Culture, Youth and Community Development; Emirates Foundation; TDIC.

Alshehabi, Omar Hesham. 2021. "Policing Labour in Empire: The Modern Origins of the Kafala Sponsorship System in the Gulf Arab States." *British Journal of Middle Eastern Studies* 48, no. 2: 291–310.

Alshehabi, Omar, Abdulhadi Khalaf, and Adam Hanieh, eds. 2015. *Transit States: Labor, Migration and Citizenship in the Gulf*. London: Pluto Press.

Anderson, Benedict. 2006. *Imagined Communities: Reflections on the Origin and Spread of Nationalism*. Rev. ed. New York: Verso.

Appiah, K. Anthony. 1994. "Identity, Authenticity, Survival: Multicultural Societies and Social Reproduction." In *Multiculturalism: Examining the Politics of Recognition*, edited by Charles Taylor, 149–64. Princeton: Princeton University Press.

ARTnews. 2009. "An Oasis in the Desert." ARTnews, 1 February. Accessed 16 March 2020. https://www.artnews.com/art-news/news/an-oasis-in-the-desert-216/.

Beaugé, Gilbert. 1986. "La kafala: un système de gestion transitoire de la main-d'œuvre et du capital dans les pays du Golfe." *Revue européenne des migrations internationales* 2, no. 1: 109–22.

Beaugrand, Claire. 2017. *Stateless in the Gulf: Migration, Nationality and Society in Kuwait*. London: IB Tauris.

Bennett, Tony. 1995. *The Birth of the Museum: History, Theory, Politics*. London: Routledge.

bin Sultan, Shaikh Zayed. 2016. "Foreword." In *Al Haraka Baraka: In Movement There Is Blessing*, 10–12. Sharjah: Maraya Productions.

Bishara, Fahad. 2017. *Sea of Debt: Law and Economic Life in the Western Indian Ocean, 1780–1950*. Cambridge, UK: Cambridge University Press.

Bose, Sugata. 2006. *A Hundred Horizons: The Indian Ocean in the Age of Global Empire*. Cambridge, MA: Harvard University Press.

Bourdieu, Pierre. 1993. *The Field of Cultural Production: Essays on Art and Literature*. New York: Columbia University Press.
Coffey, Mary K. 2012. *How a Revolutionary Art Became Official Culture: Murals, Museums, and the Mexican State*. Durham: Duke University Press.
Coutin, Susan Bibler. 2007. *Nations of Emigrants: Shifting Boundaries of Citizenship in El Salvador and the United States*. Ithaca: Cornell University Press.
Davalos, Karen Mary. 2004. "Exhibiting Mestizaje: The Poetics and Experience of the Mexican Fine Arts Center Museum." In *Museum Studies: An Anthology of Contexts*, 521–40. London: Blackwell.
Dávila, Arlene. 1999. "Latinizing Culture: Art, Museums, and the Politics of U.S. Multicultural Encompassment" *Cultural Anthropology* 14, no. 2: 180–202.
Davis Ruffins, Fath. 1992. "Mythos, Memory, and History: African American Preservation Efforts, 1820–1990." In *Museums and Communities: The Politics of Public Culture*, edited by Ivan Karp, Christine Kreamer, and Steven Lavine, 506–611. Washington, DC: Smithsonian Institution Press.
Derderian, Elizabeth. 2020. "Challenging Terms: Contemporary Art and the Disciplining of Novelty in the UAE." *Museum Anthropology* 43, no. 2 (Nov.): 79–93.
Diop, Abdoulaye, Trevor Johnston, and Kien Trung Le. 2015. "Reform of the Kafala System: A Survey Experiment from Qatar." *Journal of Arabian Studies* 5, no. 2: 116–37.
Duncan, Carol. 1995. *Civilizing Rituals: Inside Public Art Museums*. New York: Routledge.
Elsheshtawy, Yasser. 2008. *The Evolving Arab City: Tradition, Modernity and Urban Development*. Hoboken: Taylor & Francis.
———. 2010. *Dubai: Behind an Urban Spectacle*. New York: Routledge.
Exell, Karen. 2016. *Modernity and the Museum in the Arabian Peninsula*. London: Routledge.
Foster, Robert John. 2002. *Materializing the Nation: Commodities, Consumption, and Media in Papua New Guinea*. Bloomington: Indiana University Press.
Fuller, Nancy. 1992. "The Museum as Vehicle for Community Empowerment: The Ak-Chin Indian Community Ecomuseum Project." In *Museums and Communities: The Politics of Public Culture*, edited by Ivan Karp, Christine Kreamer, and Steven Lavine, 327–65. Washington, DC: Smithsonian Institution Press.
Gardner, Andrew M. 2010. *City of Strangers*. Ithaca: Cornell University Press.
Gomberg-Munoz, Ruth. 2017. *Becoming Legal: Immigration Law and Mixed-Status Families*. New York: Oxford University Press.
Grewal, Zareena. 2014. *Islam Is a Foreign Country: American Muslims and the Global Crisis of Authority*. New York: New York University Press.
Hamdan, Lamees. 2009. "Epilogue." *It's Not You, It's Me*, edited by Tirdad Zolghadr, 140–44. United Arab Emirates Pavilion, Dubai.
———. 2011. "Commissioner: Dr. Lamees Hamdan." In *Second Time Around*, edited by Vasif Kortun, 7–10. United Arab Emirates Pavilion, Dubai.
Ho, Engseng. 2006. *The Graves of Tarim: Genealogy and Mobility across the Indian Ocean*. Berkeley: University of California Press.
Kanna, Ahmed. 2011. *Dubai, the City as Corporation*. Minneapolis: University of Minnesota Press.

Karp, Ivan, ed. 2006. *Museum Frictions: Public Cultures/Global Transformations.* Durham: Duke University Press.

Kortun, Vasif. 2011. *Second Time Around: The Pavilion for the UAE at the 54th International Art Exhibition / La Biennale di Venezia.* Published by United Arab Emirates Ministry of Culture, Youth and Community Development; Emirates Foundation; TDIC.

Krieger, Zvika. 2008. "The Emir of NYU." *New York Magazine*, 10 April. https://nymag.com/news/features/46000/.

Kuo Wei Tchen, John. 1992. "Creating a Dialogic Museum: The Chinatown History Museum Experiment." In *Museums and Communities: The Politics of Public Culture*, edited by Ivan Karp, Christine Kreamer, and Steven Lavine, 285–326. Washington, DC: Smithsonian Institution Press.

Lavine, Steven. 1991. "Art Museums, National Identity, and the Status of Minority Cultures: The Case of Hispanic Art in the United States." In *Exhibiting Cultures: The Poetics and Politics of Museum Display*, edited by Ivan Karp and Stephen Lavine, 79–87. Washington, DC: Smithsonian Institution Press.

Le Renard, Amélie. 2019. *Le privilege occidental: Travail, intimité, et hiérarchies postcoloniales à Dubaï.* Paris: Sciences Po Press.

Levitt, Peggy. 2015. *Artifacts and Allegiances: How Museums Put the Nation and the World on Display.* Berkeley: University of California Press.

Lionnet, Francoise. 2004. "The Mirror and the Tomb: Africa, Museums, and Memory." In *Museum Studies: An Anthology of Contexts*, edited by Bettina Messias Carbonell, 92–103. London: Blackwell.

Lloyd, David, and Paul Thomas. 1998. *Culture and the State.* New York: Routledge.

Longva, Anh Nga. 1997. *Walls Built on Sand: Migration, Exclusion, and Society in Kuwait.* Boulder: Westview Press.

Lori, Noora. 2019. *Offshore Citizens: Permanent Temporary Status in the Gulf.* Cambridge, UK: Cambridge University Press.

Macdonald, Sharon. 2006. *A Companion to Museum Studies.* Malden, MA: Blackwell.

MacGilp, Alexandra. 2016. "Curator's Foreword." In *Maraya in Residence 2015*, 10–11. Sharjah: Maraya Productions.

Marzio, Peter. 1991. "Minorities and Fine-Arts Museums in the United States." In *Exhibiting Cultures: The Poetics and Politics of Museum Display*, 121–27. Washington, DC: Smithsonian Institution Press.

McClellan, Andrew. 1994. *Inventing the Louvre: Art, Politics, and the Origins of the Modern Museum in Eighteenth-Century Paris.* Cambridge, UK: Cambridge University Press.

McLeod, Malcolm. 2004. "Museums Without Collections: Museum Philosophy in West Africa." In *Museum Studies: An Anthology of Contexts*, 455–60. London: Blackwell.

Moghadam, Amin. 2013. "The Other Shore: Iranians in the United Arab Emirates, Between Visibility and Invisibility." In *Cultural Revolution in Iran: Contemporary Popular Culture in the Islamic Republic*, edited by Annabelle Sreberny and Massoumeh Torfeh, 247–65. London: I. B. Tauris.

Myers, Fred R. 2002. *Painting Culture: The Making of an Aboriginal High Art.* Durham: Duke University Press.

Nasar, Hammad. 2017a. "Rock, Paper, Scissors: Notes on Play." In *Rock, Paper, Scissors: Positions in Play*, edited by Hammad Nasar and Michele Robecchi, 10–27. National Pavilion United Arab Emirates la Biennale di Venezia: Pureprint, UK.

Nasar, Hammad. 2017b. "Lantian Xie." In *Rock, Paper, Scissors: Positions in Play*, edited by Nasar and Robecchi, 230–51.

Pieprzak, Katarzyna. 2010. *Imagined Museums: Art and Modernity in Postcolonial Morocco*. Minneapolis: University of Minnesota Press.

Prior, Nick. 2002. *Museums and Modernity: Art Galleries and the Making of Modern Culture*. New York: Berg.

Ross, Andrew, ed. 2015. *The Gulf: High Culture/Hard Labor*. New York: OR Books.

Salamandra, Christa. 2004. *A New Old Damascus: Authenticity and Distinction in Urban Syria*. Bloomington: Indiana University Press.

Sharjah Art Foundation. N.d. "About: Mission and History." Accessed 24 March 2020. http://sharjahart.org/sharjah-art-foundation/about/mission-and-history.

UAE Pavilion. 2015. "Artists: 1980–Today: Exhibitions in the UAE." *UAE Pavilion—2015*. https://nationalpavilionuae.org/art/2015-2/artists/.

———. 2017a. "Artists." *United Arab Emirates National Pavilion—2017*. https://nationalpavilionuae.org/art/2017-2/artists/.

———. 2017b. "Gallery." *United Arab Emirates National Pavilion—2017*. https://nationalpavilionuae.org/art/2017-2/gallery/.

———. 2017c. "Rock, Paper, Scissors: Positions in Play." *United Arab Emirates National Pavilion—2017*. https://nationalpavilionuae.org/art/2017-2/.

United Arab Emirates Government. 2018. "Tolerance in the UAE." *Government.ae* website. Accessed 6 February 2018. https://government.ae/en/about-the-uae/the-uae-government/government-of-future/tolerance-in-the-uae.

Vora, Neha. 2013. *Impossible Citizens: Dubai's Indian Diaspora*. Durham: Duke University Press.

———. 2018. *Teach for Arabia: American Universities, Liberalism, and Transnational Qatar*. Stanford: Stanford University Press.

Vora, Neha, and Natalie Koch. 2015. "Everyday Inclusions: Rethinking Ethnocracy, Kafala, and Belonging in the Arabian Peninsula." *Studies in Ethnicity and Nationalism* 15, no. 3: 540–52.

Warehouse 421. 2017. "Foreword." In *Bayn: The In-Between*, 22–23. Sharjah: Maraya Productions.

Watenpaugh, Heghnar. 2004. *The Image of an Ottoman City: Imperial Architecture and Urban Experience in Aleppo in the 16th and 17th Centuries*. Boston: Brill.

Winegar, Jessica. 2006. *Creative Reckonings: The Politics of Art and Culture in Contemporary Egypt*. Stanford: Stanford University Press.

———. 2008. "The Humanity Game: Art, Islam, and the War on Terror." *Anthropological Quarterly* 81, no. 3: 651–81.

Zolghadr, Tirdad. 2009. "It's Not You, It's Me—Pavilion as Pavilion." In *It's Not Me, It's You*, edited by Tirdad Zolghadr. United Arab Emirates Pavilion for the 53rd Venice Biennale: Dubai.

CHAPTER 2

The Gulf as an Unhomely Home
Reconfiguring Citizenship and Belonging in Diasporic Narratives on Second-Generation Migrants

Nadeen Dakkak

Contrary to common images of the Arab Gulf States as alienating places where migrant experiences are completely determined by overarching structures of exclusion, diasporic migrant communities have long established an entrenched presence with various forms of belonging. As cultural responses to this unacknowledged presence, works of fiction make visible the multiplicity of migrant experiences and subjectivities in the region. Writers can offer counternarratives that contest the tendency to homogenize the Gulf's noncitizen population. This chapter seeks to contribute to the development of a more nuanced understanding of migration to the Gulf through a comparative analysis of second-generation experiences in two novels: Haji Jaber's *Samrawit* (2012) and Deepak Unnikrishnan's *Temporary People* (2017). Both are inspired by their authors' own personal experiences and present different possibilities of belonging among Eritreans in Saudi Arabia and Indians in the United Arab Emirates (UAE), respectively. Jaber was born in Eritrea before moving as a child with his parents to Jeddah because of political conflict during the country's war of independence from Ethiopia. He started his writing career following his first visit to Eritrea as an adult, *Samrawit* being his first novel. Similarly, Unnikrishnan was raised in Abu Dhabi, which was where his parents had migrated to from Kerala in the 1970s, and *Temporary People* is his debut work of fiction. The success and popularity of these two books indicate the urgent need for new representations of Gulf migration and for emergent writing voices among second-generation migrants. I bring them together in this chapter to demonstrate how recent migration literature from the Gulf has been negotiating ideas of cosmopolitanism, belonging, and national imaginaries.

Critiquing the fact that long-term residents in the Gulf do not tend to be approached as diasporic subjects as in other migration contexts, this chapter reads Jaber's and Unnikrishnan's works as manifestations of the hybrid identities and multiple attachments that many migrants and their descendants create in their Gulf homes.[1] I show that the novels do not celebrate possibilities of belonging at the expense of addressing issues of discrimination and exclusion, but rather depict a reality where both kinds of experiences coexist (Vora and Koch 2015). Indeed, the "difference between 'feeling at home' and staking claim to a place as one's own" (Brah 1996: 190) suggests that belonging and exclusion are simultaneous in diasporic experiences, neither negating the possibility of the other. Jaber's and Unnikrishnan's works criticize exclusive citizenship and restrictive migration policies because they prevent characters from staking claims to places in the Gulf. The novels also contest this reality of exclusion by demonstrating the inability of characters to liberate themselves from the effect which their unhomely Gulf homes have had on their identities and tongues, an effect that ultimately makes them diasporic subjects and demands an appreciation of their experiences.[2]

Samrawit takes the form of a memoir that registers its protagonist's personal quest for a clearer understanding of his identity as an Eritrean in Saudi Arabia. It combines elements of nostalgic storytelling with an evident commitment to document the struggles of Eritreans in the diaspora and in Eritrea itself. Omar, a journalist in a Saudi newspaper, like Jaber before he left Saudi Arabia, reflects through first-person narration on his life in a city that does not recognize his belonging to it as well as on the first visit he makes to Eritrea, the country whose passport he holds but which he has never seen. The novel begins during this visit before taking us back to Omar's childhood in Jeddah, the struggles and exclusions that he and his Eritrean friends faced, and how he increasingly began to feel the need to escape this reality and reconnect with his homeland as an adult. In Eritrea, he meets and falls in love with Samrawit, a Lebanese-Eritrean visiting from France who accompanies him on the journey to his home city, but whose inability to marry him because of religious differences epitomizes divisions among Eritreans at home and in the diaspora and the failure of his quest, thus pushing him to return to Jeddah. *Samrawit* is thus a novel of homecoming, an attempt by Omar to find himself in the place that his parents and grandparents constructed in his imagination along the years. Yet despite the fact that the novel is part of Jaber's overall literary "project" of "shedding light on Eritrea," as he states in an interview that discusses his later work, it is at the same time heavily critical of Saudi Arabia's unwillingness to integrate its long-term residents or acknowledge their diasporic identities (Jaber 2019). My reading is centered on how this critique is conveyed through the novel's emphasis on affective relations with place. This aspect even marks the structure of the book. *Samrawit* begins with alternating chapters on Jeddah and Eritrea, and ends with chapters where memories of Jeddah infiltrate Omar's attempt to connect with Eritrea by visiting his ancestral home. His persistent recollection of these memories reflects the integral role that Jeddah has played in shaping his identity.

On the contrary, Unnikrishnan's *Temporary People* is more episodic in the way it is divided into many loosely connected or disconnected narratives set mostly in Abu Dhabi and India. It differs from *Samrawit*'s realist style of autobiographical writing in its combination of realism with surreal and magical elements. Unnikrishnan also addresses themes of temporariness, invisibility, and alienation among the migrant labor force that builds Gulf cities but remains on the margin. Such themes are particularly conveyed through his utilization of the short narrative form, which effectively humanizes marginal figures, despite only having the ability to document snippets of their temporary and invisible lives. *Temporary People* is divided into three books, each consisting of around ten chapters with narratives that vary in their length, form, and storyline. While some are centered on the struggles of migrant workers and the families they left behind, others are more focused on the cultural diversity and everyday intercultural and linguistic exchanges that both shape cosmopolitan spaces in Abu Dhabi and set the parameters of exclusion and belonging. In line with this chapter's interest in fictional works that engage with ideas of belonging and citizenship, I focus in particular on "Moonseepalty" from the second book, a realist narrative centered on the childhood experiences of the second-generation kids, described in another story as the "in-betweens" (20). Like *Samrawit*, the story is written from the adult perspective of one of these kids and combines nostalgia for the days in which Abu Dhabi felt like home with painful recollections of discrimination and exclusion. I argue that "Moonseepalty" contests the logic behind the exclusion of Indian second-generation migrants and asserts their right to claim belonging to Abu Dhabi by virtue of their everyday affective relations with place.

Jaber's and Unnikrishnan's narratives differ in their readership (Arabic versus English) and the literary traditions within which they can be situated, a topic that falls beyond the scope of this chapter. However, I bring them together because they both make vivid the role of lived experience and the everyday in shaping the identity of migrants and their feelings of belonging to the places they inhabit. My analysis of the claims they stake to the Gulf draws on phenomenological perspectives and urban research that privilege quotidian experience in the understanding of human relationship to place, namely human geographer Yi-Fu Tuan's work on topophilia (1990) and his conceptualization of space and place (2003), and Yasser Elsheshtawy's research on Gulf cities (2019). I argue that literary works that assert the role of lived experience as a legitimate form of belonging constitute a major step in the direction of contesting the rigid conceptualizations of citizenship that are used to justify exclusion.

At the same time, belonging and exclusion occur simultaneously within one space and as part of a single individual's own relationship with the Gulf. Accordingly, both narratives reveal the process of nurturing feelings of attachment through everyday experience to be fraught with exclusionary and alienating forces that inevitably turn the Gulf into an unhomely home. Gulf spaces are shaped by hierarchical power relations that are dependent on multiple factors, such as ethnicity, nationality, class, religion, and gender. The Indian second-generation characters in Unnikrishnan's "Moonseepalty" are especially vulnerable to the effect that such exclusionary forces have on their sense of identity and their relationship to the places they identify as home. My analysis focuses in particular on the role of language in facilitating exclusion, for it is one of the primary means by which power relations between different ethnicities and nationalities in the story become enacted on the ground. By contrast, fluency in the local dialect facilitates the inclusion of Omar in *Samrawit* where, alongside everyday experience, cultural and linguistic assimilation enables Eritrean characters to stake claims to Jeddah. I compare the different kinds of belonging that are manifest in these Arab and non-Arab narratives in order to challenge how "legitimate" forms of belonging and feelings of "deservingness" are often associated with assimilation at the expense of everyday experience (Akinci 2020: 2314), thus creating further exclusion through hierarchies among migrants. Omar's access to the local culture through language enables him to perform a kind of belonging to Jeddah that differs from the one performed in Unnikrishnan's story. However, my analysis demonstrates the legitimacy of the claims that non-Arab second-generation characters stake to Abu Dhabi. In countries where integration is hindered through structural exclusion and an enforced temporariness, lived experience and everyday place-making are at the center of how belonging is defined in the two narratives.

Gulf Migrants as Diasporic Subjects

The experiences of migrants in the Gulf do not tend to be understood as similar to those of diasporic subjects in other contexts. They are not seen as facing similar emotional challenges and dilemmas to those often associated with migrant communities in more common immigration countries, particularly in the West. Diasporic subjects have been theorized as experiencing "hybrid forms of identity" because of the impossibility of positioning themselves or of feeling completely at home in one place (Braziel and Mannur 2003: 5). The fact that neither migrants nor their descendants become naturalized or acquire permanent residency in the Gulf is a primary reason behind the lack of such an approach. Much of the scholarship on Gulf migration has also tended to focus on low-paid workers, the challenges they face, and the politics of exclusion in Gulf societies. Recent studies have argued for the need to go beyond such an approach that produces migrants as deprived of agency in the face of policies that are too often seen as determining all aspects of life in the Gulf. A number of studies have argued for the necessity of examining possibilities of inclusion and belonging (Ahmad 2012; Vora 2013; Vora and Koch 2015), and others have attempted to examine the experiences of middle- and upper-class migrants as well as the second generation (Ali 2011; Vora 2013; Wang 2015; Hosoda 2016; Shah 2017; Akinci 2020). Yet there is still very little done to explore the lives of these individuals and the impact of their long-term presence on both the Gulf and their identities.

My contention in this chapter is that even if concepts such as diaspora and transnationalism are employed when approaching migrant experiences, especially the second generation (Ali 2011; Vora 2013), rarely do they appear in studies that focus on Arab migrants in particular. Scholarship on the experiences of Arab migrants in the Gulf is scarce, despite decades of long-term residence (Babar 2017; Shah 2017; Akinci 2020). Their identities, perception of home, and the attachments they have created in the region along the years are largely unexamined. In addition to close geographical proximity, shared aspects of language, culture, and religion play a vital role in giving Arab migrants a sense of affinity and familiarity with the Gulf.[3] This familiarity sets the region apart from other non-Arab immigrant destinations and makes the experiences of Arab migrants different from those of non-Arab migrants. However, I show in the final section of this chapter that cultural affinity does not mean that Arab migrants in the Gulf do not face the challenges and dilemmas encountered by diasporic subjects elsewhere, or by their non-Arab counterparts in the same countries. While their presence could be met with a higher degree of acknowledgment because of their ability to assimilate, this acknowledgment does not take the form of legal inclusion or completely protect them from experiencing social exclusion.

My argument that long-term Arab and non-Arab residents ought to be considered diasporic is not unaware of the limitations of such an understanding in the context of the Gulf. Avtar Brah defines "diasporic journeys" to be "essentially about settling down, about putting roots 'elsewhere'" (1996: 179). Central to its meaning is the process of settlement that "involve[s] the re-articulation of multiple locations, temporalities and identifications in the effort to create new terrains of belonging within the place of migration" (Fortier 2010: 1). These definitions suggest that the semipermanent migrants of the Gulf cannot be considered diasporic, since inflexible policies mean that the majority would continue to perceive themselves as temporary, despite their long-term residence, and may not necessarily make the effort to create "new terrains of belonging." Nonetheless, the ambiguity of the term "diaspora" makes it inclusive of different kinds of dislocations in contemporary times (Braziel and Mannur 2003: 4). Indeed, the concept is no longer restricted to traditional immigrant communities, which typically undergo processes of assimilation and whose relationship to the homeland is imbued with feelings of nostalgia and dreams of an impossible return.

Diaspora has become broader in the age of globalization, with technological advances in travel and communication enabling even diasporic communities in Western immigration states to maintain stronger connections with the homeland (Tölölyan 1996: 20). These connections may even lead to a lesser degree of assimilation, especially in host states that endorse a multicultural model of social integration (Tölölyan 1996: 20-21). The experiences of diasporic subjects in the Gulf are accordingly not very different from other contexts, especially at a time when "multiple belonging" with all its "paradoxes" is "a condition that non-diasporan nationals also face in the transnational era" (Tölölyan 1996: 8). Even if they do not have access to legal rights and even if social integration is discouraged in the Gulf States, acculturation and other kinds of belonging do inevitably take place. As a result, migrants in these states face similar psychological and emotional dilemmas that contribute to the shaping of their identities and affective relations with place in both home and host countries. Their experiences exhibit what Jumana Bayeh calls in her work on Lebanese diasporic literature a "diasporic aesthetic or sensibility" that is characterized by ambiguity, loss, and double consciousness (2014: 8). Bayeh's understanding of this sensibility pushes for a loosened definition of diaspora that appreciates the links between different kinds of dislocation, as experienced by immigrants, refugees, migrant workers, and other displaced subjects (2014: 8-9).

According to Brah, diasporas in the plural refer to "places of long-term, if not permanent community formations, even if some households or members move on elsewhere" (1996: 190). We can thus understand diaspora as a kind of space that emerges from the settlement of communities in a new geographical place, and that it is not fixed but constantly changing. There is, for example, a long-term Eritrean presence in Jeddah and a long-term

Indian presence in Abu Dhabi even if the communities that have produced this presence are in a state of flux because of the continuous movement of Eritreans and Indians in and out of these cities. One way of understanding this presence is by considering the role of permanently temporary migrant communities in shaping the urban spaces they inhabit (Collins 2011: 322). After all, this "permanent temporariness" does not only refer to the temporary status of migrants who can never settle down in the host country, but "the reference to permanence also highlights the continual presence of temporary populations in particular places even as individuals arrive and depart and the need to pay attention to their involvement in various aspects of everyday life" (Collins 2011: 322). The everyday contributions of migrants to the places they build and inhabit suggest that the impact of their presence on the Gulf is not fleeting but long term, even if their own status is temporary. Furthermore, the connections that migrants establish in the Gulf can coexist with a continued sense of belonging to their home country, as we see in the novels. For many migrants in the Gulf, an extended period of migration leads to the formation of a diasporic subjectivity that enables them to nurture feelings of attachment to the places they inhabit alongside their own national and cultural affiliations.

Diaspora becomes then a useful tool for rethinking the affective relationship between individuals and the different nation-states to which they are connected, because it makes it possible to appreciate the psychological and emotional implications of different expressions of belonging without economic determinism (Braziel and Mannur 2003: 7; Vora 2013: 27). Although migrants in the Gulf are not typically expected to have diasporic identities because of their exclusion from citizenship or permanent residency, their experiences can be described as diasporic. Employing diaspora in the context of the Gulf questions the legal, scholarly, and public definitions of this concept as well as the tendency to marginalize experiences of "South-South migration" (Vora 2013: 23). In other words, in order to fully appreciate the kinds of belonging that migrants perform and the attachments they create in the Gulf, the concept of diaspora itself needs to be reevaluated. An expanded and more inclusive understanding of diaspora allows it to become a tool for approaching the experiences of subjects in countries that do not adopt the same conceptions of citizenship that are common in Western countries and that dominate studies on migration.

I want to argue in my reading of Jaber's and Unnikrishnan's works that fiction can critically counter the tendency to marginalize experiences of migrant belonging in the Gulf by depicting spaces that are shaped by diasporic subjects. Such spaces are in their turn integral for shaping the identity of their migrant inhabitants, for they are constantly evoked and reconstructed in nostalgic recollections by characters who become separated from their

Gulf homes, spatially or temporally. In Jaber's *Samrawit*, Omar cannot recall memories of Jeddah and the Al-Nuzlah neighborhood where he grew up without evoking the presence of many Eritreans who have contributed to shaping the place and were in turn shaped by it (87).[4] Al-Nuzlah itself has an Eritrean feel to it, "as if it's a miniature copy of that absent place" (13). It is a neighborhood marked by the feelings of *ghurba*, or estrangement, that have accompanied aging parents along the years and that constantly infiltrate the days of the second generation, reminding them of the ancestral country that their parents have left behind (13).[5] A combination of estrangement and belonging makes the Eritrean community's presence in Jeddah diasporic par excellence, and endows its members with a diasporic subjectivity that is characterized by multiple affective relations with different places, notwithstanding their temporary status and their precariousness in the face of exclusion.

Temporary People's depiction of the diasporic Indian presence in the UAE also makes visible the traces migrants leave in the Gulf. In "Akbaar: Exodus," a chapter in the form of a news column documenting the "mandatory retirement" and departure of thousands of South Asians from the Emirates, a deep-rooted sense of belonging is established through decades of residence in Hamdan Street in Abu Dhabi (83). Vasudevan and his wife Devi are among the returnees after almost thirty-eight years. As they sit quietly in the airport, "[t]hey smell like their apartment. Their empty apartment smells like them. Old" (86). The couple's entrenched presence in the country is mediated through their intimate relationship with the place they inhabit. Each of them has a tangible and long-lasting effect on the other, their identities entirely shaped and reshaped through years of contact. However, their own effect on the place is on the verge of disappearance, for we are told that in July, "their building, one of the oldest on Hamdan Street, decrepit like a smoker's lungs, will be razed" (86). The fragility of the roots they establish, or indeed their own precarity, reflects the fragility of place in a country constantly reconstructing itself—a "crane country," as the narrator of "Moonseepalty" describes it (143). Seen as temporary, these diasporic communities and the effect their presence has had on the Gulf are deliberately erased, leaving no physical traces except in the memories of those who can remember and document. The relationship between such unappreciated forms of belonging and the kind of urban modernization adopted by Gulf cities is a point to which I return by reference to Elsheshtawy's work (2019) on the notion of transience and its connection to the invisibility of migrants. Yet I wish to emphasize here the way in which both Jaber and Unnikrishnan prioritize intimate connections between migrants and inhabited physical place in their attempt to document and make visible the traces they leave behind. As a result, this process of placemaking through everyday lived experience forms the base for understanding how migrants can rightfully stake claims to the Gulf.

Lived Experience as a Form of Belonging in the Gulf

Omar in *Samrawit* begins his narrative by stating the sorrowful, albeit taken-for-granted, fact that he is neither completely Saudi nor completely Eritrean (11). He did not grow up to be completely Eritrean because he was always too preoccupied by following the games of Al-Ahli, listening to the music of Abadi, and watching the last episode of *Laylat Hurub*, all of which are cultural references signifying the extent to which his existence is entrenched in the culture of Saudi Arabia (12). Omar reflects on how integral Jeddah has been to the shaping of his character and his entire existence during the self-discovery trip he makes to Eritrea with the hope of reconnecting with his family's roots. Jeddah, he writes, "was visible in my language, the tone of my voice, and even my smile" (85). His love for the city can be described as topophilic, a term that Tuan defines "broadly to include all of the human being's affective ties with the environment" (1990: 93). Topophilia, or "the human love of place" (1990: 92), is dependent on both the "role of culture in conditioning people's environmental perception and values" and on "the effect of the physical setting on perception, attitudes and world view" (1990: 75). The constant changes that both culture and the environment undergo result in an ever-changing relationship between humans and places, for neither of them has a fixed identity. Like any other place, Jeddah is experienced differently by individuals at certain historical moments. That it becomes identified as home by Omar and other characters suggests the extent to which their personal daily experiences, comprising elements from Jeddah's own cultural milieu and their own practices, are integral to shaping both the identity of the city and their own identities as its inhabitants. Omar's topophilic relationship with Jeddah challenges the dominant perception of migrants as temporary outsiders who do not establish forms of belonging in the Gulf.

The role of lived experience in creating feelings of belonging is also evident in the novel's emphasis on the emotional significance of Al-Nuzlah in the imaginary of Eritreans, as well as other national groups in Jeddah. Omar writes that for many Eritreans from the second generation, Al-Nuzlah is the only home they have known along the years; its streets harbor their friendships and childhood memories (86). Until he starts questioning his identity and gradually begins to seek refuge in his Eritrean roots, Al-Nuzlah is his immediate answer when asked about where he is from, for it is the place that reflects his sense of self (85). Omar also writes that Al-Nuzlah was a neighborhood where the differences between Saudis and non-Saudis could melt, and where his Saudi friend Riyad constantly flaunted his knowledge of the Eritrean vocabulary he had learned (86). In his adult years, his bedouin friend and coworker at the newspaper, Adel, is another figure who, Omar says, is exactly "like us," meaning the Eritreans of Jeddah, and whose love for Al-Nuzlah and its ethnic restaurants makes Omar nostalgic for days in which the differences between Saudis and the "foreign" migrants did not seem that visible (112-14). The novel's depiction of the social relations and cultural exchanges that connect Saudis and non-Saudis challenges the perception of "the citizen/noncitizen binary" as necessarily determining the way a Gulf city such as Jeddah is experienced (Vora and Koch 2015: 544). The rich image Jaber paints of the city can even be read as a tribute to the people who have turned it into an accommodating place, notwithstanding the official laws that create inherent inequalities among different individuals and communities.

Samrawit represents Jeddah as a "diaspora space" that "is 'inhabited,' not only by those who have migrated and their descendants, but equally by those who are constructed and represented as indigenous" (Brah 1996: 205). "Diaspora space" is a term Brah uses to contest the categories of "inclusion" and "exclusion" by which the relationship between the "self" and the "other" and the status of "insider" and "outsider" are shaped (1996: 205). That *"the native is as much a diasporan as the diasporan is the native"* in the diaspora space reveals the necessity of recognizing the effective presence of migrants (1996: 205—emphasis in original). By representing the entirety of Jeddah as a "diaspora space" shared by migrants and locals alike, *Samrawit* makes it impossible to draw the boundaries between what is inside and what is outside, what is native and what is foreign. Jaber accordingly contests national imaginaries and narratives of authentic identity that form the basis for social exclusion and discrimination against the migrant "other."

Jeddah is indeed known for its rich cultural diversity and its openness, characteristics that make Omar proclaim that "Jeddah is enough" when asked about life in Saudi Arabia (48).[6] Yet from the specific perspective of Eritreans, Jeddah is not only a place that gave them refuge after they left war-torn Eritrea. "This city was not the home of others who graciously did us the favor of allowing us to stay in its margins. Rather, we were its people who resembled it in every way" (85). *Samrawit* thus stakes claim to the places that Eritreans identify as home, making them ultimate "diaspora spaces" where the boundaries between inside and outside collapse. In this way, the novel challenges restrictive categories of belonging through origins and national identity. Omar's feelings of belonging are rooted in lived experience and performed encounters with specific geographical places rather than being derived from an abstract idea of national belonging. He explains that he has fallen in love not with the Kingdom of Saudi Arabia but with Jeddah in particular (12). He then corrects himself by saying that even Jeddah was not completely his own, for it is only Al-Nuzlah that has marked the extent of his love and power over the place (13). The role of the everyday manifests itself in the construction of the meaning of home and in the kind of belonging that Omar and others establish in the places they inhabit.

The fact that Jaber and Unnikrishnan place emphasis on experience does not mean that migrants in general cannot nurture forms of belonging in their Gulf host countries at the level of national identification. Even if they do not want, or are unable, to publicly identify themselves as "Saudi" or "Emirati," it is common among many migrants to express support and allegiance to the rulers and their nationalist visions, or to participate in symbolic national celebrations, both of which could be encouraged by the public discourse that expects migrants to express their gratitude and loyalty to the country that has been generous enough to host them (Koch 2016).[7] This chapter chooses to examine literary depictions of forms of attachment that do not exercise such nationalist tropes precisely because they assert the role of experience in giving migrants the right to stake claims to the places they inhabit. Lived experience and the everyday challenge official or nationalist conceptualizations of citizenship and belonging. As I show in the next section on assimilation, uncritical expressions of nationalist sentiments can be problematic in the way they affirm essentialist definitions of what it means to claim legitimate belonging in the Gulf.

In *Temporary People*, belonging is similarly depicted as grounded in specific geographical locales where it ensues from everyday lived experience rather than from any kind of national identification. In "Moonseepalty," the story of a group of Indian teens for whom Fridays in their Abu Dhabi neighborhood consist of playing football in the empty parking lot of the Municipality building, home is not the UAE, nor even the Emirate itself. It is the more tangible places that shape daily experiences and memories, places that the narrator evokes in his attempt to paint a picture of what belonging meant for him in his childhood years: "I can't recall this gone world without the cranes, without my parents or the old haunts. I then remember football, where I learned the game best, the school grounds, how my body and mind needed the ball so much, and how I now miss it. I then think of Moonseepalty, where football was a religion" (143). As a physical and a collective social activity that is grounded in place, football allows these teens to establish an intimate connection with the spaces they inhabit and to turn them into emotionally valuable places (Tuan 2003: 6). Such intimate experiences inform their sense of identity and give them the right to stake claims to the places they inhabit without the need to be legitimized by any form of national belonging that takes the UAE's history or culture as its base. In his critique of patriotism, Tuan argues that "a strong attachment to the homeland . . . can form without the memory of heroic battles won and lost, and without the bond of fear or of superiority vis-à-vis other people. Attachment of a deep though subconscious sort may come simply with familiarity and ease, with the assurance of nurture and security, with the memory of sounds and smells, of communal activities and homely pleasures accumulated over time" (2003: 159).

Experience and everyday spatial and social encounters allow individuals to form a deep sense of belonging to place, even if they are not seen to belong to it in countries where nationality law adopts the principle of *jus sanguinis*, and even if both the place they experience and their own status are temporary.[8] From the beginning of their establishment as modern nation-states, "the territorial referent has never been the main criterion for inclusion or exclusion from citizenship" in the Gulf States, which instead prefer "ethnocultural markers of identity, irrespective of the place of residence" (Beaugrand 2018: 9). The fact that migrants arrive to the Gulf with preexisting national affiliations gives them no sense of entitlement over their rights as long-term residents and even leads them to internalize the logic of discrimination and exclusive citizenship (Beaugrand 2018: 25, 139). Yet, as Jaber's and Unnikrishnan's novels reveal, affective human relationships with place do not have to conform to the policies that dictate who has the right to belong and who is to remain ultimately excluded.

Recent scholarship has rightly highlighted the need to look at the urban practices of migrants in order to appreciate their experiences of belonging in the Gulf. In his documentation of instances of "informality" in which the built environment in Gulf cities is "appropriated" in accordance with its inhabitants' needs, Elsheshtawy argues that migrants do create a place that "offers a sense of comfort" despite temporariness, so that "for a fleeting moment some permanence takes hold" (2019: 6). Personalizing space and performing practices and behaviors that do not conform to the design of modern urban spaces in Gulf cities can be understood as an assertion of authority over place. "By imbuing these sites with what they like to do, rather than what is expected of them, [migrants] ascertain a presence, and thus a form of longevity. It is a way to make a space homely, rather than being unhomely" (2019: 46). Elsheshtawy's emphasis on the role of "everyday, ordinary urbanity" in turning the Gulf into a homely place for a large section of its migrant population corresponds to the way in which both Jaber and Unnikrishnan depict belonging as naturally formed through the second generation's experience of inhabiting place (2019: 69). The two narratives additionally demonstrate how such an approach makes it possible to destabilize and reconfigure the conceptualization of citizenship that does not allow for nuanced understandings of belonging. One other way of understanding the kind of belonging manifest in the narratives is through the concept of "urban citizenship," which Vora employs in her research on Dubai's Indian diaspora. Following Michel de Certeau, she examines how "legal categories of citizenship may not map onto forms of lived urban citizenship that take place at the scale of everyday life" (2013: 40).

However, in the same way in which placemaking occurs in response to the experience of growing up or living in places that become infused with memories, *Samrawit* and "Moonseepalty" suggest that feelings of belonging are simultaneously fragile. Attachment is subject to change as a result of the changing nature of the places and the experiences from which it is derived. When the aspects that shape the narrator's experience of belonging in "Moonseepalty" cease to exist, the place no longer feels the same, even if the temporary rootedness it had granted to the second generation remains ingrained in the memory of the narrator in his adult years. "I don't know what home looks like anymore," he says. "Parents have died and I've stopped playing since I tore my ACL" (142). Home is fragile not only because it is rooted in a place that is constantly changing, as we have seen in "Akbaar: Exodus," but also because it is shaped through daily experiences and interactions that are in themselves fragile in the face of transience. While this fragility of home is arguably a universal condition that is not specific to cities that, like Abu Dhabi, "have embraced transience as their *raison d'être*," it is especially in such spaces that feelings of belonging become difficult to maintain (Elsheshtawy 2019: 10).

Elsheshtawy argues in his critique of urban modernization in the Gulf that the aim of such temporary cities is indeed "to minimize physical attachment to place and to discourage setting down roots" (2019: 12). However, rather than focus on the effect of transient urbanization on the affective relationship between characters and place, I show how both Unnikrishnan and Jaber represent the fragility of home as a direct result of the unequal power relations that are experienced by diasporic subjects in the same places they identify as home. In other words, the process of nurturing feelings of attachment through everyday experience is simultaneously fraught with exclusionary forces that constantly turn homely places into unhomely and alienating spaces. By presenting narratives in which the belonging of second-generation migrants remains unacknowledged and fragile in the face of exclusion, the writers question the discourse that marginalizes the role of experience in building affective relationships with place in favor of a more rigid understanding of belonging as dependent on ethnocultural origins and nationalist sentiments.

Everyday Exclusions and Inclusions

In "Moonseepalty," the claims that the Indian narrator and his friends stake to the ground where they play football are subject to power relations dependent on the social hierarchy that privileges the voices of some neighborhood residents but not others. Football—a significant part of Omar's childhood in *Samrawit* as well—becomes a means of asserting a group's authority over place and its sense of ownership and legitimate belonging. On Fridays, by evening time, the narrator says, "the parking lot would have transformed into dozens of makeshift playgrounds, swaths of asphalt claimed by gangs of boys speaking multiple tongues. For a few hours we were all temporary inhabitants of Moonseepalty, an ephemeral, football-mad province of many complex cultural parts powered by nationality or race, where all of us pretended to be footballing warlords, ruling with our feet, manically protecting our tarred kingdoms" (144).

The ephemerality of Moonseepalty is not unlike the transient nature of Abu Dhabi itself and other Gulf cities where temporariness characterizes both the status of migrants and the constantly changing urban environment. This small transient space is represented as strictly hierarchical, with ethnicity, nationality, class, and other categories shaping the relations between different native and migrant communities, often determining their access to advantages and their varying levels of exclusion or inclusion. When the patrolling police comes to break up the games, it is the Arabs who get to continue playing, unlike the narrator and his friends whose vulnerability vis-à-vis state authority, as well as the "Arabee boys" (146) who are too intimidating to play against, becomes even more accentuated when they play cricket, a game "which made your nationality glow in the dark" (144).[9] It is not simply the citizen/noncitizen binary that shapes the way Abu Dhabi is experienced here. The hierarchy between Arabs and non-Arabs produces further exclusion and redefines the meaning of belonging by endowing some migrants with more legitimate claims to place. The contestations of power that occur in the parking lot of the municipality reflect how identity, belonging, and exclusion are negotiated by migrants at the scale of everyday encounters with place and people.

The importance of the hierarchy between Arab and non-Arab migrants is revealed in the degree to which their presence and claims to belonging are either prioritized or marginalized.[10] The story emphasizes the role of language as one of the primary means by which power relations between different ethnicities and nationalities become enacted on the ground. Lack of fluency in the local Arabic heightens the marginality of the Indian characters and makes them more vulnerable to discrimination and exclusion in the same space in which their feelings of belonging and their memories of Abu Dhabi are formed.[11] In one such instance, when they are forced to cease playing and hide from the police, one Arab kid walks "boldly towards the waiting patrol car, like his father owned the world" (146). He simply resumes playing with the rest of his gang after he "shook hands, exchanged pleasantries, and negotiated in clipped Arabic" with the officers (146). Language grants power to the Arab kid who is able to negotiate with authority and deprives the narrator and his friends of the ability to do the same, even if both of them are ultimately subjected to similar exclusionary policies and perceived as temporary outsiders in a country they can never legally belong to. The experiences of non-Arabic speaking migrants in the Gulf differ from those of Arab migrants, who mostly face fewer challenges because of linguistic, cultural, religious, and even ideological affinities (Babar 2017; Akinci 2020). Even if lived experience through performed encounters with specific geographical places enables both the Indian and the Arab kids to establish a rooted sense of belonging that makes them feel entitled to play football in the same place, they do not receive similar treatment, nor is their presence as outsiders perceived in the same way. The kind of attachment the narrator and his friends have to the place is accordingly affected by this knowledge, with their sense of identity and masculinity becoming a reflection of the power relations in which they are involved. As the narrator writes, "We didn't like Arabees but we rarely told them that. We wanted to talk back, we wanted to fight, we wanted tungsten gonads. We wanted all that but we didn't want to get into trouble" (152).

The additional level of marginalization to which the Indian teens are subjected is especially evident in how language becomes a tool of exclusion and discrimination; but in this case, at the hands of authority itself. At the center of the story is an incident of linguistic and physical violence that epitomizes unequal power relations in Moonseepalty. When Tits, one of the Indian kids, frantically asks the police to run after two Somali boys who stole his bike, he faces sarcasm and hostile demands to speak in Arabic (149). The issue of his stolen bike is completely unacknowledged and his appeal for the help of the police officer turns into a situation in which his own right to be present in the country becomes questionable through the officer's persistent demand for Tits to show his identity card (148-49). He decides to take revenge on the gang of boys who stole his bike, but he is betrayed by the friends who encouraged him to start the fight and is severely injured as a result. Tits eventually leaves the school and is never seen again until the narrator meets him by coincidence years later, recognizes the mutilation that was caused by his injury, and faces his revenge for having betrayed Tits in the fight. It is not just miscommunication that denies Tits the assistance that could have returned his bike and prevented the situation from escalating into violence. The linguistic exchange that occurs between him and the police essentially deprives him of agency and affirms his marginality in a country that does not recognize his presence. This exchange brings Tits, but also the friends who were too afraid to stand by his side, face-to-face with the reality of their exclusion in the place to which they feel most connected. Any form of belonging that these second-generation migrants nurture in the city they identify as home is challenged and destabilized by such daily alienating encounters. Tits' revenge on the narrator after all these years is not a response to his betrayal per se, but an expression of anger and frustration at the conditions of marginalization in a city that deprived him and his friends of the ability to fight.

The discrimination experienced by the Indian second-generation migrant characters in "Moonseepalty" may suggest that assimilation would potentially pave the way for more positive experiences of belonging where migrants are less vulnerable to daily encounters with social exclusion. In migration studies, "assimilation" is generally understood as "[t]he process by which immigrants become similar to natives—leading to the reduction (or possibly the disappearance) of ethnic difference between them" (Bartram, Poros, and Monforte 2014: 15). Assimilation, in this sense, does not occur in the context of the Gulf because the naturalization of migrants is an exception, and this group is generally a majority vis-à-vis a dominant native minority. Moreover, exclusionary policies deliberately hinder possibilities of integration, creating boundaries between what is perceived as a homogeneous local society and culture with specific ethnocultural origins, and the different cultures embodied by different migrant communities. Therefore, assimilation in this chapter refers to some migrants' adoption of the local dialect or other cultural practices in a way that enables them to pass as Gulf locals, to receive the privileged treatment usually reserved for citizens, or to avoid direct instances of exclusion or discrimination. This is a selective kind of assimilation because it does not entail giving up one's original language/dialect or culture, hence the formation of multiple identifications and layers of belonging as part of the migrant's diasporic subjectivity.

Omar's experience in *Samrawit* highlights how linguistic, cultural, and even religious assimilation enables him and other Eritreans to grow an entrenched presence in Jeddah and to stake claims to its distinctive dialect and culture. His authentic Jeddah dialect allows him to pass as a Saudi on many occasions and to put Saudis themselves in embarrassing situations when they share with him their negative attitude toward migrants without being aware of his origins (36–37). Moreover, cultural and religious affinities allow him and many other Eritreans to feel "Saudi" alongside their Eritrean sense of identity, further facilitating their inclusion (13). In this sense, the experience of Arab or Arabic-speaking migrants becomes easier because their linguistic and cultural affinities make them less vulnerable to exclusion at the scale of everyday encounters with place and people, even if their citizenship status ultimately makes them outsiders. Assimilation in the Gulf can be performed deliberately in order to acquire a position of power or be admitted into exclusive social circles (Akinci 2020: 2318–20). However, in the case of Omar and other Eritreans in *Samrawit*, assimilation happens inevitably as part of the intercultural exchanges or the "acculturation" that occurs in many Gulf spaces (see Bartram, Poros, and Monforte 2014: 8). Therefore, it is necessary here to acknowledge the many differences between Jeddah and Abu Dhabi (in terms of demographics, urban organization, etc.) that could make the former a space where assimilation is more likely to occur for migrants as a consequence of growing up in a multicultural social milieu that accommodates both Saudis and non-Saudis.[12]

Omar's ability to form a Saudi identity and to claim Saudi dialect as his own challenges both the perception of migrants as outsiders and the nationalist rhetoric that represents Saudi identity as the exclusive possession of citizens. Recent ethnographic research on the second generation, especially in the UAE, also acknowledges forms of assimilation among noncitizens as contestations of the exclusivity of national identity, arguing for the need to explore placemaking not only through urban belonging, but also as a "state-based affinity" (Vora and Koch 2015: 544). Akinci, for example, argues that performances of "Emiratiness" among some second-generation Arab migrants have "the potential to blur the boundaries between migrants and citizens and complicate the official and popular equation of citizenship (as legal membership) to national identity (cultural belonging) in the Emirates" (2020: 2321). Vora's Indian interlocutors, however, disavow belonging to the UAE and see themselves as ultimately Indian. "Urban citizenship," rather than "nationalist sentiment toward the UAE," is what defines their feelings of belonging to Dubai, a situation that Vora understands as an indication of the systematic "production of parochialized South Asian identities" among youth in the diaspora (2013: 154). Like Akinci, she rightly argues that this disavowal of belonging among many migrants reinforces state logic of exclusion, suggesting the necessity of acknowledging expressions of national belonging that destabilize ethnocultural conceptualizations of citizenship.

At the same time, assimilation can reproduce essentialist understandings of belonging as coupled with national identity and citizenship when it is understood as the only means of endowing migrants with the right to stake legitimate claims to the Gulf. Through the assertion of lived experience and the prioritization of urban belonging over assimilation as the basis of such claims, both "Moonseepalty" and *Samrawit* redefine the meaning of belonging and citizenship and push for the need to reconfigure these concepts and how they are practiced in the Gulf. As we have seen, Unnikrishnan reveals the inherent injustice in the hierarchy between migrants who should have equal claims over the places they inhabit. His story challenges the way in which ethnic and linguistic affinities are associated with feelings of entitlement over place by documenting the entrenched presence of second-generation Indian migrants. These characters have strong feelings of urban belonging to Abu Dhabi despite the fact that they do not possess Arab ethnocultural markers of identity. They lack the Arab and Islamic affinities that give many long-term Arab residents feelings of "deservingness" in the Gulf (Akinci 2020: 2314). In other words, Unnikrishnan's writing destabilizes deterritorialized conceptions of citizenship by asserting the primary role of territory and the affective relationship between individuals and place in shaping belonging and identity (Beaugrand 2018).

Samrawit takes this critique further by showing how assimilation provides an illusory and temporary feeling of belonging to the Eritrean protagonist who experiences social exclusion and inclusion simultaneously. During a phone interview with an academic who describes migrants in derogatory terms, Omar confesses his Eritrean origins. The academic offers a confused and apologetic response in which he associates fluency in the local dialect with the right to "Saudiness" and elevates Omar's status above that of other migrants (37). "Mashallah, you speak authentic Jeddawi," he says. "Why haven't you applied for the nationality then? But that's not what I meant. You are the son of this country. I meant the foreigners, while you are the son of this country" (37). Ironically, the word "foreigners" or *ajanib* is also generally used to refer to migrants who, like Omar, are born and raised in the Gulf and who may or may not necessarily speak the local dialect or be fortunate enough to pass as locals and avoid direct experiences of discrimination. The academic's response is recounted in sarcastic terms to show how his attitude reflects essentialist definitions of local identity and culture. In another instance, Omar recalls the time when he became part of a local religious circle and his religious mentor admonished him for wearing his *ghutra* (traditional Arab headdress) by tying it around his head. "Wear it the way the people of this country wear it," he tells him (105). Omar writes with frustration that it was not only the *ghutra* that needed to conform to how things are done by the locals (105). In line with many scholarly critiques of normative and ethnocentric usages of assimilation (Bartram, Poros, and Monforte 2014: 16), the novel questions this understanding of cultural assimilation as the one legitimate means of developing a sense of belonging, receiving inclusion, or staking claims to Gulf spaces. Assimilation affirms what is perceived as an authentic and homogeneous culture that is incapable of accommodating difference, hence the novel's critical representation of the kind of belonging it facilitates.[13]

Omar's experience of inclusion as illusory is further confirmed by the fact that it is not his own presence in Saudi Arabia that is acknowledged, but merely his ability to assimilate and pass as a Saudi. Omar asserts that he was not able to live completely as a Saudi because "three decades were apparently not enough," not even with the "letters of the alphabet sneaking into [his] mouth" (12). Jeddah has provided him along the years with "a feeling of completeness that is nonetheless fake" (13). Despite the fact that assimilation occurs throughout Omar's childhood years, the novel suggests its futility because his belonging is ultimately met by a hostile rejection. As an adult, he is reluctant to come face-to-face with the reality that members of his migrant community are not recognized by the only home they have known (84). The novel suggests that Jeddah has changed after it embraced Omar and other Eritreans during their childhood and teen years. The city does not reciprocate the love that Eritreans and other diasporic communities have for it, nor does it offer them any life chances in return for the years they spend in its neighborhoods, such as university education, for example, or the opportunity to join a football club: "Jeddah has become too harsh on its children, turning them into mere foreigners" (87). Like the many friends who decide to immigrate elsewhere or who lose hope of accomplishing any of their dreams in a country that does not recognize them, Omar reacts to this rejection by deciding to visit Eritrea for the first time, attempting to find an alternative sense of belonging and security in the memories of his exiled parents. The failure to find himself in Eritrea reveals the impossibility of liberating himself from his diasporic subjectivity and the impact on his identity of living as a non-Saudi in Jeddah.

Through its critical representation of a deep sense of belonging that does not take the form of assimilation, *Samrawit* demonstrates that the migrant "other" can and has the right to establish a rooted presence that needs to be acknowledged by virtue of lived experiences rather than any obligation to perform a national identity built upon exclusion and illusive homogeneity. Jaber decouples the feelings of belonging that Omar has for Jeddah from any national or cultural affiliations and, instead, connects these feelings to everyday social and spatial encounters that Omar continues to evoke in his nostalgic recollections of his childhood days. Even though assimilation makes him less vulnerable to discrimination on a daily basis, his precarious legal status leads him to experience Jeddah as an unhomely home in the same way in which the Indian kids in "Moonseepalty" experience Abu Dhabi as a place that is simultaneously homely and unhomely.

Conclusion

My analysis of Jaber's *Samrawit* and Unnikrishnan's "Moonseepalty" has illustrated how the various levels of exclusion among second-generation migrants emerge from the rigid conceptualizations of legal belonging that do not acknowledge the reality of their lives in the Gulf. Exclusive citizenship laws treat all migrants and their descendants as temporary subjects because they are seen as ultimately attached to their countries of origin. In reality, the lived experiences of these diasporic subjects have led them to establish roots and connections that make their presence integral to the Gulf, even if it becomes invisible after their departure. Omar nostalgically laments an older Jeddah by recounting the fate of many of his Eritrean friends who immigrated to other countries, leaving invisible traces in their former homes and in his memory (87). Similarly, "Moonseepalty," and *Temporary People* more generally, document transient lives in a place that actively erases traces of its former inhabitants. Both narratives represent diasporic subjects who are capable of nurturing forms of belonging to the Gulf that coexist with, and sometimes even completely surpass, their attachment to their home countries. Even if the second generation can neither escape their diasporic subjectivities nor acquire a more secure legal belonging to their Gulf homes, both Jaber and Unnikrishnan grant visibility to these fleeting experiences of belonging. They depart from common narratives of alienation and exploitation among low-paid workers and stake claims that give migrants the right to call Gulf spaces their own. Following Brah, diasporas are "permanent community formations," even if their spaces are constantly witnessing the departure and arrival of new individuals (1996: 190). Literary depictions can contest the image of diasporic migrant communities as merely transitory by registering their "permanent" presence and by demanding an urgent reconfiguration of citizenship, identity, and belonging in the Gulf.

This chapter has additionally compared Arab and non-Arab experiences in order to assert the necessity of examining the diasporic identities of Arab migrants, thus countering the tendency to marginalize or completely overlook their experiences in much of the scholarship on the Gulf. Cultural affinities make Arabic-speaking migrants such as Omar in *Samrawit* less vulnerable to daily experiences of exclusion, but this does not mean that they cannot be also understood as diasporic, not least because they occupy a precarious status in the Gulf. Both Jaber and Unnikrishnan depict a reality where the presence of Arab and non-Arab long-term residents is similarly unacknowledged in the face of rigid conceptualizations of citizenship and belonging.

Nadeen Dakkak is a postdoctoral fellow at the Institute for Advanced Studies in the Humanities and Alwaleed Centre for the Study of Islam in the Contemporary World at the University of Edinburgh. She completed her PhD in English and Comparative Literary Studies at the University of

Warwick in 2021, where her research examined migration to the Arab Gulf States in Arabic fiction. She has published "Migrant Labour, Immobility and Invisibility in Literature on the Arab Gulf States" in *Mobilities, Literature, Culture*, edited by Marian Aguiar, Charlotte Mathieson, and Lynne Pearce (Palgrave Macmillan, 2019), and has a forthcoming article in the *Journal of Arabian Studies* on Mia Alvar's *In the Country*.

NOTES

1. Although it is beyond the scope of this chapter to situate these two texts within the wider literary scene of modern and contemporary fiction on migration and diaspora in Arabic and English, I want to propose that novels addressing belonging and identity among migrants in the Gulf States can be similarly approached as examples of this genre because they evoke the same motifs and tackle themes that speak to diasporic subjects in other contexts, even if they also can be understood as forming a category of their own because of the particularity of the Gulf as a migrant-receiving region. See Neuwirth, Pflitsch, and Winckler (2010) and Al Maleh (2009) for examples of studies that examine Arab literature on migration in other contexts.
2. My ideas here are loosely informed by Homi Bhabha's notion of "the unhomely" in his essay "The World and the Home" (1992), which is itself influenced by Freud's notion of "the uncanny."
3. It is beyond the scope of this chapter to dwell on other reasons that could explain why Arab migrants in the Gulf are not seen as diasporic, but it is important to point out that the popular pan-Arab ideology has historically strengthened this sense of affinity and viewed inter-Arab migration positively rather than a potential threat to national and cultural identity. The conception of citizenship, national identity, and belonging as well as emigration policies in emigration countries also affect how Arab migrants perceive their identity in relation to their Gulf host country and the extent to which they maintain ties with the homeland. As an example of such emigration policies in Egypt, see Tsourapas (2019). Because this chapter addresses the experiences of Eritreans in *Samrawit*, see Hirt and Mohammad (2018) on the control that the Eritrean state imposes on its diaspora in the Gulf.
4. All quotations from *Samrawit* are my own translation from Arabic.
5. Like thousands of other Eritreans, Omar's parents and grandparents left Eritrea because of violent political conflicts during the war of independence from Ethiopia. After the war, the new regime's authoritarianism and its control over Eritreans at home and abroad prevented the return of many to their former homes. For more on the Eritrean diaspora in the Gulf, see Hirt and Mohammad (2018).
6. On the diversity of Jeddah and the historical reasons that have made it different from and even more accommodating than other Saudi and Gulf cities, especially the Islamic pilgrimage, see Freitag's introduction in *A History of Jeddah* (2020).
7. Such nationalistic performances of gratitude and loyalty are evident in other novels that are arguably critical of the role of noncitizens in maintaining the status quo

in authoritarian Gulf States, such as Mohamed El-Bisatie's *Drumbeat* (2015) and Benyamin's *Jasmine Days* (2018), both of which are set in fictional Gulf cities.
8. *Jus sanguinis* is citizenship by law of blood while *jus soli* is citizenship by law of the soil.
9. The term "Arab" is inclusive of Emirati nationals as well as Gulf and non-Gulf Arab migrants. While the story does not specify the exact nationality of the Arabee boys, the social hierarchy that elevates the status of Arabs above non-Arabs means that the Indian teens occupy a weaker position and are vulnerable to exclusion in relation to both nationals and Arab nonnationals. Given the fact that there are numerous factors separating Emirati and non-Emirati residential areas, and because "Arabee" is used later in the story to refer to the Somali boys who steal Tits' bike (mentioned later), my reading of power relations between the different ethnic groups in the story understands the "Arabee boys" to be Arab migrants rather than nationals.
10. On the differences in policy toward Arab and non-Arab migrants, see Kapiszewski (2006) and Babar (2017). Also see Longva (1997) on the Arab/non-Arab hierarchy in the context of Kuwait and how it affects the level of exclusion to which migrants are subjected.
11. In migration studies, language or linguistic assimilation is one of the primary factors that determine the migrant's chances of inclusion in the host society. It is accordingly at the center of the immigration country's policies of integration. Even though the situation is different in the Gulf because no integration through assimilation is aimed for, language remains a factor that determines levels of exclusion/inclusion at the scale of everyday social encounters. See Shah (2017: 153).
12. I do not have the space to dwell on such differences in this chapter, but it is important to note that even if citizenship laws and migration policies are the same, possibilities of acculturation or cultural assimilation vary from one Gulf country to another, depending on numerous factors that could make the host society more accommodating for migrants. Saudi Arabia in general differs in many ways from other Gulf countries not only because it has hosted large migrant communities for a longer period of time, but also because it has facilitated the assimilation of these communities, primarily through religion, which has allowed a form of integration to occur between Saudis and migrants from different nationalities. For example, assimilation through the adoption of Salafist Islamic practices and through joining local religious groups is part of Omar's experience in *Samrawit*. See Shaker (2019) for an insight into the experiences of multigenerational migrants in Saudi Arabia.
13. Citizen attitudes toward migrants' adoption of the local dialect or local cultural practices also vary and can be seen as complex and contradictory. On the one hand, as evident in the example of the academic's response, it can be welcomed and perceived positively as an affirmation of the superiority of local culture and as evidence of the country's generosity and acceptance of migrants. On the other hand, this adoption may be seen as an unwelcome, if not threatening, transgression of the boundary separating citizens and foreigners, which in turn could lead second-generation migrants to refrain from performing local identities and to affirm their difference (Akinci 2020: 2315).

REFERENCES

Ahmad, Attiya. 2012. "Beyond Labor: Foreign Residents in the Persian Gulf States." In *Migrant Labor in the Persian Gulf*, edited by Mehran Kamrava and Zahra Babar, 21–40. London: Hurst.

Akinci, Idil. 2020. "Culture in the 'Politics of Identity': Conceptions of National Identity and Citizenship Among Second-Generation Non-Gulf Arab Migrants in Dubai." *Journal of Ethnic and Migration Studies* 46, no. 11: 2309–25.

Ali, Syed. 2011. "Going and Coming and Going Again: Second-Generation Migrants in Dubai." *Mobilities* 6, no. 4: 553–68.

Al Maleh, Layla, ed. 2009. *Arab Voices in Diaspora: Critical Perspectives on Anglophone Arab Literature*. Amsterdam: Rodopi.

Babar, Zahra. 2017. "Introduction." In *Arab Migrant Communities in the GCC*, edited by Zahra Babar, 1–18. Oxford: Oxford University Press.

Bartram, David, Maritsa V. Poros, and Pierre Monforte. 2014. *Key Concepts in Migration*. London: Sage.

Bayeh, Jumana. 2014. *The Literature of the Lebanese Diaspora: Representations of Place and Transnational Identity*. London: I. B. Tauris.

Beaugrand, Claire. 2018. *Stateless in the Gulf: Migration, Nationality and Society in Kuwait*. London: I. B. Tauris.

Benyamin. 2018. *Jasmine Days*. Translated by Shahnaz Habib. New Delhi: Juggernaut.

Bhabha, Homi. 1992. "The World and the Home." *Social Text* 31/32: 141–53.

Brah, Avtar. 1996. *Cartographies of Diaspora: Contesting Identities*. London: Routledge.

Braziel, Jana Evans, and Anita Mannur. 2003. "Nation, Migration, Globalization: Points of Contention in Diaspora Studies." In *Theorizing Diaspora*, edited by Jana Evans Braziel and Anita Mannur, 1–22. Oxford: Blackwell.

Collins, Francis Leo. 2011. "Transnational Mobilities and Urban Spatialities: Notes from the Asia-Pacific." *Progress in Human Geography* 36, no. 3: 316–35.

El-Bisatie, Mohamed. 2015. *Drumbeat*. Translated by Peter Daniel. Cairo: American University in Cairo.

Elsheshtawy, Yasser. 2019. *Temporary Cities: Resisting Transience in Arabia*. London: Routledge.

Fortier, Anne-Marie. 2010. "Diaspora." In *Cultural Geography: A Critical Dictionary of Key Concepts*, edited by David Atkinson, Peter Jackson, and David Sibley, 182–87. London: I. B. Tauris.

Freitag, Ulrike. 2020. *A History of Jeddah: The Gate to Mecca in the Nineteenth and Twentieth Centuries*. Cambridge, UK: Cambridge University Press.

Hirt, Nicole, and Abdulkader Saleh Mohammad. 2018. "The Lack of Political Space of the Eritrean Diaspora in the Arab Gulf and Sudan: Torn between an Autocratic Home and Authoritarian Hosts." *Mashriq and Mahjar* 5, no. 1: 101–26.

Hosoda, Naomi. 2016. "Middle Class Filipinos and the Formation of Diasporic National Communities in the United Arab Emirates." In *International Migration in Southeast Asia: Continuities and Discontinuities*, edited by Kwen Fee Lian, Md Mizanur Rahman, and Yabit bin Alas, 39–56. Singapore: Springer.

Jaber, Haji. 2012. *Samrawit*. Beirut: al-Markaz al-thaqāfī al-'arabī.

———. 2019. "Eritrean Novelist Haji Jaber: On Writing the Stories of the Falasha Jews." Interview by M. Lynx Qualey. *Arablit*, 21 January. Accessed 15 March 2020. www.arablit.org/2019/01/21/eritrean-novelist-haji-jaber-on-writing-the-stories-of-the-falasha-jews/.

Kapiszewski, Andrzej. 2006. "Arab Versus Asian Migrant Workers in the GCC Countries." United Nations Expert Group Meeting on International Migration and Development in the Arab Region, Population Division, Department of Economic and Social Affairs, United Nations Secretariat, Beirut. Accessed 22 March 2021. https://www.un.org/en/development/desa/population/events/pdf/expert/11/P02_Kapiszewski.pdf.

Koch, Natalie. 2016. "Is Nationalism Just for Nationals? Civic Nationalism for Noncitizens and Celebrating National Day in Qatar and the UAE." *Political Geography* 54: 43–53.

Longva, Anh Nga. 1997. *Walls Built on Sand: Migration, Exclusion, and Society in Kuwait*. Boulder, CO: Westview Press.

Neuwirth, Angelika, Andrea Pflitsch, and Barbara Winckler, eds. 2010. *Arabic Literature: Postmodern Perspectives*. London: Saqi.

Shah, Nasrah. 2017. "Kuwait Is Home: Perceptions of Happiness and Belonging among Second Plus Generation Non-Citizens in Kuwait." *Asian Population Studies* 13, no. 2: 140–60.

Shaker, Annas. 2019. "Belonging in Transience: Multi-Generational Migrants in Saudi Arabia." Migrant-Rights.org. Accessed 9 August 2020. www.migrant-rights.org/2019/10/belonging-in-transience-multi-generational-migrants-in-saudi-arabia/.

Tölölyan, Khachig. 1996. "Rethinking *Diaspora(s)*: Stateless Power in the Transnational Moment." *Diaspora: A Journal of Transnational Studies* 5, no. 1: 3–36.

Tsourapas, Gerasimos. 2019. *The Politics of Migration in Modern Egypt: Strategies for Regime Survival in Autocracies*. Cambridge, UK: Cambridge University Press.

Tuan, Yi-Fu. 1990. *Topophilia: A Study of Environmental Perception, Attitudes, and Values*. New York: Columbia University Press.

———. 2003. *Space and Place: The Perspective of Experience*. Minneapolis: University of Minnesota Press.

Unnikrishnan, Deepak. 2017. *Temporary People*. New York: Restless.

Vora, Neha. 2013. *Impossible Citizens: Dubai's Indian Diaspora*. London: Duke University Press.

Vora, Neha, and Natalie Koch. 2015. "Everyday Inclusions: Rethinking Ethnocracy, *Kafala*, and Belonging in the Arabian Peninsula." *Studies in Ethnicity and Nationalism* 15, no. 3: 540–52.

Wang, Yuting. 2015. "'Global Citizenship' and the Dislocated Generation in the United Arab Emirates." In *Challenges to Citizenship in the Middle East and North Africa Region*. LSE: Middle East Centre. Volume 2, 70–85. Accessed 22 March 2021. http://eprints.lse.ac.uk/id/eprint/61773.

CHAPTER
3

Navigating the Cosmopolitan City
Emirati Women and Ambivalent Forms of Belonging in Dubai

Rana AlMutawa

Raisa, a twenty-two-year-old Emirati woman, was standing with her husband and friends at the valet of a popular five-star hotel in Jumeirah. It was 11 p.m., and they were waiting for their cars after having had dinner at one of the hotel's restaurants. The hotel was frequented both by Emiratis and wealthy residents and tourists, but today—only in the valet area—it was different. Raisa noticed that they were surrounded by Westerners dressed in their evening wear, while she and her friends stood out in their abayas. Raisa said it was the first time she had felt odd in her own country.

Raisa and her friends were no strangers to socializing in spaces where they encountered people of different nationalities. Their favorite restaurants were at Dubai International Financial Centre (DIFC), where a minority of Emiratis and a much larger group of Westerners, Arabs, South Asians, and other elites went to socialize, dine, and/or drink at upscale places such as Zuma or BOCA. The restaurants in posh hotels and DIFC differed from the ones found in shopping malls or on the city's streets because they served alcohol, had a larger Western clientele, and were significantly more exclusive. Many of these restaurants became like lounges in the evening, playing the loud music one might find at a bar or nightclub. Because DIFC is known for its nightlife, some women also go there in evening wear, as they would to the hotel in Jumeirah where Raisa found them. In these spaces, Raisa and her friends may have been minorities, as Emiratis usually are—considering they constitute only 8 percent of Dubai's population (Dubai Statistics Center 2020)—but they were still there. Raisa felt comfortable there.

Places such as DIFC may be considered cosmopolitan enclaves wherein practices of consumption allow their users to engage with limited forms of difference—what one might refer to as a homogeneous form of cosmopolitanism (Raco 2003; Binnie et al. 2006: 25). One can find people of different ethnicities and nationalities in places such as DIFC, but those without sufficient economic (and cultural) capital are directly or indirectly excluded from such spaces. Raisa and her friends generally feel comfortable in places such as DIFC because they have the economic and cultural capital that allows them to enjoy these places. At different times, however, they feel that this upscale cosmopolitanism becomes too foreign.

Various scholars have described how Dubai's middle-class and upscale cosmopolitan spaces specifically cater to Western lifestyles and tastes, thereby excluding those without affinity to Western cultural norms (Ali 2010; Vora 2013; Kanna and Hourani 2016; Kathiravelu 2016). Indeed, these spaces promote exclusions, not only for low-income residents but even for my (Emirati) upper-middle-class interlocutors. However, I argue that some inclusions and exclusions are temporal and situational (Yuval-Davis 2007). Raisa and my other interlocutors feel excluded in the city's upscale developments at times, but they also make meanings and experience belonging in them during other times. This ambivalent experience is shared by the middle-aged Emirati women to whom I spoke as well.

Understanding these complex negotiations of space allows us to also move beyond some academic narratives that implicitly or explicitly depict the cosmopolitanism in the new parts of the city as entirely segregated and impenetrable, a narrative that results in binaries of Western/Emirati or foreign/local spaces (Acuto 2010; Bayat 2013; Cooke 2014; AlShehabi 2019; Elsheshtawy 2019, 2020). For instance, AlShehabi (2019) describes the newly built parts of Gulf cities as follows: "a society is created out of separate 'cantons,' in which each group lives in complete isolation from the rest of the parties, and where none of them are connected through national, cultural or political affiliations." Meanwhile, in some narratives, Dubai's inhabitants are portrayed as invisible in a city built for outsiders: "The built-in user . . . is more and more the anonymous corporate elitist or the opulent transient tourist . . . rather than [Dubai's] mostly invisible inhabitants" (Acuto 2010: 282).

While recognizing the limitations and exclusivity of these classed spaces is indeed essential, this discourse fails to acknowledge the social and cultural negotiations that take place in these settings, ones which allow us a better understanding of segregation and exclusion, but also of the forms of interaction that take place there. Furthermore, as I have argued elsewhere, the dominant discourses about urbanity in the Gulf also propagate a problematic binary discourse of supposedly "authentic, local" spaces (or, at times, authentically cosmopolitan spaces) contrasted with alienating, "tourist" spaces (AlMutawa 2019; 2020).[1] Discourses of authenticity that delineate some spaces as fake and others as authentic severely constrain our understanding of how inhabitants make meanings in them (AlMutawa 2019; 2020). These discourses are also often normative, used to depict the development of newly built cities, such as in the Gulf, as just a façade "covering up a lack of modernity underneath" (Koch 2012: 2,446; Smith 2016).

My interlocutors' attitudes toward the city's upscale cosmopolitan spaces—and the top-down developmental model—cannot be understood through a binary that sees them as either supportive of or opposing these developments. Rather, they have ambivalent, complex, and contradictory relationships toward the city's spectacles. While they feel alienated and marginalized in some settings, they also experience belonging, have cherished memories, and engage in cultural contestations within the spectacular urban landscapes.

This chapter highlights these points by first exploring the cosmopolitan subjectivities of my interlocutors. Second, I show that while upper-middle-class Emirati women feel comfortable in the city's middle-class and upscale developments, they also feel out of place in them when they embody a more homogeneous (and in this case Western) cosmopolitanism. However, these discomforts are also experienced temporally and situationally, deconstructing a binary of Western/non-Western or Emirati/non-Emirati spaces. In the final section, the binary gets further blurred, as I show how some of the Emirati women who describe feeling alienated in spaces associated with Westerners specifically seek them out when they want to get away from their community and experience a sense of anonymity. Meanwhile, Emiratis' increasing use of some of these locations shows how they reappropriate them over time, marking them as spaces where they go to see each other and be seen.

With this aim, I draw on ethnographic research that took place between 2017 and 2019. My ethnography includes interviews with over one hundred citizens and noncitizens, men and women of different age groups, most of whom can be considered as upper middle class. However, for this chapter, I focus on thirty-two interviews with Emirati women, mainly in their twenties and thirties (although some are over forty), who also belong to the upper middle class. Despite feeling marginalized at times in these upscale cosmopolitan spaces, their class background colors their experiences and allows them to create a sense of belonging in them in ways that low-income inhabitants cannot.

The majority of my interviews were audio-recorded and then transcribed. When interviewees did not want to be recorded, I wrote notes by hand during the interview and typed them up at home. The average length of interviews was about two-and-a-half hours, with the shortest interview being one hour and the longest being five hours. I also employed social media, particularly Instagram and Twitter, for this research. I used these two social media platforms because they are popular among Gulf citizens (although not necessarily with the same audiences, as Twitter is considered more "serious"); they are used both by men and women; and they are used both by the younger and older generations (from teenagers to adults in their sixties).

As an Emirati woman who grew up in Dubai, I had no difficulty finding interviewees and being connected through a snowball effect. Accompanied by my interviews were observations and walks I took to different parts of the city—mostly they were in middle-class and upscale developments—shopping malls, the beach and public parks, and new mixed-use spaces (such as City Walk, the Canal, Jumeirah Beach Residence, the Marina). Some of those were Emirati-dominated spaces, others were mixed in terms of ethnic (and at times class) background, and others were spaces often associated with Westerners (such as the Marina area).

Cosmopolitan Subjectivities

Understanding the subjectivities of my interlocutors allows better insight into their attitudes toward Dubai's development trajectory, including the ritzy projects that are aimed at attracting foreigners and tourists. Raisa, who worked at a multinational company, spoke positively about the "Year of Tolerance," and expressed a belief in Dubai as an inclusive place for all. In many ways, she appeared to fit the characteristic of a "flexible citizen," which Kanna defines as Emiratis who "engage in an active, often creative alignment of Emirati and neoliberal values" (2010: 135). As supporters of Dubai's neoliberal vision and development trajectory, flexible citizens "constitute a committed cadre of the city-corporation state and Sheikh Muhammad's future vision for a polity in which capital is dominant" (Kanna 2010: 143). While Kanna argues that flexible citizens are cosmopolitan and endorse neoliberal ideas, he explains that they also embrace some "traditional" aspects of their Emirati identity to varying degrees.

Kanna also depicts citizens with "neo-orthodox" tendencies, those who are critical of the city's rapid development and the influx of foreigners. However, he finds that flexible citizens generally reject neo-orthodox voices, which they regard as "stifling and rigid": "It is not uncommon for younger Emiratis, especially from among the neoliberal managerial class, to orient themselves towards a perceived multinational modernity beyond the confines staked out by these voices" (2010: 135). Kanna contends that a neo-orthodox criticism, such as of the demographic imbalance, also represents veiled criticism of Dubai's developmental model.

Kanna provides nuance by showing varieties within the group he labels "flexible citizens," such as in how they differ in their attachment to "traditional" values. While some individuals may indeed easily fit the characteristics of a flexible citizen, this term (including his contrasting of it with neo-orthodox voices) inadvertently glosses over various nuances. In such depictions, flexible citizens generally appear to endorse and support the state's development projects (with some reservations), while neo-orthodox voices produce veiled critiques of it. Applying this method, one might therefore expect a flexible citizen to be generally comfortable in Dubai's new cosmopolitan spaces and those with neo-orthodox tendencies to be alienated by them. The reality is often more complex.

Mizna, a middle-aged Emirati woman, exhibited neo-orthodox tendencies, arguing that Dubai's developments were being built for Westerners and foreigners while citizens were being sidelined and alienated in their own land. However, Mizna also enjoyed going to the "Western" areas in the city, saying she thoroughly enjoyed these places because she felt as if "she wasn't in Dubai anymore." A similar sentiment was shared by other middle-aged Emirati women regarding Western-dominated spaces. While they heavily criticized women in skimpy outfits or the presence of alcohol in these places, they frequented these places that they considered "higher-class" or that made them feel as if "they're in Europe," highlighting their aspirations—like flexible citizens—to be part of a global and cosmopolitan (and elite) world.

Meanwhile, although she did not fit many characteristics of a "flexible citizen," Mizna wholeheartedly accepted some of the neoliberal values that Kanna describes this group to endorse, such as the importance of being entrepreneurial and "open-minded" or the positive association of studying and traveling abroad with self-discovery and self-sufficiency. Similarly, many of my interlocutors did not fit into either category—that of flexible citizen nor the neo-orthodox. There were Emiratis who did not have the "entrepreneurial spirit" that flexible citizens are supposed to have, who worked in "typical" government jobs and refused to adapt to the changing neoliberal market, but who enjoyed the city's changes and the "Western" spaces of consumption such as those at DIFC. Are they considered flexible citizens? There were Emirati parents with neo-orthodox tendencies who complained about the loss of Arab and Muslim values but sent their children to schools with weak (or nonexistent) Arabic and Islamic Education classes because they believed these schools otherwise provided outstanding education and cultivated better cultural experiences. While some may have more neo-orthodox tendencies than others, and Kanna's category of flexible citizens certainly applies to some of them, the categories did not sufficiently depict the subjectivities of my interlocutors or their positionalities toward the city's development trajectory.

At a more mundane level, when I asked Muna, a thirty-one-year-old Emirati researcher, how she and the women she knew felt about going to the beach, her answer illuminated attitudes toward modesty and women's dress that made it difficult to entertain categorizations (among Emiratis and even non-Emiratis). Rather, individuals had layered and complex attitudes that exhibited different subjectivities at once that cannot be categorized by resorting to binaries such as "traditional" and "liberal." Talking about the beach and how Emirati women use it, Muna said:

> I think because there are options that are ladies-only—like for example Wild Wadi Ladies' night and Dubai Ladies' Club [private beaches]—if they [Emirati women] really care about modesty, they would go to these places. There are some people, they don't care about modesty, but they care about reputation, so for them, they would hide under the cloak of anonymity, and they would go to places that are more Western-oriented and where they won't see anyone they know; and yes, of course, some of them wear bikinis and some of them wear slightly more conservative [swimsuits]. . . . But by the way, the Ladies' Club nowadays, it's not really so private anymore; there are so many projects around it that directly look over it, so I think most of the people now who go there, honestly, they're not so bothered with no one seeing them; they just don't want to be around men. It's just a more conservative option. There are so many jet skis and there are so many boats nearby that people can really see your figure and what you're wearing from a distance. But I see a lot of Emiratis there, and a lot of Arabs there [wearing swimsuits], and also a lot of people who . . . prefer staying in their hijab and long clothes.

The variety of preferences that Muna recounted demonstrates that these women experience the city in different ways. Those who choose not to wear swimsuits at Dubai Ladies' Club (DLC) because of the lack of privacy, and those who cannot afford to go to private clubs, for instance, may find that the city does not cater to them as much as it does to Western forms of cosmopolitanism. They may feel more excluded in the city than the other women. But in which category do we place women who go to DLC knowing they might be seen? The quote exemplifies the complexity of Emirati (and non-Emirati) women's attitudes toward the city's urban spaces, even among women who may otherwise be considered cosmopolitan "flexible citizens" or more "traditional" individuals with neo-orthodox tendencies. It also demonstrates that inhabitants do not necessarily experience different parts of the city through binaries such as Western/non-Western, as I show in the next sections.

Varieties of Cosmopolitanism

Many academics have depicted the ways in which Dubai's upscale developments target Westerners. They argue that the imagined consumer of the city's new developments "is a wealthy white European or American" (Vora 2013: 49), and that the target "for high-end properties [in Dubai] is largely Westerners" (Ali 2020: 40–41). It is this catering to Western lifestyles and social norms that attract some of them to the city. "British citizens felt welcome in Dubai because of a collective, active effort to carve out zones of British cultural comfort" (Kanna and Hourani 2016: 616). While recognizing the ways the new parts of the city cater to Westerners (and the marginalization of those without economic and Western cultural capital) is vital, my interlocutors do not necessarily experience the spaces catering to Western tastes simply as Western spaces. Rather, the types of cosmopolitanism found in upscale Dubai vary temporally and situationally. Indeed, the politics of belonging—and therefore the carving of who belongs and who does not—is situated temporally, intersectionally, and spatially (Yuval-Davis 2007).

While Raisa and my other interlocutors have the cosmopolitan cultural capital that allows them to feel at home in these upscale restaurants and hotels, even they may sometimes feel excluded when the cosmopolitanism that takes place there becomes too "Western." Speaking of the gated communities in Dubai, Kathiravelu says that while these middle-class developments are used by residents of various ethnicities and nationalities, "the homogenizing effects of gated communities thus embed migrants in a space that is discursively and culturally white, but which passes as neutral" (2016: 144). This depiction applies to many of Dubai's upscale developments beyond gated communities.

Many of the Emirati women I spoke to enjoy the city's upscale cosmopolitan spaces, yet their occasional discomfort also stems from their feeling that Western social norms are overwhelmingly dominant there. I should specify that many of these practices that I refer to here as Western forms of cosmopolitanism, such as drinking alcohol or forms of dress considered revealing for women, are certainly not only practiced in the West. However, I refer to them in that way because they reflect contemporary practices associated with Western social norms, and because my interlocutors described them as such. The dominance of these social norms in some parts of the city does not necessarily mean that non-Westerners are more comfortable in "non-Western" spaces, but rather that there are temporal and situational dimensions to the Western forms of cosmopolitanism in many parts of the city. For example, Raisa felt comfortable in the hotel in Jumeirah she frequented, except on that evening when she saw that she and her friends were the only Emiratis (and Arabs or Muslims) among Westerners. In some lounges and restaurants, such as Caramel lounge at DIFC, there is a temporal difference in terms of the clientele during the daytime and the evening, wherein there are more Emirati attendees during the day than in the late evening. Such realities highlight the need to deconstruct binaries of Western/non-Western or foreign/local spaces while still recognizing that Western forms of cosmopolitanisms do get privileged in some of these environments (Ali 2010; Vora 2013; Kanna and Hourani 2016; Kathiravelu 2016).

Raisa's story of feeling out of place wearing the abaya among women dressed in more revealing outfits was shared by many of my other interlocutors. Muna gave a similar example—not about an upscale development but about the public beach: "Sometimes I get a little bit shocked when I see butts, and stuff like that, in front of me, like when people are wearing very small swimsuits," she said. However, she clarified that it was not necessarily their swimsuits that made her uncomfortable, but rather seeing them in contradistinction with her wearing her abaya: "I feel uncomfortable when I'm wearing my abaya around all of these people that are super, super naked."

Other Emiratis I spoke to recounted similar experiences of their discomfort in a place where they felt they stood out while wearing the national dress. On one end, the national dress cements the difference between citizens and noncitizens (Khalaf 2005; Kanna 2010; AlMutawa 2016; Akinci 2020). Because of its visibility, non-Emiratis clearly notice who is Emirati or not, and vice versa, leading my interlocutors to occasionally feel out of place when they find that they are the only ones wearing it. This may imply exclusion based on a citizen/noncitizen binary, wherein my interlocutors feel marginalized in spaces where they are clearly the only Emiratis there. While this sort of anxiety does exist, my interlocutors are also very comfortable in cosmopolitan spaces in other circumstances. For instance, Assaf (2020) highlights the shared urban cosmopolitanism between Emiratis and Arab noncitizens in Abu Dhabi. Similarly, many of my interlocutors feel at ease with the cosmopolitanism in places such as Dubai Mall, which includes a mix of Arabs, South Asians, East Asians, Westerners, and Emiratis.

What becomes clear in these examples is that my interlocutors feel discomfort in places that are dominated by a certain group and their social norms (whether this group be Westerners, South Asians, or another group that they feel is different from them). This indicates that it is also the cultural homogeneity of a space (e.g., its Western-ness or its South Asian-ness rather than its cosmopolitanism) that makes them feel out of place. When Emirati women compare themselves to a majority of women in more revealing outfits, they are pointing out the dominance of Western forms of cosmopolitanism. In these cases, they are not feeling excluded (just) because they are minority citizens, but rather because of the homogeneous forms of (non)cosmopolitanism that make them feel as if they stand out as marginal. Therefore, the presence of non-Emirati women in hijabs or women dressed modestly ameliorates this discomfort and makes them feel less out of place.

These scenarios are akin to those of South Asian British Muslims in the UK who moved from Asian-dominated spaces in England to white suburban spaces, and for whom "the presence of 'any Asian face' (irrespective of origin or religion) was often deemed to be a comfort" (Phillips 2006: 33). For my interlocutors, seeing other (non-Emirati) women dressed more modestly puts them more at ease. This demonstrates that their experiences of marginalization are not necessarily based on citizen/noncitizen dynamics (although they very well may be at other times), but about what forms of cosmopolitanism (or lack of) they are interacting with.

The public beach provides various examples of my Emirati interlocutors' experiences of exclusion through the dominance of "Western" social norms. The majority of Emirati women use the public beach as a space for leisure—but not for swimming. I realized it was not always this way: Maysoon, an Emirati friend, surprised me by saying that her female relatives used to go to the beach and enter the sea in their clothes (the *jallabiyya*, essentially a long, traditional dress), something they would not do today when most of the women surrounding them are dressed in swimsuits. I had never experienced swimming at the public beach, nor did I remember seeing women from my social circles doing so. Maysoon's comment made me realize there was a lifestyle I had missed out on. Some non-Emiratis also noticed a difference. Shireena, a Filipina-Pakistani woman, similarly mentioned the transformations she felt took place on the public beach:

> I remember the wave of Russians that came through that changed Dubai overnight. . . . I remember: I was fifteen; we went to the beach. It's now La Mer—before it was just an open beach. [laughing] . . . And you know, back then, like, we didn't go to the beach in swimming costumes, right? Like, we would wear like tights, a shirt or whatever, you know. I mean, I make fun of these people now. [laughing] . . . I don't make fun of them. . . . It's just, it's funny, but this was us back then. . . . I remember, you know, the waves of Russians coming in, and they'd be in the shower, and they'd be topless taking a shower.

Whether it was really Russian women who contributed to the change in the beach scene is not something I can comment on. However, Shireena's quote points to the "Westernization" of the beach through the changing social norms there.[2] The beach scene Shireena describes prior to the influx of Russians and/or Westerners was still cosmopolitan. There were not only Emiratis there, but other non-Westerners such as Shireena and her friends, who were South Asian and Arab. While these individuals did not wear the same types of dress as Emiratis did, they did share the similarity of dressing more modestly. Maysoon said that the women in her family went to the beach and swam with their clothes on, which did not seem out of place among other (non-Emirati) women entering the water also fully clothed. The beach was a cosmopolitan space at that time, but it represented a different type of cosmopolitanism. As a larger number of Westerners came to Dubai, the type of cosmopolitanism in that place changed, and with it the social norms of that place. Like many other Emirati women, the women in Maysoon's family now felt they would stand out if they went swimming in their clothes.

Some women, Shireena being an example, appear to have with time altered their own dress codes to adjust to the city's changing social scene. Others may continue to go to the beach and enjoy swimming there in modest dress. But for many Emiratis, these options are not socially acceptable, and their use of the public beach is often limited to walking or exercising there (but not swimming). Because some of them felt they stood out wearing the abaya on the beach (in addition to its being less convenient to exercise in), they sometimes go instead wearing hoodies. "Even when the weather is hot . . . [the hoodie] is like the negotiated outfit that's not an abaya but not unconservative, so you'd see a lot of teenagers and young women . . . maybe twenties and thirties, wearing hoodies even if the weather is hot because it gives them more mobility," Muna said. She contrasted the walking path on the beach to the walking path in Khawaneej, the latter being a place where many Emiratis live and where women rarely wear a hoodie even when engaging in the same activities they would on the beach. Wearing a hoodie to feel less out of place, however, is not necessarily something they are "pressured" to do to fit in. Many simply find that the hoodie is the appropriate thing to wear at the beach, just as getting dressed up and wearing the abaya is seen as the appropriate form of dress for the mall. Meanwhile, many women still do go to the beach and walk there wearing the abaya. This is very common, especially with the opening of upscale food trucks on the beach, some of which are very popular with Emiratis.

What this indicates is that the changing population dynamics in the city also lead to changing social norms among Emiratis, even those that appear minuscule: Emirati women who used to go swimming in their clothes stopped feeling comfortable doing so as the dynamics of the beach changed. Meanwhile, it became more socially acceptable for young Emirati women to wear something other than the national (or traditional) dress at the beach, a practice that may otherwise be considered taboo. I elaborate on these changing social norms later in this chapter. These changes result in a sense of alienation and loss for some of my interlocutors, but they also indicate that cultural negotiations are taking place.

In this section, I have demonstrated that my Emirati interlocutors' experiences in the city's upscale developments are tied to the types of cosmopolitanisms found there. Many of my interlocutors generally felt comfortable in middle-class and upscale cosmopolitan spaces. When they experienced discomfort there, it was usually because they felt that a certain group and their social norms were dominating a place, creating a homogeneous (rather than cosmopolitan) space and making Emiratis stand out. In the cases I have explored, it is Western forms of cosmopolitanism that are dominating, resulting in Emiratis feeling out of place. However, the types of cosmopolitanism in upscale Dubai vary temporally and situationally. This reality allows us to move beyond depictions of Dubai's cosmopolitan enclaves as entirely impenetrable, and which elide the negotiations that take place in these settings. As I show in the next section, my Emirati interlocutors use these "Western" spaces to gain a sense of anonymity, while others increasingly use them and reappropriate them as "local" spaces, changing the dynamics that take place there and further blurring the binary of Western/local spaces.

Making Belonging in "Western" and "Tourist" Places

> Depending on my mood, sometimes I get this feeling that I really don't want to go to Dubai Mall because I will see everyone [Emiratis]. I always comment on my sister because she says, "Ewww, I don't want to go there, it's all locals [Emiratis]"; and I say, "Why—then what are you?" . . . But I get what she means, you want to escape. . . . I think I've never been to [Galleria Mall] in my life without saying hello to people [Emiratis]. And it's fine, we don't mind it. But there are days where I'm not in the mood. . . . Because when I go there, I need to make sure I'm dressed up; I need to make sure that I look presentable. Other times, I'm not in the mood. I remember once going to Marina in a hoodie and sneakers, and I'm enjoying myself. That's something I wouldn't be able to do here [City Walk]. . . . I remember I went ziplining once. . . . You know the Dubai Mall zipline . . . it ends in Dubai Mall. I was wearing my shayla [headscarf], but I was wearing jeans [without an abaya]. So, when I got out at Dubai Mall, I was really uncomfortable. I mean, per-

sonally I'm fine with it, I'm not even *mit-hajba* [wearing a hair veil]. . . . But me being in Dubai Mall and not dressed, I thought a lot, maybe someone will see me, maybe someone will say something, maybe, you know. So, I've done also the same zipline in Marina [an area associated with Westerners]. Here is when I was in my hoodie and I don't care, and I was comfortable, and I enjoyed that ten times more. . . . [But] in Dubai Mall we immediately got our abayas.

Raisa, who earlier commented about feeling excluded in a Western-dominated space in Dubai, expressed her preference for them at other times when she did not want to encounter members of her community. The comment her sister made about not wanting to go somewhere because "it's all locals" is not uncommon. Like Raisa, some of the other Emiratis I spoke to wanted to go to spaces they associated with Westerners, such as the Marina area, to get a sense of anonymity and comfort. This was a way for them to go out without feeling the need to dress up or behave in a certain way—particularly as they felt scrutinized in Emirati-dominated spaces—and without bumping into people they know and having to constantly say hello. Wilson (1992) argues that one of the attractions of the modern city, for women as much as anyone, is the possibility for people to lose themselves in the crowd. While modern cities can be solitary, they provide anonymity for inhabitants (Tonkiss 2005). Yet Dubai does not provide anonymity for my Emirati interlocutors (or noncitizen interlocutors who have extended family in the UAE). Rather, it is certain spaces in Dubai—such as Western-dominated spaces—that provide them this anonymity.

For those who did not want to wear the shayla and abaya but knew they would be criticized either (or both) by family or by society, going to Western-dominated spaces allowed them to do so without fear of being seen by members of their community. It permitted them a sense of freedom because in those places you "don't feel like you're in Dubai anymore," and therefore are unburdened by the social norms you must abide by elsewhere in the city. Similarly, Emirati women who do not feel comfortable smoking *sheesha* in Emirati-dominated spaces choose to go to certain hotels or to areas of the city where many the people there are Westerners and/or tourists, and where they feel that no one knows who they are.

Parallels are found in other settings as well. Nonheterosexual Bangladeshi-British men in London frequent some of the coffee shops dominated by white cosmopolitans in their gentrifying neighborhood in Spitalfields, as the atmosphere there lends itself to providing "cover for men from less privileged social groups" from their own communities (Brown 2006: 141). Meanwhile, young British Muslim women from South Asian backgrounds tend to want to move to the middle-class and white suburbs of the city because it allows them to "occupy social, cultural, and spatial position on the margins of the community, which affords some freedom from perceived social strictures and conventions" (Philips 2006: 35). These British-South Asian men and women are also marginalized in these white spaces. White middle-class cosmopolitans have gentrified the areas that the Bangladeshi diaspora live in, while the South Asian-British women faced racism in predominantly white spaces. In fact, racism was one reason that many of these individuals preferred to remain in their own communities. Yet some of them found pleasures outside of it for various reasons. Exclusionary spaces, therefore, may be used in various ways for different purposes, and inhabitants create ambivalent forms of belonging within them.

Similarly, upscale coffee shops play important roles for upper-middle-class women in Cairo because these women can use them to engage in behavior they are otherwise not able to participate in elsewhere in the city: this includes the way they dress and their socializing in mixed-gender settings (de Koning 2009; Peterson 2011). The exclusion of others (low-income Egyptians) marks these coffee shops as "decent" places to engage in performances that are otherwise deemed "inappropriate." In Chennai, young women go to "afternoon clubs" where they can similarly socialize among peers and engage in activities that would be considered improper in other settings (Krishnan 2018). Comparably, Emirati women from Dubai find that the city's spaces they associate with Westerners provide them a sense of anonymity that is liberating in some ways.

Not all those who reject Emirati-dominated spaces do so to transgress social norms. Many simply seek a place where they do not feel constantly under watch. Cafés dominated by Emirati men were particularly uncomfortable for some Emirati women. Alia, an Emirati woman in her late twenties, talked about how anxious she was when she passed a coffee shop in which all she "could see was white" (men wearing the "national dress"), saying that she probably would have not felt this way if these men were of different nationalities. This is a very common reaction among Emirati women to spaces dominated specifically by Emirati men.

Similarly, when I asked Bayan, my ex-colleague and friend, about her trip to Kuwait, one of the things she commented on was the high ratio of Kuwaitis to non-Kuwaitis. On one hand, she viewed this positively, saying that it was nice to go out and see so many citizens. This contrasts with many places in Dubai. On that day, for instance, we were sitting in Dubai Mall, where Emiratis are a (visible but small) minority. When I asked her to compare her experiences in both cities, however, Bayan said that she could not imagine living in a place where there were so many Emiratis. Bayan went to an Emirati-only university for her undergraduate degree and was not necessarily uncomfortable in such settings, but she found herself to be more at ease in leisure spaces where there were many non-Emiratis, and where she felt less watched. While some citizens prefer going to places where they can see other Emiratis, others may opt for more "cosmopolitan" spaces to which they have become accustomed through schools, universities, workplaces, or other institutions.

Like Raisa, who enjoyed being in Marina Mall with her hoodie, these spaces associated with Westerners can sometimes give Emiratis an ability to get away from environments they find suffocating. Some Emiratis avoid Emirati-dominated spaces because they feel they are centered on *khaga* (showing off) and appearances. In places like Marina Mall, however, they feel that no one knows who they are, and no one cares either. Indeed, the possibility of going somewhere and not constantly bumping into people they know and stopping to say hello is reason enough for some of them to enjoy these places.

Just as some Emirati women go to these Western places without abayas, it has become increasingly common to see women wearing abayas in spaces normally considered "Western." Kanna and Hourani (2016) describe how Dubai's forms of bourgeois gratification, which they said includes malls, gated communities, resorts, and bars, are created to please Western tastes. They qualify this by adding that Emiratis do use some of these spaces as well, although they refer to their usage of these spaces as "ironic" (Kanna and Hourani 2016: 615). They are correct to note that what makes these spaces popular among both Westerners and Emiratis is that they are sanitized spaces that exclude "unwanted others" (such as the working-classes). However, by describing them solely as Western spaces that "carve out zones of British cultural comfort" based on an imperial legacy (Kanna and Hourani 2016: 616), we also miss out on their meanings among other groups, including Emiratis. Changing Emirati socializing patterns and social norms are also elided in these narratives. Muna recalled a time when she became aware of these changing social dynamics: "I remember the first time I was [in Caramel lounge] with my sister, I saw the bar, that it was exposed, and that there were a lot of drinks in the area, and I was telling Sumaya [her sister], 'Oh, is it *'ady*, [normal]? Like, people [Emiratis] are okay with it now?'"

Muna expected Emiratis not to go to places where alcohol was so visibly displayed. Indeed, even some of those who socialize in such places may still be critical of the exhibition of alcohol and women dressing in revealing outfits (particularly parents, for instance, who may be dragged there by younger family members). This was even more so the case when types of establishments were still new. With time, however, things changed. "There were all sorts of people, including Emiratis, wearing abaya and shayla [at Caramel]. And I think with Zuma and Petite Maison, and Caramel, they [have] become 'it spots' and somehow that makes it okay for anyone to go there; like it's not *'ayb* [shameful] anymore for some people because it's an 'it spot,'" Muna said. She not only saw younger Emiratis in these establishments but families as well, although the latter tended not to go to the lounges such as Caramel, but rather to the upscale restaurants in hotels: "It's not just couples or a group of girls or a group of guys [who go there]. It's like a whole family with an older dad and traditional looking mom going there with their children," she said. Despite this, these places are characterized by their exclusivity, and it is their segregation from most of society that gives them their appeal to many of those who use them.

These exclusive places also become sites for the negotiation of social norms—albeit among a restricted group—as can be seen from Muna's reaction to seeing other Emiratis there (AlMutawa 2020). As opposed to other places such as Marina, where some Emiratis go to avoid being seen by other members of the Emirati community, places such as Caramel or Zuma that were once associated with Westerners or cosmopolitan elites become locations where some Emiratis also go to see and be seen: they are not spaces to hide but rather to display oneself to other Emiratis. They come to have different meanings among citizens over time.

The fact that some Emirati women, including those wearing the shayla and abaya, go to places like hotel lobbies and restaurants is a more recent development. In her book about women in Abu-Dhabi, Bristol-Rhys (2010) claims that the spaces catering to Westerners and tourists such as hotel restaurants were not acceptable spaces for Emirati women. Perhaps this is reflective of the attitudes from over a decade ago, as well as possibly reflecting different attitudes and behaviors in different emirates. To be sure, these spaces are certainly not enjoyed or even visited by all Emiratis. Some women may face repercussions from their families for going there, and there are Emiratis who cannot afford them. Others may not face these restrictions but feel uncomfortable in such places, nonetheless.

However, because these are not bars or nightclubs (although some of them may have similar atmospheres in the evening with loud music and dim lighting), they are regarded as more respectable. While Emiratis who attend nightclubs or bars normally attempt to keep this socializing practice private, attending restaurants such as the one Muna described is not necessarily something Emiratis are secretive about. Many of them post photos of these places on Instagram and Snapchat, indicating that these are places they want to be seen in or associated with. They are no longer taboo for some segments of Emirati society, but rather spaces in which to perform social distinction. This is not to say that many people, including those who go to these restaurants and lounges, do not complain that the city is too "Westernized." Rather, it demonstrates that these places become embedded with new or different meanings over time.

This chapter has demonstrated that upscale cosmopolitan spaces in Dubai are exclusive and inclusive in various ways. It is not uncommon to hear many Emiratis (and non-Emiratis) referring to these places as "built for Westerners." Such comments are made both by those who may feel uncomfortable in such spaces, but more importantly, they are also made by some Emiratis who do use and enjoy them. In fact, it is their association with "Westerners" that attracts some non-Western residents (even including older and more "traditional" Emiratis) who view these places as high end or who use them to obtain a degree of anonymity. Over time, Emirati social norms and attitudes towards these places also change. Some "Western" spaces become used more and more by Emiratis, rendering them no longer spaces of anonymity but spaces where Emiratis go to see and be seen. These changing dynamics highlight the need to go beyond common dichotomies, such as Western/local spaces, that omit the negotiations and cross-interactions that take place there.

Conclusion

This chapter has explored the cosmopolitan subjectivities of my female Emirati interlocutors, arguing that going beyond common categorizations allows us better insight into Emirati women's complex relationships to the city. I have demonstrated that my interlocutors' ambivalent experiences toward high-end developments are tied to the types of cosmopolitanisms found there. Upper-middle-class Emirati women generally feel comfortable in middle-class and elite cosmopolitan spaces (AlMutawa 2020). However, the types of cosmopolitanism in upscale Dubai vary temporally and situationally. When my interlocutors feel uncomfortable, it is usually because they find that a certain group and their social norms are dominating a place, creating a homogeneous (rather than cosmopolitan) environment. In the cases I explored, my interlocutors felt that Western forms of cosmopolitanism are dominant, leading them to visibly stand out. Yet many Emirati women feel both belonging and exclusion in such places. This is evident in the way some of them use parts of the city that they associate with "Westerners" to get a sense of anonymity, which allows them to enjoy the city both in transgressive ways (such as smoking sheesha or engaging in activities otherwise deemed inappropriate) and nontransgressive ways (such as enjoying the comfort of not having to bump into people they know and say hello). Furthermore, some of these "Western" spaces are being increasingly used by Emiratis. Rather than being spaces of anonymity, they become ones where citizens go to see and be seen by members of their community (AlMutawa 2020). This changes the dynamics of these spaces and further blurs the binary of Western/local spaces. Moving beyond common narratives about Dubai's cosmopolitan enclaves allows us to better understand the exclusions that manifest there, as well as the forms of belonging and negotiations that take place.

Rana AlMutawa is an Emirati assistant professor emerging scholar of social research and public policy at NYU Abu Dhabi. She completed her PhD at the University of Oxford, St Antony's College. Her current research focuses on urban studies, belonging, and everyday life in the UAE. She was formerly a Managing Editor of Gulf Affairs, a nonpartisan journal at St Antony's College, and taught a course on the societies and cultures of the Middle East at the University of Oxford. Prior to that, she was an instructor and researcher at Zayed University in Dubai, where she researched national identity and gender in the Gulf. She has published her work in *Arab Studies Journal*, *Urban Anthropology*, and other journals.

NOTES

1. For example, Elsheshtawy (2020) contrasts two less-regulated low-income areas in the UAE as an example of "true urbanity" and cosmopolitanism against middle-class areas of "bland cosmopolitanism" (813–14).
2. While Russians may be regarded as part of the East by Europeans and US Americans, for my non-Western interlocutors they are regarded as Western in their appearance, culture, and behavior.

REFERENCES

Acuto, Michele. 2010. "High-Rise Dubai Urban Entrepreneurialism and the Technology of Symbolic Power." *Cities* 27, no. 4: 272–84.

Akinci, Idil. 2020. "Culture in the 'Politics of Identity': Conceptions of National Identity and Citizenship among Second-Generation Non-Gulf Arab Migrants in Dubai." *Journal of Ethnic and Migration Studies* 46, no. 11: 2,309–25.

Ali, Sayed. 2010. *Dubai: Gilded Cage*. New Haven: Yale University Press.

AlMutawa, Rana Khalid. 2016. "National Dress in the UAE: Constructions of Authenticity." *New Middle Eastern Studies* 6: 1–13.

———. 2019. "'The Mall Isn't Authentic!': Dubai's Creative Class and the Construction of Social Distinction." *Urban Anthropology* 48, no. 1–2: 183–224.

———. 2020. "'Glitzy' Malls and Coffee Shops: Everyday Places of Belonging and Social Contestation in Dubai." *Arab Studies Journal* 28, no. 2: 44–75.

AlShehabi, Omar. 2019. "Right to the City" [Alhaq fee almadina]. Gulf Centre for Development Policies. Accessed 22 March 2021. https://gulfpolicies.org/2019-05-18-07-30-16/2019-05-18-10-21-49/1592-2019-07-02-11-59-19.

Assaf, Laure. 2020. "'Abu Dhabi is my Sweet Home': Arab Youths, Interstitial Spaces, and the Building of a Cosmopolitan Locality." *City* 24, no. 5-6: 830-41.

Bayat, Asef. 2013. *Life as Politics: How Ordinary People Change the Middle East*. Stanford, CA: Stanford University Press.

Binnie, Jon, Julian Holloway, Steve Millington, and Craig Young, eds. 2006. *Cosmopolitan Urbanism*. London: Routledge.

Bristol-Rhys, Jane. 2010. *Emirati Women: Generations of Change*. London: Hurst Publishers.

Brown, Gavin. 2006. "Cosmopolitan Camouflage: (Post-)Gay space in Spitalfields, East London." In *Cosmopolitan Urbanism*, edited by Binnie, Holloway, Millington, and Young, 130-45.

Cooke, Miriam. 2014. *Tribal Modern: Branding New Nations in the Arab Gulf*. Oakland: University of California Press.

De Koning, Anouk. 2009. *Global Dreams: Class, Gender, and Public Space in Cosmopolitan*. Cairo: American University in Cairo Press.

Dubai Statistics Center. 2020. "Number of Population Estimated by Nationality—Emirate of Dubai (2020-2018)." Dubai Statistics Center, Government of Dubai. Accessed 22 March 2021. https://www.dsc.gov.ae/Report/DSC_SYB_2020_01_03.pdf.

Elsheshtawy, Yasser. 2019. *Temporary Cities: Resisting Transience in Arabia*. London: Routledge.

———. 2020. "Urban Enclaves and Transient Cosmopolitanism." *City* 24, no. 5-6: 805-17.

Kanna, Ahmed. 2010. *Dubai: The City as Corporation*. Minneapolis: University of Minnesota Press.

Kanna, Ahmed, and Najib Hourani. 2016. "'A Group of Like-Minded Lads in Heaven': Everydayness and the Production of Dubai Space." *Journal of Urban Affairs* 36, no. 12: 605-20.

Kathiravelu, Laavaanya. 2016. *Migrant Dubai: Low Wage Workers and the Construction of a Global City*. Basingstoke: Palgrave Macmillan.

Khalaf, Sulayman. 2005. "National Dress and the Construction of Emirati Cultural Identity." *Journal of Human Sciences* 11: 230-67

Koch, Natalie. 2012. "Urban 'Utopias': The Disney Stigma and Discourses of 'False Modernity.'" *Environment and Planning A* 44: 2,445-62.

Krishnan, Sneha. 2018. "Clubbing in the Afternoon: Worlding the City as a College-Girl in Chennai." *City, Culture and Society* 19: https:doi.org/10.1016/j.ccs.2018.09.001.

Peterson, Mark Allen. 2011. *Connected in Cairo: Growing up Cosmopolitan in the Modern Middle East*. Bloomington: Indiana University Press.

Phillips, Deborah. 2006. "Parallel Lives? Challenging Discourses of British Muslim Self-Segregation." *Environment and Planning D: Society and Space* 24, no. 1: 25-40.

Raco, Mike. 2003. "Remaking Place and Securitising Space: Urban Regeneration and the Strategies, Tactics and Policies of Policing in the UK." *Urban Studies* 40: 1,869-87.

Smith, Benjamin. 2016. "The Sheikh of Araby Rides a Cadillac": Popular Geoeconomic Imaginations, Positional Anxiety and Nouveau Riche Territories." *Environment & Planning D: Society & Space* 34, no. 3: 564-80.

Tonkiss, Fran. 2005. *Space, City and Social Theory: Social Relations and Urban Forms*. Cambridge, UK: Polity Press.

Vora, Neha. 2013. *Impossible Citizens: Dubai's Indian Diaspora*. Durham: Duke University Press.
Wilson, Elizabeth. 1992. *The Sphinx in the City*. Berkeley: University of California Press.
Yuval-Davis, Nira. 2007. "Intersectionality, Citizenship and Contemporary Politics of Belonging." *Critical Review of International Social and Political Philosophy* 10, no. 4: 561–74.

PART II

Aspirational Gulf

CHAPTER
4

Dubai as Heterotopia?
The Aspirational Politics of Everyday Cosmopolitanism in Gulf Space

Jaafar Alloul

The lives of my interviewees, moving between Europe and the Gulf, were not free of the moral contention surrounding places like Dubai. Take Maryam, for instance, a thirty-eight-year-old Belgian-Moroccan female who had worked in Dubai's private sector for a period of six years before returning to Belgium, where I first met her in early 2015. She claimed to have often received very negative comments in Brussels—her hometown—about moving to the Gulf. She rebuffed such skepticism, however, by microreferencing to me her family history and (earlier) class location: "Some people used to say that by going [to the Gulf], I would contribute to injustice and exploitation, because of the labor regimes on site. . . . but come on! In the end, I just wanted to improve my condition; get a better life. Why is that different from what our parents did, coming to Belgium from Morocco? . . . I mean this is, in a way, just the *renewed migration*. The only difference is that we refer to ourselves as expats." Maryam thus legitimized her overseas status position by framing her own mobility pursuits within a broader sequence of intergenerational labor migration, thus grounding her individual efforts as born out of the social necessities of a working-class condition. However, in so doing, she conveniently left out the fact that the current Emirati "regime of mobility" (Glick Schiller and Salazar 2013) does not grant citizenship to long-term (manual) workers in the same way that some states in postwar Europe did—Belgium included—albeit under pressure of surging labor (union) movements. To date, the UAE still prefers to rotate and replenish its "excess populations" (Davis 2007) systematically with new demographic "surpluses" from Asian sending countries (De Bel-Air 2018: 13). For instance, during the 2008 financial crisis and the ensuing market downturn, the UAE simply dismissed "temporary" workers back "home," thus freeing itself (in the immediate years to follow) from the domestic upheaval (Arab Spring) faced by many other Arab states, where unemployment directly affected the national citizenry. It is precisely this government-endorsed (labor) "hierarchization" in the UAE (Jamal 2015) that had conveniently allowed "expats" like Maryam to earn a much higher salary in Dubai than the average low-wage migrant worker from the Indian subcontinent or Southeast Asia.

Yet, besides the obvious class spoils of an expatriate wage package overseas, other elements in Maryam's narrative seemed equally important in fully understanding her newly cultivated "cosmopolitan" affect for the Gulf. Over the course of her resettlement in the UAE, Maryam had also inculcated a newfound self-esteem about her Arab Muslim heritage, so derided in Europe. While she stressed that she did not think of Dubai as an Islamic place per se, she did laud that "Emiratis are really proud of their culture and don't allow anyone to offend them," citing various examples of how Western celebrities, politicians, and tourists were put to the door by local authorities for offending native sensibilities or for behaving "improperly" in public. She also referred to alleged criticism on the part of other expats on government plans to build a mosque in the middle of a tourist area in Dubai—one that is known for its nightlife—to which she added: "Instead of building just one mosque, as planned, they built two, just to make a point. And this was *not* about religion; it was about pride." After celebrating this state-enforced sanctification of (Islamic) national heritage in the UAE, she then contrasted it immediately to a radically different configuration in Europe; one that she would now have to get used to again, having returned to her native Brussels: "It's a real struggle when you're Muslim in Europe. [Wearing the veil] I can tell you that it's a daily struggle for me again. In Dubai nobody is really preoccupied with such matters. Everyone is different there, so you feel comfortable the way you are." For Maryam, the Gulf seems to have functioned as a reflexive sort of sanctuary, a mirror space in which she took temporary refuge, having been fed up with Europe, a site she associated with (nativist) closure, negative alterity, and a distressed sense of struggle in terms of everyday belonging. Her account demonstrates the need to approximate "migration aspirations" (Aslany et al. 2021: 7) in socially grounded and longitudinal ways rather than relegating the process of migration to a momentary kinetic action of which the motivations and effects are finite or short-lived. In so doing, migration aspirations may indeed provide an insightful lens into how "people make sense of their lifeworlds, their individual lives, their pasts, presents and futures" (Bal and Willems 2014: 254). Yet while Maryam frames Dubai as an uplifting place harboring a casual sort of "cosmopolitan" openness when compared to Europe, throughout this chapter I will argue due caution in jumping rapidly to overly positivist or categorical comparative claims about Gulf space in analytical terms.

As pointed out by social historians (Hanley 2008), a romantic conviviality has long been projected onto the Middle East. Furthermore, it is often the uncritical reproduction of the discourse of cosmopolitanism in cultural studies (e.g., Appiah 2006) and historiography that naturalizes its use as an analytical category. Such unscrupulous elevations of the term *cosmopolitanism* not only service conveniently the aesthetic ideal types, or analytical judgments of "taste" (Bourdieu 1977: 87), of the "benevolent" academic observer—oftentimes scholars who themselves grew up in (globally transient) elite milieus (and diplomatic households)—but also veil the ways in which cosmopolitan talk tends to mask "a colonial or quasi-colonial situation of domination," which "depends largely on the exclusion of the majority from the mixed environment reserved to a wealthy, powerful and mobile elite" (Eldem 2013: 215). I raise these criticisms here not to dismiss, for instance, the (pre-)imperial histories of cultural exchange and transcontinental (commercial) flows in the Indian Ocean (dhow) trade complex (Fuccaro 2009; Bishara 2017), but rather to substantiate that, in "playing cosmopolitan" in contemporary Dubai (Stephan-Emmrich 2017: 272), European migrants like Maryam were positioned, by and large, on the "native" side of the local class divide (Lowi 2018: 401), resulting (not unexpectedly) in a more positive appreciation of Gulf space.

The above data excerpts provide an adequate entry point to explore the (proto-paradigmatic) spatial concept of "heterotopia," theorized by Michel Foucault ([1967/1984] 1986) as being mirage-like counter places, which, through their insulating properties, may operate momentarily in defying otherwise overwhelming social forces (of domination). This contribution takes particular interest in such unsettling occurrences of "space" and the ways in which they are experienced by *some*—those who are privileged enough—as if radically inverting formerly established norms and the order of things. With the help of Pierre Bourdieu's structuration paradigm of social analysis (1977; 1984; 2005), this chapter will discuss such unsettling and oftentimes celebratory narratives of the Gulf after migration. Hence, much like Reay, Crozier, and Clayton (2009: 1,103; 1,115) do in their study on higher education in the UK with the help of their functional archetype of being "strangers in paradise," this contribution applies a spatial metaphor (heterotopia) precisely in order to unpack the complex ways in which working-class-origin climbers become learning subjects along the way, fully capable of appropriating over time the behavioral traits of the more dominant social classes and, accordingly, of coreproducing hegemonic norms themselves.

Contextualizing Migrant Affect in Gulf Space

In trying to catch up with the meteoric rise of the UAE in political and economic affairs, social science scholarship on the Gulf Arab states is slowly gaining more traction. In recent years, a series of critical studies have come to light, many of which focus on international migration to the Gulf region (Ali 2010; Kanna 2013; Vora 2013; Walsh 2014; Kathiravelu 2016; Babar 2017; Mahdavi 2019; Akinci 2020; Le Renard 2019; Lori 2019; Stephan-Emmrich 2020; Parrenas 2020; Thiollet and Assaf 2020). This body of literature has started remedying the lack of knowledge about the social lives of foreigners in the Gulf Arab states (Gardner 2011: 1). In part, however, this lacuna persists, and it has much to do with the fact that "studies of identity and belonging in Gulf monarchies tend to privilege tribal or religious affiliation" over favorably incorporated immigrant groups like European workers, who constitute the local "community of privilege" together with citizen-subjects (Lowi 2018: 401).

This study is timely, therefore, as it investigates the "affective moves" of EU laborers (with a Maghrebi background) migrating from France, Belgium, and the Netherlands to the UAE, aiming to illustrate how human mobility compounds "a particularly intense emotional and transformative experience" (Svasek 2012: 13). As such, it unpacks the subject transformations that lay enmeshed in global emplacements and replacements, profoundly social processes that is, in which "people are changing places, moving from one location to another, transforming, and being transformed" (Kalir 2020: 357).

The longitudinal ethnographic data presented below suggests that Gulf places like Dubai were deeply appreciated for their cosmopolitan homeliness and canopy-like (Anderson 2012) properties. At first sight, this may seem at odds with Dubai's "authoritarian" mode of labor segregation and controversial track record on workers' rights (Kathiravelu 2016: 30; ILO 2017). Ample studies have set Dubai aside as an "urban apartheid" (Smith 2014: 293–94); a hypercapitalist dystopia mired in "modern day slavery" (Degorge 2007: 657) and built on the "superexploitation of workers drawn from the peripheries surrounding the GCC" (Hanieh 2011: 26); and a site where low-wage workers are esthetically segregated in specially designed industrial compounds and labor camps in the desert, as if they were (merely disposable) "foreign matter" (Dresch 2006). Another strand of literature, however, has started complicating this picture. For instance, in their study on state-based affinities in the Gulf Arab states, Vora and Koch (2015: 542) document a noncitizen form of "belonging despite exclusion," fueled in part by the recent actions of the Emirati leadership to allegedly "improve working conditions for workers of all class backgrounds" (2015: 549).

Yet others, like Akinci (2020), who have closely studied the lives of (non-GCC) second-generation Arab migrant communities in Dubai, add further complexity to what we know about settlement affect in Gulf space. Her work demonstrates that Gulf-based Arabs oftentimes strive to attain Western citizenship in the medium term as part of a transnational household strategy that deals with permanent exclusion from Emirati citizenship. However, in the long term, these residents still tend to plan their itineraries around the idea of "returning to the UAE, where they feel their cultural identity is not only unproblematic but also relatively privileged when compared to other non-Western migrant groups" (2020: 2318). In a similar way, most of the European-Maghrebi interlocutors I interviewed in the Gulf also tended to frame Dubai as a place where they felt at home and wanted to stay. These alternative accounts about belonging in the Gulf do seem to challenge to a certain extent the brisk categorization of Gulf Arab states as being almost unique in their mode of exclusion (Fargues 2011) and mainly "transitory" (Khalaf, AlShehabi, and Hanieh 2014) in nature, that is, as spaces allegedly bereft of their own "affective economies" (Threadgold 2020: 40) and gravitational logic of social reproduction (Bourdieu 1977).

Dubai as Heterotopia?

The visceral impression of experiencing a highly differential dignity and self-worth after setting up life in the UAE was widespread among my interviewees. This perceived inversion of social forces confronting them in local social space, experienced over the course of their resettlement to the UAE, thus approximates some of the properties of what Foucault conceptualized as "heterotopia." In his essay "Of Other Spaces," Foucault describes heterotopias as mirage-like counter-places, which, through their insulating properties have the ability to momentarily defy established norms: "I am interested in certain ones [spaces] that have the curious property . . . to suspect, neutralize, or invert the set of relations that they happen to designate, mirror, or reflect. These spaces . . . are of two main types. First there are the utopias. Utopias are sites with no real place. . . . There are also . . . something like counter-sites, a kind of effectively enacted utopia in which the real sites . . . are simultaneously represented, contested, and inverted" ([1967/1984] 1986: 24). Foucault then goes on to formalize the main characteristics of these so-called heterotopias, namely as holding the potential of deviating momentarily yet radically from otherwise established norms; as spaces to which access is restricted in some way or form; as highly illusionary in terms of their sensorial properties; and as leaving a visceral imprint on those who immerse themselves in the inverted rites of spatial passage that they entail. The notion of heterotopia has been operationalized by architects, geographers, and anthropologists as "something particular" within a given society or cityscape. Petti, for instance, in his 2008 work on Dubai's artificial Palm Islands megaproject, applies it to theorize the envisioned social relationships preengineered to take place in them. Others, like De Boeck (2014: 254-55), thinking through the spatial ambiance of the Congolese capital of Kinshasa, write that heterotopias are "the spaces that escape from the order of things, its standard forms of classification and accumulation, if only because they constantly conjure up the aesthetic through their appeal to the imagination and the oneiric." Building on this body of work, my contribution seeks to further expand these applications of heterotopia, in particular by putting this analytical metaphor to work in the context of Gulf space writ large. In so doing, it aims to unpack the cultural symbolism that a specific group of European migrants attaches to a place like Dubai.

In concerning itself latently with how migrant aspirations develop and play out across places, this contribution will resort implicitly to a Bourdieusian (1977: 72, 82-83, 214) lens of interpretation, meaning it will approach aspirations-as-dispositions that are, at least in part, socially grounded and socially produced, and therefore inherently tied into a person's "traveling habitus" (Alloul 2021). In the current era of neoliberal governance across the Western world, aspirations are, however, increasingly defused top-down as a self-help strategy in attaining social mobility (Stahl et al. 2020: 1) despite the gradual rise in social precarity that has emerged in the wake of large-scale deindustrialization and financialization. Critics remain adamant, therefore, in stressing that the cultivation of so-called individual aspirations "cannot be divorced from their political, economic and social context" (Reay 2020: xviii). By adopting a Bourdieusian paradigm of social inquiry, this contribution thus seeks to move the study of minority subjectivities beyond an increasingly dominant mode of approaching human agency from a largely individual-existential (meta-philosophical) angle. As such, it starts from the premise that some people remain further removed from seeing their future-focused aspirations fulfilled in the span of their own life course than others (e.g., Threadgold 2020: 37). Indeed, social (class) location matters in approximating to what extent subjective aspirations are likely to remain illusory or not.

This chapter endeavors to tease out the relational working of such affective forces—forces which, for instance, entice some migrants into making the Gulf their desired home. It is precisely by attending to such intimate yet broader meaning-making processes about space, as subjectively contextualized by migrants themselves, that we may apprehend the deeper (objective) grounds (back home) that spur specific social groups to come and "reinvent themselves in Dubai" (Mahdavi 2019: 1,389). In fact, the heterotopian-like affect that underlies such future-oriented (home-making) aspirations in relation to the Gulf Arab states would not leave my interlocutors unscathed over time. As I will demonstrate below, while many managed to effectively unsettle the former (European) order of things (by engaging in the counter-technique of emigration), their subsequent status privileges in the Gulf signaled also their very own implication (through inescapable social gravity) in coreproducing locally salient hegemonic norms and social hierarchizations.

Drawing on extensive "multi-sited" ethnographic fieldwork (Marcus 1995), this study relies on eighty semistructured interviews gathered among seventy interviewees, including ten focused follow-up interviews with key respondents at different time intervals. This pool of interlocutors consisted of twenty-nine males and forty-one females, all aged between twenty-five and forty. All were EU citizens, with at least one parent[1] born in Morocco, Algeria, or Tunisia. Other sample inclusion criteria were that interviewees were either working in the UAE, had returned (temporarily) after doing so, or were actively planning to move there when meeting them. Respondents hailed predominantly from working-class milieus, and their parents were blue-collar workers. The majority of them held advanced tertiary degrees. They worked in such fields as marketing, engineering, sales, IT, finance, marketing, tourism, architecture, real estate, and corporate law.

Becoming European in the Gulf:
Whiteness as a "Passport of Privilege"

I first met Latifa in May 2016 in Dubai. She was a thirty-six-year-old woman from Brussels of Belgian-Algerian origin who had been working in the UAE for nine years, mainly in the marketing and advertising industry. She was born a Belgian citizen and graduated from the Free University of Brussels (ULB) with an MA degree in Sociology. When I asked her whether she felt satisfied about her life in the Gulf, she answered: "I am a director now and [so far] I have worked for the most famous advertising firms. The salary and lifestyle are much more than they'd be in Belgium." Latifa grew up in the Brussels suburb of Etterbeek, where she was the oldest of three siblings.

Her parents were born in the Algerian city of Oran, and her father had previously lived in France before moving permanently to Belgium. Latifa referred to her working-class background to explain why she "had a rather difficult youth," claiming that "poverty was no stranger to us." She further described her upbringing as follows:

> I was born and raised in Brussels, in Etterbeek, which was actually a middle-class neighborhood. . . . I felt like I was limited in Belgium, professionally, emotionally, etcetera. . . . I went to a Catholic school, the *Institut St. Boniface-Parnasse* [in the Ixelles suburb], with only three other Arabs—Muslims—and racist comments were very frequent. . . . [I] never felt like I belonged to Belgium. . . . I used to feel like trash when I was a kid, coming from a *much poorer* background than most of the other students at school.

As a francophone Belgian, Latifa felt connected both to Belgium and France, as well as Algeria. She had always been fond of Algeria, to the extent that she had initially sought to move there so as to help improve "my country of origin." After graduating in 2006, she moved to Algeria. Yet upon arrival, she noticed she was considered "local" rather than "European" by the international development NGOs she had singled out as prospective employers: "Even though I am a Belgian passport holder, in Algeria I was considered Algerian, which comes with an Algerian salary . . . [pause] so it wasn't economically viable for me to work there. . . . It was crazy to see that others, Germans, French . . . [pause] *de souches, tu sais* [whites, you know], would get paid better than me simply because of my proximity to Algeria! The salary I got was only a few hundred euros per month." Latifa conveyed her disappointment about Algeria to me by highlighting that she was unable to blend her Belgian citizenship, Western degree, and "cultural proximity" to the local population, thus falling short of occupying a "European" status position upon arrival. In their recruitment of staff in the field, international organizations and NGOs usually differentiate between local and international contracts, a boundary-making practice in "humanitarian mobility" (Redfield 2012) that has been criticized for reproducing global inequalities and (neo-colonial) power disparities. In referencing what a "suitable" degree of privilege in Algeria would look like, Latifa references "native" Europeans (*"de souches"*) as an almost natural benchmark in terms of her desired wage setting. This goes to show that people "imagine, plan, and undertake different types of mobility in interaction with other relevant mobile and immobile subjects" (Kalir 2020: 353). Socialized in Europe from birth, Latifa's "migratory speak" thus suggests here that she genuinely presumed a level of material comfort to go along with her move to North Africa, not least through the allocation of salary that was not local. Clearly, Latifa had certain class expectations overseas, irrespective of whether or not she had altruistic motives for Algeria.

Latifa's latent expectations about a "European" distinction overseas, discursively disclosed by her conviction that "it wasn't economically viable for me to work there," may in part be understood as deriving from her socialization in the field of tertiary education in Europe. This socialization, occurring in a field historically characterized by an ever-more "blurred and fuzzy" production of social hierarchies, infusing even more hope into the aspirations of working-class students (Bourdieu 1984: 151), would have gradually instilled into Latifa's habitus a horizon of firmly (upper) middle-class expectations, or what Bourdieu (1984: 138) called a grounded sense of "objective potentiality." Unable to appropriate a "European" wage and its implied lifestyle privileges in Algeria, however, Latifa then rerouted her emigration project to Dubai. Indeed, for her, leaving behind negative alterity in Europe by "going native" overseas was not enough. She also seems to have expected her emigration project to yield a minimum degree of social mobility. If she had remained in Algeria, she may have condemned herself in the medium-to-long term to the same (experiential) class location that her household had previously occupied in Belgium, a lived social location she equated to feeling "like trash" during her early childhood. It was this lingering condition of a perceived class entrapment that traveled with her to Algeria, characterized by a racially structured mobility deprivation in relation to other "white Europeans," whom she considered to be her peers, which Latifa sought to overcome by engaging in the same mobility strategy her parents had earlier: transcontinental migration.

The fact that Latifa left Algeria after a short (six month) stint but then decided to stay put in Dubai does beg the question of what sort of status position she would subsequently be able to occupy in the Emirati hierarchy. Rahma, a thirty-seven-year-old Dutch-Moroccan biomedical engineer born and trained in the Netherlands, aptly made sense of what a "European" status position in the UAE may entail. I first met her in May 2016 in Abu Dhabi. She had taken up an applied research position in a specialized diabetes hospital, a public Emirati institution affiliated with Imperial College London. During her time on the work floor, and by mingling with peers working in the private sector, she had gained plenty of insight into the implicit stratifications of migrant labor in the UAE. When interviewing her in a café at an Abu Dhabi mall, she phrased it as follows:

> Look, if you work for a private company over here, then Arabic language skills are a real advantage. This is mainly due to the fact that locals [read: shareholders, investors, governmental stakeholders] still prefer to talk in Arabic. This is why [in every large company] you have

this layer of Arabs who act as intermediaries. Right underneath [the Emirati elites and the Arab business intermediaries], you have all the managers, Europeans, and other Westerners. In our institute, there are also many binationals like me, people with Western degrees and Arabic language skills. These people are really well positioned too.

While few of my Euro-Maghrebi interlocutors were as proficient in Arabic as Rahma, let alone able to mobilize it professionally and with due diligence—e.g., reading, writing, and switching dialects confidently when speaking—many did cite their transcultural versatility, in some way or form, as being more of an advantage to them in the Gulf when compared to Europe. This would come in the form of passive language skills or religious-normative affinities to the official and dominant state religion of the UAE. In fact, these comparative advantages may help explain why some Euro-Maghrebi interlocutors working in the private sector would attest to receiving a markedly cold shoulder from their Levantine-Arab coworkers in the Gulf. Initially, most of my male interlocutors saw the latter group as fellow "Arab" brethren from whom they aspired to learn the insides of a local (Arab) business culture. They were surprised, however, to be categorically perceived by their Arab coworkers as potential competitors instead.

Mohammad, a pious French-Moroccan in his late twenties working for a large American consultancy company in Dubai, shed some light on this. I interviewed him in the bustling Jumeirah Beach Residence area, where he rented out a flat. He agreed to meet me for dinner after finishing a long day of work. In his narrative it was clear that some of his earlier romantic aspirations about a "natural" Arab brotherhood in the Gulf were quickly at variance with his professional experiences on the ground: "What came as a shock to me was to see Arab colleagues here, mainly Lebanese, judge me as someone who's not modern when they noticed I pray and don't drink. . . . I left France fleeing just that and here I encounter it again." Despite the fact that French-Maghrebi workers like Mohammad would often be less proficient in (a relevant) Arabic (dialect) and less frequently exposed to the inner workings of local Arab and Emirati etiquette in terms of commercial conduct in the UAE, their EU citizenship status and technical training in Europe were still very much valued in the workplace. Mohammad, who had a few years of professional experience in the corporate sector in Europe under his belt, thus foregrounded his French "technological capital" (Bourdieu 2005: 194) as being a competitive edge beneficial to more "efficiently" carrying out everyday labor: "Compared to them, who often only did a bachelor's degree in Europe or Canada, we usually deliver more quality work. . . . This makes you feel very European, because suddenly you're aware of your European education."

Mohammad's French "educational capital" (Bourdieu 1984: 295, 302) thus made him stand out positively in the Emirati labor market, where he mingled with workers from all over the world. Mohammad's perception about a pending competition between his group and Levantine Arabs may have derived from each group possessing different but highly valued assets for the private sector in Dubai. Indeed, Mohammad's Levantine coworkers may have felt threatened by the appearance of a new group, who, at least at face value, appear to harbor the potential of positioning themselves in an equally hybrid fashion in Gulf space. After all, the Lebanese are historically known to dominate the figure of (imperial) "interloper" (Arsan 2014) in many fringe and emerging markets (e.g., West Africa, Latin America), not only in GCC economies. The analytical impression that Mohammad may very well be able to transgress—at least in part—into the privileged status zone of his Lebanese coworkers is further demonstrated by his astonishment about a dual uplifting in terms of status ascension in Gulf space:

> When they notice your accent in Arabic, and that you're in fact European, it helps; the French passport always helps. But in other social dimensions of the company—and this really astonished me—being an Arab is a real advantage. I never experienced this before! It's strange, but you feel it in relation to the Indians, Pakistanis, and Filipinos. Even if your [managing] boss is Indian, the mere fact that you're Arab will make him respect you. I've really noticed it at work. . . . It's wrong, of course, but this is just to say that it's totally the opposite from France, where the word Arab is usually the worst pejorative you can find. Here, you suddenly feel proud to be Arab.

For many of my respondents it was this sort of far-reaching (racial) status accrual overseas that discouraged them from returning to Europe any time soon. Furthermore, when I talked to French, Belgian, and Dutch migrants without an Arab immigrant background in Dubai, it appeared that they resided in the UAE only for a period of three to five years on average, and still considered Europe as their "natural home."

Mohammad's perception of undergoing an increase in self-worth seemed also to confluence exponentially his opportunities in the Gulf for effectuating class ascension. Take Malika, for instance, a thirty-one-year-old Dutch female born and raised in The Hague to immigrant parents from Morocco, who worked as a sales manager for a high-end Italian furniture company in Dubai. Her narrative aptly points to an actualization in Dubai of the class aspirations underlying her transnational career-building efforts: "As you long as you pay your bills and keep your mouth shut, it's perfect. You can drive any car you want, go spend your money in the Dubai Mall and everything's fine. Just don't come here in order to change the world or to stir up their political affairs. That's not your role over here. But if you want to make money, do business, and build a career, yes, all of that is very possible here." Malika seemed well aware of her "role" in the UAE, and equally of what she could potentially achieve in that context, namely the accumulation of "international" work experience, and, by proxy, "economic capital" (Bourdieu 1986: 243. This is contrary to what Akinci (2020: 2318) describes in her work on (non-GCC) second-generation Arab migrant communities in Dubai who already possess a considerable degree of economic capital and therefore venture out (temporarily) in search of legal security (Western citizenship status) in order to sustain their specific social position of privilege in the UAE in the long term. What is important to note here, however, is that both of these groups—each possessing in some way relevant Arab "racial capital" (Alloul 2020)—seem to feel very much at ease in Gulf modernity, even to the extent of envisioning it as a long-term place of residence, and this despite the legal insecurity and (therefore) residential impermanence sometimes associated with migration to this region of the world (Vora 2013; Khalaf, AlShehabi, and Hanieh 2014).

As shown above by Latifa's Algerian experience, my interlocutors' very ability to lay claim to Europeanness overseas derives in practice not only from the symbolic capital that lays enshrined in a Western passport, but also from the normative specificities that permeate the societal rhythms of the arrival space. Indeed, it was the interplay between their "honorary license" (Western passport) and the specific social context of the UAE that jointly produced their "honorary status" (Europeanness) in the Gulf. Hence, the racial properties that lay enmeshed in EU citizenship, and the potential ways in which this interchangeable form of capital provides a "conversion grid" (Arnaut et al. 2020: 6) for racialized "whitening" processes overseas, depend equally on the concrete places in which they are mobilized. It was this sort of strategic repositioning or agentive learning along the way—sometimes after "failing" in another place—that represents some of the "hard work" (Bourdieu [1982] 2020: 135), I would argue, that lays entangled in the migratory technique mobilized by my respondents in defying, or indeed transforming, the "social laws" previously governing their aspirations in Europe. As such, migration-as-process comes to the fore here as an alternative strategy of "defending one's capital" (Bourdieu [1982] 2018: 128), if not exponentially increasing it, depending on the doxic opportunity structures permeating the space of arrival.

The mobility aspect present in the narratives of Latifa, Malika, and Noura approximates what race studies scholars have called "whiteness as a passport of privilege" (Andrucki 2013: 123). This expression is used to describe both "the transcendent power consistently bestowed on and associated with whiteness across the globe," as well as "the emergence of whiteness as a congeries of bodies characterized by their capacity to move across borders, and how this is linked both to earlier histories of [settler-colonial] movement and the current globalizing era" (Andrucki 2013: 123). It is important to note that the racialized power bestowed onto "white migrations" exceeds the dimension of it being an unstable epistemological category of classification, which may for instance be retraceable to historical records of bureaucratic classification. This neocolonial type of power also perpetuates today in the form of powerful practices, not least through the everyday circulation of mobile bodies, which by virtue of their privileged movement across borders and within local spaces, constantly reify such "imagined" constructions of race in place. Race, in this basal sense—as the primary ideational building block for racialization—represents foremost a pseudo-scientific episteme borne out of a racist European modernity, ushered in on a global scale during the expansive era of Euro-colonial enterprise (Marx 1998: 23; Lentin 2020: 6-7), after which it has become operational as an empirical modality of practiced difference across nation-states the world over.

The highly racialized status privilege that seemed to be at the disposal of legally sanctioned European bodies in the Gulf is amplified by my interlocutors' casual ability to "come and go," entering and exiting the UAE with relative ease. Take, Fouad, for instance, a French-Tunisian male in his late twenties. He was one of the young men I got to know and occasionally hung out with in Dubai. Prior to his relocation to the Gulf in 2014, he had completed a one-year internship in London. When I first met him in Dubai in early 2016, he was enrolled in a traineeship with a French multinational company, working in sales and procurement, after which he was hired as a regular employee by the same company. Although I had interviewed him extensively, it was one of his social media posts that caught my attention. Having lived in the UAE for about two years at the time of his writing, he reflected on becoming more aware over time of the comparative value of his French passport: "My colleague Maria, from the Philippines, just received her visa approval to go on holiday to Germany. Immediately, she burst out in joy, screaming, crying even, because it seemed so incredible to her. A sentiment I can't even imagine. I'm reminded that it's a simple fortune and also pure luck to hold a French passport." Unlike the joy expressed by his Filipino colleague when she was finally granted permission to travel to Europe, Fouad needed not fantasize to the same extent over being granted tourist visas, a sort of non-European sentiment he "can't even imagine." Following his labor migration to the Gulf, Fouad's travel options remained abundant. Unlike Filipino workers in the UAE, he did not experience more stasis, for instance, by the Emirati labor regime governing his entry (e.g., Parrenas 2020). In the UAE, Fouad needed only occupy himself with deciding what was next on his leisure list. In fact, every other month or so, he would simply go on a long weekend excursion to get away from the everyday stress of working in corporate Dubai. As demonstrated by the leisure habitus of Fouad, it was relatively easy for my respondents to put the cosmopolitan idea of being a global citizen (*kosmopolites*) into actual practice during their stay in Dubai. As symbolic rites of self-making, their frequent travel habits as globetrotters thus signify a profoundly racialized form of class distinction in the globalized Gulf space. As will be demonstrated in the following section, for my respondents Dubai came to represent a deeply affectionate counterspace to Europe, so much so that they would find the sort of consumerist inclusion for which Gulf cities have become famous a far more appealing and dignified social contract than what they deemed was available to them in Europe.

The Cosmopolitan Gulf: Situating Heterotopia in Comparative Mobilities

Many of the Euro-Maghrebis I met in Dubai lived in well-furnished apartments, in neighborhoods like Dubai Downtown or Dubai Marina, or the areas immediately adjacent to them, such as Jumeirah Lake Towers or Jumeirah Beach Residence. They would either live alone or cohouse with other EU nationals. Unlike many Southeast Asian (low-wage) workers in Dubai (Kathiravelu 2012: 112), they would rarely take public transport, and moved around town in their own cars. As most of my European interviewees held working-class backgrounds in terms of household origins, this type of residential preference in the Gulf signals their social climbing. One way of describing their newfound (upper) middle-class lifestyles abroad is by way of their reveling in a readily available access in Dubai to "Islamic consumerism" (Pink 2009). Many attributed everyday value to a wide-ranging consumer infrastructure in the Gulf catering specifically to Muslim sensibilities. Marwan, for instance, a thirty-three-year-old Belgian-Moroccan who lived in Dubai for about five years (2009–14) before returning to Belgium with his spouse and two children, demonstrates aptly the profound impact a sudden access to the most generic of consumer rites may have on people's everyday sense of inclusion with the following account:

> In Dubai you can lead a *normal* life as a Muslim. You can go to the mall in your *jellaba* if you like. You can eat and shop for food *everywhere* you want, and not just in specific ethnic neighborhoods. . . . When I go to the supermarket in Belgium, it's sort of boring because I restrict myself to the vegetable and fruits section [laughs], but in Dubai I can really knock myself out: buy steak, chicken, hamburgers, basically *whatever* I

want, *wherever* I want, even in McDonalds! I know that it can be crappy food, and that these are small things, but it's *so nice*, you know!

Interestingly, Marwan equated the idea of a "normal life as a Muslim" with an overseas socialization into a more mainstream consumer culture. In Dubai he was able to casually "participate" in consumer modernity in any given hypermarket, even when dressed in traditional Maghrebi garments. No longer having to restrict himself to specific "ethnic neighborhoods" or particular sections of the supermarket in his native Flanders, Marwan felt like he was able to move around with less restraint and more anonymously in the Gulf—his *jellaba* no longer drawing attention, suspicion, or disdain. Others, like Munir, a twenty-eight-year-old French-Moroccan working in corporate law and sales in Dubai, echoed Marwan's consumer conviviality, stating that "everyone here thinks of advancing his or her career, of having a good time, of going to the beach, of enjoying oneself: a society of consumption, everything is within your reach to consume." Rather than applying to all immigrant workers in Dubai, as Munir so generously claims, the privilege of everything being "within your reach" in the Gulf emerges from the specific class location of a person's European expatriate group. The fact that he characterizes his resettlement experience as near frictionless and one that is marked by self-gratifying rites of "conspicuous consumption" (Veblen [1899] 2016) is analytically significant. It goes to show the ways in which Dubai has come to occupy today a lived, imagined, and broadly circulated consumer "model" for a widely aspired-to "Muslim modernity" (Stephan-Emmrich 2020: 298) under contemporary global capitalism.

Following Bourdieu's (1977: 79) sociological *Outline of a Theory of Practice*, we may argue here that place-specific shifts in habitus, along with the spatial affects they arouse dialectically, carry with them the relational indexes of differential power, and therefore, momentarily denote the agent's specific locus within the social hierarchy: "It is because subjects do not, strictly speaking, know what they are doing that what they do has more meaning than they know. . . . That part of practices which remains obscure in the eyes of their own producers is the aspect by which they are objectively adjusted to other practices and to the structures to which the principle of their production is itself the product." The claim of equating Gulf space with a decreased sense of spatial friction was a recurrent theme in the narratives of my Euro-Maghrebi respondents. For instance, when in 2016 I interviewed Samir, a thirty-two-year-old French-Algerian male working for the Dubai Department of Tourism and Commerce Marketing, he described to me how, over the course of his studies and early professional internships in France, he was worn down by a subtle yet unabating racialization in key spaces of everyday socialization:

> The first time I really experienced the difference was the moment when I got my *bacc* [high school degree] and needed to look for a school. . . . The second time I felt this sense of difference . . . was when I started looking for internships [in the final year of university]. I looked for six months while most others [of my class] did for about two weeks because they all had had contacts. But I had prepared for this . . . by doing small nonobligatory traineeships during my schooling; because I knew that I'd be starting with a handicap. . . . I always felt it in the business environment in France, small jokes that would indicate my difference. That's how you feel *it*.

Annoyed by this everyday racialization ("it") in the workplace, Samir then decided to leave for the UK instead, where he spent eight years working in the sales and marketing sector of the automobile industry, before moving on to the UAE in mid-2013. When recounting to me his subsequent move to Dubai, he signaled how his former (French) status deficiency ("it") appeared not only to have been neutralized—much like it had been in the UK—but also that after moving geographically even further away from France, it felt as if his earlier status "handicap" was even inverted in the Gulf: "Here, it's gone. I really feel that I belong to this place. I feel a lot more connected. I don't feel out of place at all. I feel like I've been here my whole life. There is no friction at all for me! I don't know; it's a weird feeling. It's so natural; an inner tranquility, from the inside." Samir's evocation of feeling "no friction at all" in Dubai suggests that he occupies a more privileged (racial) status position in the UAE when compared to France, standing out less negatively in his new hometown. Samir claims that "it" remains more positively charged in the UAE, superseding in experience the strict realm of his work experience in the field of marketing and tourism. In fact, he states that he feels "no [phenomenological] friction at all," almost as if he were a native of the country. He equates this transformation of status following his onward migration with a form of personal liberation, that is, with a certain sense of "tranquility" with geographical place and "connection" to social space. Moreover, this gradual reconfiguration also allowed him to determine for himself to what extent he wished to practice his religiosity (through daily prayers, for example), both in private as well as in the (public) workspace, something that would have been unimaginable to him in his native France.

Given that Dubai is known to be a highly monitored and "nearly crime-free, consumer-oriented society" (Ali 2011: 556), the city's "inclusive" properties were expressed by my respondents not only in relation to its consumer rites but equally in terms of everyday safety, especially by female interlocutors. Many such French and Belgian respondents recounted instances of physical harassment in Europe, perpetrated by males of both the in- and out-group. It was Sarah, a thirty-two-year-old Belgian-Moroccan accountant-turned-flight attendant for Emirates, who highlighted the gendered probability of everyday physical violence with which racialized bodies in Europe are confronted. When I met Sarah in Dubai in early 2016, she had spent more than three years in the Gulf, insisting—in near heterotopian vein—that life had immediately become easier for her after moving. When she recalled the months leading up to her departure from Belgium—a time during which she still wore the veil—she stated:

> Upon arrival [in Dubai] . . . I could go where I wanted. I could carry out my prayers if I wanted to. No racist comments, which I used to get a lot in Belgium. I remember once passing someone . . . [long pause] I remember . . . [pause] when I used to go to Antwerp more often [coming from Brussels], a Belgian man who passed me, all of a sudden just spat in my face. My [female] friend and I were completely shocked. Such things would never happen to me over here . . . being Muslim over there seemed like a taboo, as if it's the worst thing you could possibly be. I couldn't stand it any longer.

What had been shocking to Sarah was not only undergoing this sort of denigrating violence in public life in Europe, but also the unexpectedness by which it could occur, eclipsing her ability to shield herself mentally from a perpetrator's act. Sarah's experience lends anecdotal evidence to the longitudinal observations of social historians (Traverso 2016: 94, 96) who claim that modern racism in continental Europe has now undergone a transfer of object, with anti-Semitism having morphed into current day Islamophobia. At first sight, then, my respondents' narratives approximate Elijah Anderson's (2012) notion of the "cosmopolitan canopy," described as a spatial experience during which otherwise salient racial divides (permeating wider society) are suspended temporarily, instead revealing a fragile moment of sudden "civility." Anderson highlights the deep appreciation that young African American males—who are used to having their skin color "associated with poverty, danger, and distrust" (2012: 2)—tend to feel for such fragile spaces of suddenly perceived civility. These spaces, which may be at once geographical as well as social, entice highly racialized subjects in particular, mainly because they represent a glimpse into the potentialities of a future social ambiance hitherto still elusive in their broader experience with society. I would argue that the narratives of my respondents about the perks of an anonymous consumer respectability and alter-civility in Dubai echo some of the mirage-like properties of Anderson's notion of cosmopolitan canopy, at least when juxtaposing them to a former sense of constant racial interpellation in Europe.

My interlocutors' "progressive sense of place" (Massey 1993) in the Gulf, along with their fraught social biographies in Europe, seem to have resulted in a heterotopian perception of Dubai as being a "safe haven against the violence of society, legal or illegal" (De Cauter and Dehaene 2008: 296). It is precisely by contrasting across space two seemingly distinct ontologies that may help unearth in more nuanced ways the situated logics (Bourdieu [1982] 2018: 92, 128) from which they spring. In trying to develop the notion of heterotopia, Foucault ([1967/1984] 1986: 27) uses the key metaphor of the boat-as-heterotopia, which he not only ties to the idea of being an emotionally *insulating* vessel in troubled times, but also attributes the function of propelling its passengers in pursuit of their (colonial-like) mobility aspirations overseas. The wrought histories of European colonial enterprise, and the (industrialized) metropole's ad hoc need to expose its excess populations (Oxley 1996) onto overseas "dumping grounds" (Bourdieu 1984: 150), do resonate with the idea of contemporary Dubai-as-counterspace. Indeed, the narratives of many interlocutors seemed to denote reflexively such mirror functions: Gulf space as insulating them physically and emotionally from a former social condition of (classed, raced, and gendered) turbulence in Europe while equally propelling them in the UAE into actualizing some of their deeply held aspirations.

Based on some of the interview narratives presented above, one may be tempted to shortsightedly frame Dubai as if it were only a harmonious space, a cosmopolitan home in which my interlocutors sought refuge, far removed from the haunting specter of the "iconic ghetto" (Anderson 2012: 3) racially policing their class (im)mobility in Europe. Indeed, many of my interviewees would affectionately frame Dubai as their deracialized "safe heaven" or as a "home in diversity." However, these narratives about Dubai are very *classed* too, insofar as they hide the uplifting process of having undergone a positive reracialization (as "white" Europeans) overseas, albeit one with a different outcome. In Dubai my respondents remained very insulated from being overtly confronted with the discomforts of the local underclass (e.g., the sight of abject poverty or everyday exposure to petty crime), segregated out of sight by an authoritarian mode of labor governance (Dresch 2006; Zizek 2011; Smith 2014). In resettling to the UAE, my interviewees became part and parcel of a small and very privileged group of European workers who, in direct or indirect ways, started taking part in profiting from the labor exploitation confronting the bulk of the (Asian) resident population (De Bel-Air 2018: 13). Hence, it remains key to contextualize (Western and Arab) narrative claims about "inclusionary assemblages" (Vora and Koch 2015: 544, 549) in the Gulf, as (ideologically) flowing from a very specific "expatriate" milieu—or "traveling habitus" (Alloul 2021)—as well as being immediately contingent upon a very particular migrant hierarchization and citizenship "tiering" (Jamal 2015) by hand of the Emirati authorities on the ground.

It is precisely by drawing up such a "contextualized ethnography of whiteness," within and across national borders that classist processes of racialization become visible as implicit power "structures of privilege and control" (Hendriks 2017: 697). In this sense, "playing cosmopolitan" in Dubai is also about complex and transnational politics "of belonging and longing" (Stephan-Emmrich 2017: 274), not least in terms of the displaced class aspirations and racial self-cultivations that such a display of agency harbors. Indeed, a Fanonian ([1963] 2001: 32) social psychology may be at work here: in building a new "home" overseas, my interviewees may very well have internalized over time and appropriated (unconsciously) the (former) "master's tools," contributing all too easily in new modes of (settler-colonial-like) social reproduction. Such *dominant* dispositions of a new-found and "naturalized" character overseas (Bourdieu [1982] 2020: 137) were most certainly reflected in the narratives of my interlocutors in the UAE. Take Rahma, mentioned above, who expounded a *sanitized* discourse on the Gulf, by leaving out any accountability that might befall her privileged "expatriate" group in the UAE:

> Many people have an opinion about the fact that locals earn twice as much as nonlocals. The same goes for the [plights of the] non-expat group, which doesn't have many rights. They can only work here and earn some money, and that's basically it. . . . However, when you then talk to some of them, you get the impression that they have a much better life over here than in their country of origin. Okay, maybe they only make 1 EUR an hour or so, but maybe they can still build some kind of life with that. For them, this [UAE] is probably better than that [country of origin]. So, it's relative. My opinion is that as long as people are treated rather decently, it's all fine.

While the historical development of racial capitalism (Robinson 1983) has had a truly global reach (Gilroy 1993), its articulations remain place-specific, thus also engendering the continuation of a largely global playing field of radically divergent life opportunities for those who are willing or forced to venture out. This echoes race studies scholars Neely and Samura's (2011: 1934) insight that "the making and remaking of space is also about the making and remaking of race," a dimension equally relevant in the context of the transcontinental migration of mobile bodies, sometimes racialized differently across places. When analyzed from this vantage point, then, Dubai's neocolonial ambiance—still very much entangled with the "European man's" (Fanon 1963) global financial and security architectures (Blumi 2018; Hanieh 2018)—may very well resemble that of older colonial destinations in the New World. It is worth citing the work of migration scholar Robin Cohen (2006: 153), who in his analysis of British migration in the nineteenth century was quick to point out that it used to be "perfectly possible for English and Irish convicts to become landowners and gentlemen farmers in Australia." It demonstrates that a drive for upward mobility in the social order has long functioned as an (infra-colonial) emigration motive, especially for symbolically stained European publics that would have otherwise remained stuck in their abject social positions.

It becomes clear that many of my respondents were discouraged to return "home" because the Gulf had facilitated *a whole series of actualized inversions* in terms of spatial affect and inculcated aspirations, some of which lay outside of the immediate (economistic) purview of strictly material gains and financial stability. For them, migration-as-process was not only an immediate strategy of "defending one's capital" (Bourdieu [1982] 2018: 128) in light of a perceived racial "handicap" on the labor market in Europe (cf. Samir, above), but equally represented a longer-term strategy of redefining "home" altogether.

Given its starkly neocolonial ambiance, Dubai could be seen as representing an "extreme type" of heterotopia (Foucault [1967/1984] 1986: 27), radical in its potential to invert the status fortunes of those willing enough to "populate" and "manage" its space. I argue, therefore, that sanitized narratives about the Gulf only become legible analytically when attending to the racialized class positionalities that they denote. Indeed, cosmopolitan distinction is not free from the determinate social bases from which it arises (Calhoun 2002: 873). Despite a long intellectual tradition of neo-Kantian moralism seeking to advance and naturalize a more "universalist" notion of cosmopolitan identification as if it were a desired alternative ontology in an otherwise "troubled" world (e.g., Appiah 2006), in critical sociology there is less room for a "pure" or "disinterested" affect, floating freely as an isolated "individual consciousness," merely there for the perks of philosophical extrapolation (Bourdieu, as cited in: Jenkins 2002: 128). Hence, cosmopolitan affect, as the dispositional judgments of taste that often flow from a racialized class habitus, needs always to be contextualized relationally in the place-specific "affective economy" (Threadgold 2020) that coproduces it.

Conclusions

This contribution has explored the heterotopian-like affect for the Gulf permeating the narrative metaphors of EU laborers with a Maghrebi background in Dubai. In pursuit of an alternative critique of the affective belonging of noncitizen groups in the UAE, this contribution argues for a denaturalization of "cosmopolitanism" as if it were a neutral category of practice. In a two-pronged manner, it argues for an analytical reading of this affect metaphor that goes beyond the mere individual-existential level. First, the interview data and ethnographic materials presented above ground the idea of a frictionless homecoming in Dubai in relational opposition to the burdensome condition of a former stigmatization in Europe, thus mindful of the consequential mobility aspirations that spring from it.

Second, highly sanitized claims about a cosmopolitan inclusiveness in Gulf space are foregrounded to be (ideologically) contingent upon a very specific and numerically exclusive "expatriate" milieu in the UAE; that is, part of the dispositional armory of those who are socialized into a much more dominant group following international migration. It was my respondents' legal privileges as European expats in the UAE, their cultural proximity to the dominant "native" group within local racial hierarchization in Dubai, as well as their long-aspired normalization as anonymous consumers included into a more readily available "Islamic" market infrastructure in the Gulf that made their aggregate experience of Gulf space approximate that of an appealing counter-modernity, nearing a fragile but ideal-type heterotopia. In sum, it was not in spite of, but precisely because of Dubai's neoliberal and neocolonial ambiance—conducive to such an insulating alter-civility—that many of my respondents were allowed to reinvent themselves gradually as global citizens, or *kosmopolites*.

Jaafar Alloul holds a joint PhD degree from the University of Amsterdam and KU Leuven. He is currently a postdoctoral research fellow at KU Leuven and Nanyang Technological University (NTU) Singapore, focusing on the sociology of migration, diversity, and citizenship regimes in Qatar. Next to labor migration, urban ethnography, political Islam, and transnational class making, one of his longstanding research foci is the economic, social, and cultural development of the Gulf Arab states. His work has appeared in *Middle East Critique*, *The Journal of Immigrant & Refugee Studies*, *Mobilities*, and *Transitions: Journal of Transient Migration*.

NOTE

1. All but one respondent had two parents with North African heritage.

REFERENCES

Akinci, Idil. 2020. "Culture in the 'Politics of Identity': Conceptions of National Identity and Citizenship among Second-Generation non-Gulf Arab Migrants in Dubai."

Journal of Ethnic and Migration Studies 46, no. 11: 2309-25. https://doi.org/10.1080/1369183X.2019.1583095.

Ali, Syed. 2010. *Dubai: Gilded Cage*. New Haven: Yale University Press.

———. 2011. "Going and Coming and Going Again: Second-Generation Migrants in Dubai." *Mobilities* 6, no. 4: 553-68.

Alloul, Jaafar. 2020. "Leaving Europe, Aspiring Access: Racial Capital and Its Spatial Discontents among the Euro-Maghrebi Minority." *Journal of Immigrant & Refugee Studies* 18, no. 3: 1-13. https://doi.org/10.1080/15562948.2020.1761504.

———. 2021. "'Traveling Habitus' and the New Anthropology of Class: Proposing a Transitive Tool for Analyzing Social Mobility in Global Migration." *Mobilities*. https://doi.org/10.1080/17450101.2021.1885833.

Anderson, Elijah. 2012. *The Cosmopolitan Canopy: Race and Civility in Everyday Life*. New York: W. W. Norton & Company.

Andrucki, Max. 2013. "The Visa Whiteness Machine: Transnational Motility in Post-Apartheid South Africa." In *Geographies of Privilege*, edited by W. Twine and B. Gardener, 121-34. New York: Routledge.

Appiah, Kwame Anthony. 2006. *Cosmopolitanism: Ethics in a World of Strangers*. New York: W. W. Norton & Company.

Arnaut, Karel, Jean-Michel Lafleur, Nadia Fadil, Jeremy Mandin, and Jaafar Alloul. 2020. "Leaving Europe: New Crises, Entrenched Inequalities and Alternative Routes of Social Mobility." *Journal of Immigrant & Refugee Studies* 18, no. 3: 1-9. https://doi.org/10.1080/15562948.2020.1759751.

Arsan, Andrew. 2014. *Interlopers of Empire: The Lebanese Diaspora in Colonial French West Africa*. London: C. Hurst & Co. Publishers.

Aslany, Maryam, Jorgen Carling, Mathilde Balsrud Mjelva, and Tone Sommerfelt. 2021. "Systematic Review of Determinants of Migration Aspirations—QuantMig Deliverable 2.2." Southampton: University of Southampton.

Babar, Zahra. 2017. "Introduction." In *Arab Migrant Communities in the GCC*, edited by Zahra Babar, 1-18. London: C. Hurst & Co.

Bal, Ellen, and Roos Willems. 2014. "Introduction: Aspiring Migrants, Local Crises and the Imagination of Futures 'Away from Home.'" *Identities* 2, no. 13: 249-58. http://dx.doi.org/10.1080/1070289X.2014.858628.

Bishara, Farid. 2017. *A Sea of Debt Law and Economic Life in the Western Indian Ocean, 1780–1950*. Cambridge, UK: Cambridge University Press.

Blumi, Isa. 2018. *Destroying Yemen: What Chaos in Arabia Tells Us about the World*. Oakland: University of California Press.

Bourdieu, Pierre. 1977. *Outline of a Theory of Practice*. Cambridge, UK: Cambridge University Press.

———. 1984. *Distinction: A Social Critique of the Judgement of Taste*. London: Routledge.

———. 1986. "The Forms of Capital." In *Handbook of Theory and Research for the Sociology of Education*, edited by John Richardson, 241-58. Westport: Greenwood.

———. 2005. *The Social Structures of the Economy*. Cambridge, UK: Polity Press.

———. (1982) 2018. *Pierre Bourdieu: Classification Struggles; General Sociology. Volume 1: Lectures at the Collège de France 1981–1982*. Translated by Peter Collier, edited by

Patrick Champagne, Julien Duval, Franck Poupeau, and Marie-Christine Rivière. Cambridge, UK: Polity Press.

———. (1982) 2020. *Pierre Bourdieu: Habitus and Field; General Sociology*. Volume 2: *Lectures at the Collège de France, 1981–1982*. Translated by Peter Collier, edited by Patrick Champagne, Julien Duval, Franck Poupeau, and Marie-Christine Rivière. Cambridge, UK: Polity Press.

Calhoun, Craig. 2002. "The Class Consciousness of Frequent Travelers: Toward a Critique of Actually Existing Cosmopolitanism." *The South Atlantic Quarterly* 101, no. 4: 869-97. https://doi.org/10.1215/00382876-101-4-869.

Cohen, Robin. 2006. *Migration and Its Enemies: Global Capital, Migrant Labour and the Nation-State*. Burlington: Ashgate.

Davis, Mike. 2007. *Planet of Slums*. New York: Verso.

De Bel-Air, Françoise. 2018. "Demography, Migration and the Labour Market in the UAE." *GLMM Explanatory Note* 1: 1-31. https://gulfmigration.org/media/pubs/exno/GLMM_EN_2018_01.pdf.

De Boeck. Filip. 2014. *Kinshasa: Tales of the Invisible City*. Leuven: Leuven University Press.

De Cauter, Lieven, and Michiel Dehaene. 2008. "The Space of Play: Towards a General Theory of Heterotopia." In *Heterotopia and the City*, edited by Lieven De Cauter and Michiel Dehaene, 287-96. London: Routledge.

Degorge, Barbara. 2007. "Modern Day Slavery in the United Arab Emirates." *The European Legacy* 11, no. 6: 657-66. https://doi.org/10.1080/10848770600918307.

Dresch, Paul. 2006. "Foreign Matter: The Place of Strangers in Gulf Society." In *Globalization and the Gulf*, edited by John Fox, Nada Mourtada-Sabbah, and Mohammed AlMutawa, 200-22. London: Routledge.

Eldem, Edhem. 2013. "Istanbul as a Cosmopolitan City: Myths and Realities." In *A Companion to Diaspora and Transnationalism*, edited by Ato Quayson and Girish Daswani, 212-30. Hoboken: Wiley-Blackwell.

Fanon, Frantz. (1963) 2001. *The Wretched of the Earth*. London: Penguin.

Fargues, Philippe. 2011. "Immigration Without Inclusion: Non-Nationals in Nation-Building in the Gulf States." *Asian and Pacific Migration Journal* 20, no. 3-4: 273-92. https://doi.org/10.1177/011719681102000302.

Foucault, Michel. (1967/1984) 1986. "Of Other Spaces." *Diacritics* 16, no. 1: 22-27. https://doi.org/10.2307/464648.

Fuccaro, Nelida. 2009. *Histories of City and State in the Persian Gulf: Manama Since 1800*. Cambridge, UK: Cambridge University Press.

———. 2013. "Preface: Urban Studies in the Arabian Peninsula: Six Thoughts on the Field." *Arabian Humanities* 2. https://doi.org/10.4000/cy.2530.

Gardner, Andrew. 2011. "Gulf Migration and the Family." *Journal of Arabian Studies* 1, no. 1: 3-25. https://doi.org/10.1080/21534764.2011.576043.

Gilroy, Paul. 1993. *The Black Atlantic: Modernity and Double-Consciousness*. Cambridge, MA: Harvard University Press.

Glick Schiller, Nina, and Noel Salazar. 2013. "Regimes of Mobility Across the Globe." *Journal of Ethnic and Migration Studies* 39, no. 2: 183-200. https://doi.org/10.1080/1369183X.2013.723253.

Hanieh, Adam. 2011. *Capitalism and Class in the Gulf Arab States.* London: Palgrave Macmillan.

———. 2018. *Money, Markets, and Monarchies: The Gulf Cooperation Council and the Political Economy of the Contemporary Middle East.* Cambridge, UK: Cambridge University Press.

Hanley, Will. 2008. "Grieving Cosmopolitanism in Middle East Studies." *History Compass* 6, no. 5: 1346–47. https://onlinelibrary.wiley.com/doi/abs/10.1111/j.1478-0542.2008.00545.x.

Hendriks, Thomas. 2017. "A Darker Shade of White: Expat Self-Making in a Congolese Rainforest Enclave." *Africa* 87, no. 4: 683–701. https://doi.org/10.1017/S0001972017000316.

ILO/International Labour Organization. 2017. "Employer-Migrant Worker Relationships in the Middle East: Exploring Scope for Internal Labour Market Mobility and Fair Migration." *White Paper of the ILO Regional Office for Arab States* 9789221306771: 1–26.

Jamal, Manal. 2015. "The 'Tiering' of Citizenship and Residency and the 'Hierarchization' of Migrant Communities: The United Arab Emirates in Historical Context." *International Migration Review* 49, no. 3: 601–32. https://doi.org/10.1111/imre.12132.

Jenkins, Richard. 2002. *Pierre Bourdieu.* London: Routledge.

Kalir, Barak. 2020. "Afterword: On Transitive Concepts and Local Imagination: Studying Mobilities from a Translocal Perspective." In *Mobilities, Boundaries, and Travelling Ideas*, edited by Manja Stephan-Emmrich and Philipp Schröder, 349–60. Cambridge, UK: Open Books Publisher.

Kanna, Ahmed. 2013. "'A Group of Like-Minded Lads in Heaven': Everydayness and the Production of Dubai Space." *Journal of Urban Affairs* 36, no. 2: 605–20. https://doi.org/10.1111/juaf.12074.

Kathiravelu, Laavanya. 2012. "Social Networks in Dubai: Informal Solidarities in an Uncaring State." *Journal of Intercultural Studies* 33, no. 1: 103–19. https://doi.org/10.1080/07256868.2012.633319.

———. 2016. *Migrant Dubai: Low Wage Workers and the Construction of a Global City.* New York: Palgrave Macmillan.

Khalaf, Abdulhadi, Omar AlShehabi, and Adam Hanieh, eds. 2014. *Transit States: Labour, Migration and Citizenship in the Gulf.* London: Pluto Press.

Lentin, Alana. 2020. *Why Race Still Matters.* Cambridge, UK: Polity Press.

Le Renard, Amélie. 2019. *Le Privilege Occidental: Travail, Intimité et Hierarchies Postcoloniales à Dubai.* Paris: Presses de Sciences Po.

Lori, Noora. 2019. *Offshore Citizens: Permanent Temporary Status in the Gulf.* Cambridge, UK: Cambridge University Press.

Lowi, Miriam. 2018. "Identity, Community and Belonging in GCC States." *Sociology of Islam* 6: 401–28. https://doi.org/10.1163/22131418-00604004.

Mahdavi, Pardis. 2019. "The Personal Politics of Private Life in the United Arab Emirates (UAE): Sexualities, Space, Migration and Identity Politics in Motion." *Culture, Health & Sexuality* 21, no. 12: 1,381–93. https://doi.org/10.1080/13691058.2018.1564938.

Marcus, George. 1995. "Ethnography in/of the World-System: The Emergence of Multi-Sited Ethnography." *Annual Review of Anthropology* 24: 95–117. https://doi.org/10.1146/annurev.an.24.100195.000523.

Marx, Anthony. 1998. *Making Race and Nation: A Comparison of the United States, South Africa, and Brazil*. Cambridge, UK: Cambridge University Press.

Massey, Doreen. 1993. "Power-Geometry and a Progressive Sense of Place." In *Mapping the Futures: Local Cultures, Global Change*, edited by Jon Bird, Barry Curtis, Tim Putnam, George Robertson, and Lisa Tickner, 59–69. London: Routledge.

Neely, Brooke, and Michelle Samura. 2011. "Social Geographies of Race: Connecting Race and Space." *Ethnic and Racial Studies* 34, no. 11: 1,933–52. https://doi.org/10.1080/01419870.2011.559262.

Oxley, Deborah. 1996. *Convict Maids: The Forced Migration of Women to Australia*. Cambridge, UK: Cambridge University Press.

Parrenas, Rhacel. 2020. "The Mobility Pathways of Migrant Domestic Workers." *Journal of Ethnic and Migration Studies* 47, no. 1: 3–24. https://doi.org/10.1080/1369183X.2020.1744837.

Petti, Alessandro. 2008. "Dubai Offshore Urbanism." In *Heterotopia and the City*, edited by Michiel Dehaene and Lieven De Cauter, 287–96. London: Routledge.

Pink, Johanna. 2009. *Muslim Societies in the Age of Mass Consumption: Politics, Culture and Identity Between the Local and the Global*. Cambridge, UK: Cambridge Scholars Publication.

Reay, Diane. 2020. "Foreword." In *International Perspectives on Theorizing Aspirations: Applying Bourdieu's Tools*, edited by Garth Stahl, Derron Wallace, Ciaran Burke, and Steven Threadgold, xiv–xx. New York: Bloomsbury.

Reay, Diane, Gill Crozier, and John Clayton. 2009. "Stranger in Paradise: Working Class Students in Elite Universities." *Sociology* 43, no. 6: 1,103–21. https://doi.org/10.1177/0038038509345700.

Redfield, Peter. 2012. "The Unbearable Lightness of Ex-pats: Double Binds of Humanitarian Mobility." *Cultural Anthropology* 27, no. 2: 358–82. https://doi.org/10.1111/j.1548-1360.2012.01147.x.

Robinson, Cedric. 1983. *Black Marxism: The Making of the Black Radical Tradition*. London: Zed Press.

Smith, Richard. 2014. "Dubai in Extremis." *Theory, Culture & Society* 31, no. 7–8: 291–96. https://doi.org/10.1177/0263276414547775.

Stahl, Garth, Derron Wallace, Ciaran Burke, and Steven Threadgold. 2020. "Introduction: Using Bourdieu to Theorize Aspirations." In *International Perspectives on Theorizing Aspirations: Applying Bourdieu's Tools*, edited by Garth Stahl, Derron Wallace, Ciaran Burke, and Steven Threadgold, 1–17. New York: Bloomsbury.

Stephan-Emmrich, Manja. 2017. "Playing Cosmopolitan: Muslim Self-Fashioning, Migration and (Be-)Longing in the Tajik Dubai Business Sector." *Central Asian Affairs* 4, no. 3: 270–91. https://doi.org/10.1163/22142290-00403001.

———. 2020. "iPhones, Emotions, Mediations: Tracing Translocality in the Pious Endeavours of Tajik Migrants in the United Arab Emirates." In *Mobilities, Boundaries, and*

Travelling Ideas: Rethinking Translocality Beyond Central Asia and the Caucasus, edited by Manja Stephan-Emmrich and Philipp Schröder, 291–318. Cambridge, UK: Open Book Publishers.

Svasek, Maruska. 2012. "Affective Moves: Transit, Transition and Transformations." In *Moving Subjects, Moving Objects: Transnationalism, Cultural Production and Emotions*, edited by Maruska Svasek, 1–40. New York: Berghahn Books.

Thiollet, Hélène, and Laure Assaf. 2020. "Cosmopolitanism in Exclusionary Contexts." *Population, Space & Place* 27: 1–16. https://doi.org/10.1002/psp.2358.

Threadgold, Steven. 2020. "Bourdieu Is Not a Determinist: Illusio, Aspiration, Reflexivity and Affect." In *International Perspectives on Theorizing Aspirations: Applying Bourdieu's Tools*, edited by Garth Stahl, Derron Wallace, Ciaran Burke, and Steven Threadgold, 36–50. New York: Bloomsbury.

Traverso, Enzo. 2016. *The End of Jewish Modernity*. London: Pluto Press.

Veblen, Thorstein. (1899) 2016. *The Theory of the Leisure Class*. New York: Pantheon Classics.

Vora, Neha. 2013. *Impossible Citizens: Dubai's Indian Diaspora*. Durham: Duke University Press.

Vora, Neha, and Natalie Koch. 2015. "Everyday Inclusions: Rethinking Ethnocracy, Kafala, and Belonging in the Arabian Peninsula." *Studies in Ethnicity and Nationalism* 15, no. 3: 540–52. https://doi.org/10.1111/sena.12158.

Walsh, Katie. 2014. "'It Got Very Debauched, Very Dubai!' Heterosexual Intimacy amongst Single British Expatriates." *Social & Cultural Geography* 8, no. 4: 507–33. http://dx.doi.org/10.1080/14649360701529774.

Zizek, Slavoj. 2011. *Living in the End Times*. New York: Verso.

CHAPTER
5

A Strangeness One Can Occupy
Clothes and Their Codes in the Photographs of Gulf Migrants from Kerala

Mohamed Shafeeq Karinkurayil

In his 1958 travelogue *Hajj Yatra* (The Hajj Journey), C. H. Muhammad Koya, who would later rise to prominence as the towering leader of the Indian Union Muslim League and would even serve as the Chief Minister of the south Indian state of Kerala, has this to say about fashion in Makkah:

> The Arab men are male honey bees [sic] who spend three quarters of their life drinking Suleimani, bantering and smoking hookah. Their women lot are even lazier. They just cook for one meal a day. They buy some bread from the stall for mornings and evenings. For them the evenings are for shopping. They wander about in lipstick and polish [sic] on their hands, and dresses that would rival those in Paris. Had the Saudi government not compelled them to wear a black veil on top of these, there wouldn't be much difference in fashion between Paris and Arabia. (Koya 2011: 77)

The lethargic Arab male is the stuff of Orientalism, but we see how the idea of an unchanging ahistorical time is immediately offset by the idea of a fashion sense that rivals the Mecca of fashion, Paris. When set against this horizon, laziness acquires the languor of urban cool, and consumerism its modality of being. Hijab then becomes the self-restraint of a government whose concomitant existence with the West is to be kept under wraps. The plenitude that is possible under the veil slips into the plenitude of the possibilities of the veil. On the one hand, the veil performs the claim of national difference and distinction from Paris and what it represents; by being visible *as a veil* to the onlooker, it strikes at individual claims to difference. But on the other hand, the veil becomes the possibility of experimenting with the West while retaining national difference. The realm of the private becomes the space in which to experiment with universality, while maintaining a national peculiarity in the outer world's domain.

The Arabian Peninsula has been a familiar place to Kerala since ancient times, as both of them belong to the Indian Ocean network where ideas, texts, and people circulated along the trade routes. Local beliefs assert that the first Muslim from what is present-day Kerala dates back to the Prophet's own lifetime (seventh century) (see Prange 2018: 1–2). Kozhikode, the largest city in north Kerala, was established as a trading port in the twelfth century (Kooria and Pearson 2018; on the Islamic cosmopolis of the Indian Ocean, see Ricci 2011). Arabs were the dominant merchant class until the arrival of the Portuguese in the late fifteenth century. As the home to Makkah and Madinah and other places of significance in Islamic history, Arabia is within the horizon of affective geography for the Muslims of Kerala. The Hajj pilgrimage is part of the community's annual routine, when some of its members undertake the journey to the sacred sites. Poetry, literature, folk songs, and so on have indexed Arabia in terms of the sacred and the affects that sacrality can induce. Overwhelming religious imagery meant that the Arabian Gulf was lost as a lived space of the here and now, an imagery that Koya's travelogue set out to correct (Shafeeq K. 2015). It was only decades after Koya's observations, closer to the 1980s, with large-scale migration and the widespread use of photography, that the Gulf became unmoored from an exclusively sacred chronotrope and became moored in the here and now.

Sartorial Practice and Citizenship

The large-scale migration of labor from the south Indian state of Kerala to the Arabian Gulf began in the 1950s and 1960s, when the demand for labor in the wake of the discovery of oil could not be matched by existing labor suppliers from Iraq and Iran. The vast majority of the early laborers were undocumented. By the mid-1970s, the process was formalized, and the result was a phenomenal boom in the number of migrants from Kerala (Ilias 2018: 69–70). Of the various districts in Kerala, Malappuram, a Muslim majority district, contributed the most—15.3 percent of all the migrants to the Gulf from Kerala in 1998 (the earliest figures available are from 1998) (Zachariah and Irudaya Rajan 2012: 37). Muslims in general have a higher percentage of migrants among the different communities—41.1 percent of the total number of migrants from Kerala in 1998 (Zachariah and Irudaya Rajan 2012: 46).

It is a well-acknowledged fact that what distinguishes migration to the Arabian Gulf from relocation to similar targets of economic migration—North America, Western Europe, Malaysia, Singapore, Australia—is the impossibility of ever becoming a citizen in the Gulf states. This is central to the experience because it results in circular migration: the option to settle and be part of a diaspora does not exist. The temporary nature of migration conditions both ends of the migration circuit. Non-belonging is reinforced through structural means. Existing scholarly literature has pointed out that the racial distinction between the native and migrant is crucial to nation-building processes in the Arabian Gulf (Gardner 2010; Fargues 2011; Sater 2013). This special situation has led scholars to look at other avenues of citizenship in the global city, that is, visibility and participation in public life, such as conspicuous consumption (Vora 2013). In this chapter, I wish to put forward a different proposition: that the foreclosure of citizenship in the Gulf need not foreclose a discussion as to how the Gulf might indeed be, for migrants, an object in the discursive struggle for citizenship back home.

One of the peculiarities of nation-building in India has been that, owing to colonial consolidation, the state arrived before the nation, and the nation was incumbent on the state to translate its people into the register of modern states: "In the absence of other forces—such as great revolutionary social classes like the bourgeoisie or the proletariat that played such an important role in European social transformations—it was the state which almost entirely arrogated to itself the power of proposing, directing, and effecting large-scale social change" (Kaviraj 2010: 210). The process has been studied in the mode of passive revolution, where a nonhegemonic bourgeois class wages a protracted war of positions in order to outwit the power-wielding traditional classes and finally bring forth a bourgeois nation (Chatterjee 1986). This means that, though citizenship in India was theoretically based on universal suffrage, at the discursive level the state—a bourgeois project—recognized within the borders of the state a sphere of population groups who would have to be trained in the discourse of modern nationalism, which was built on ideas of rationality and individualism. This project of extending the discursive universe of citizenship thus identified citizenship with modernity, against which was grouped what was identified as the hindrance to development: atavistic ideologies embodied in the population groups. Modernity had to come through outside interference and through state bureaucracy.

At the same time, the centralized planning, redistributive logic, and simultaneous expansion of the apparatus of the Indian state, which was the prime purveyor of patrimonies, also meant that in order to exert pressure to gain resources, one had to form associations, which were more often than not on the lines of existing fault lines of religion and caste. This led to the frustration of the neat divisions between tradition and modernity that the state discourse had hitherto maintained (Kaviraj 2010: 221-32). Looking from the other side, one could also say that the early postcolonial state not only tried to impress rationality but also the spiritual culture of the ruling elite, transcoding their caste particularity as an ethos of spiritual life, which met with resistance from the subaltern caste groups that had a history of antagonistic indebtedness to modernity (Pandian 2002). Thus, politics since the 1970s has been characterized by the prominence of identity politics and the unraveling of the hegemony of the statist position, thereby leading to the vernacularization of politics (Kaviraj 2010: 226) and to alternative registers of negotiation with the state by communities that are not necessarily rooted in preexisting identities (Chatterjee 2004).

This transactional logic puts pressure on communities to walk the tightrope between claiming universality and particularity. On the one hand, claiming modernity ensues projecting that one is universal enough to be abstracted to the category of citizen; but on the other hand, to be efficient as a pressure group (in governmental logic), one also has to be visible as a particular group. This is, inter alia, a business of perception management. It is in this vein that I read the migrant photographs as a quest for citizenship in the register of alternative claims to modernity. By displaying special access to a world that is commonly perceived as "modern," the migrant photographs lay claim to modernity and demand inclusion in the discursive universe of citizenship while bypassing the prescribed route, which is via the state institutions. At the same time, this different route of modernity could itself be the sign of particularity, that which separates these groups from the others. It is important to note that citizenship was technically an already given fact, and the discursive struggle for citizenship is fought on a less concrete and more ideological level, where one's self-projection as a rightful claimant is aimed as much at oneself as at other communities that make up the polity.

Sartorial choice is of importance in this universe of appearances because the choice of clothing deploys crosscutting currents of discourse of identity. Clothing is not a matter of individual choice alone but is of dense historical significance and is linked to ideas of modernity and citizenship (in terms I have previously referred to) in Kerala. The sartorial codes in migrant photographs, which include those taken in India as well as in the Gulf, will be seen as meaningful actions at such a historical juncture. This chapter will show that clothing was deployed to mark one's place within the hierarchical social structure. The spectacle of the Gulf photographs allowed migrants, often hailing from humble backgrounds, a conspicuous prominence among their home audience in Kerala. This was deployed at times to claim distinction of place within the hierarchical structure and on other occasions, ironically, to shun the extra visibility that comes with being a cultural minor, which means being particular. The photographs, as records of sartorial choices as well as indices of other space-times, served as markers that claimed a place within the Kerala polity, through visibility as a population group as well as the enviable invisibility of being part of the mainstream.

The relationship between the imaginary construction of a nation and the role of photography in elaborating the nation's formation, through sartoriality, is usually overlooked. Bethke (2019) undertook a rare study in the context of Israel, based on photographs available in public archives and belonging to various movements. Considering nation, photography, and sartoriality in the sphere of family photographs requires us to study clothing as projected by photographs as a practice that establishes social distinctions and imagines alternate futures without necessarily being accompanied by a categorically ideological and political program. In other words, body itself is to be taken as the site of cultural resignification, unsettling established binaries and seeking to redefine nation and discursive citizenship (Dhareshwar and Niranjana 2000).

The primary source of this study is photographs that I collected from migrants or their family members as part of my wider fieldwork on Gulf migration. I collected some 120 photographs from eleven migrants (or their families) who made their first forays into the Gulf in the late 1970s and early 1980s, generally referred to as the first generation of migrants, because they were the first after the present Gulf states were formed and after migration between these states and India was formalized. The participants in my study were Muslim male migrants and their families from the district of Malappuram, in northern Kerala. The interviews were conducted over the course of two years, in 2018 and 2019, in Malayalam and in the local dialect. The choice of my participants was based on a snowballing sample.

My aim was to collect a few photographs that would depict migrants' representation of the Gulf—the landscapes, the urbanscape, the workplace, places of stay, and so on. The idea was to study how they represented themselves and the Arabian Gulf. What I discovered in the process was that, as far as my collection goes, migrants hardly ever photograph landscape. Most of the images are photographs of people—friends, relatives, coworkers. They are almost always strategically placed among high rises or with modern amenities in the vicinity, including cars, televisions, or neat and well-equipped office spaces. I soon understood the need to widen my collection to photographs from Kerala from around the same time to see how they related to those taken in the Gulf. Over the course of my fieldwork, I realized the potential of these photographs to be a resource of memory against the temporariness that characterizes the Gulf migrant situation (see Karinkurayil 2021), as well as looking at how the Gulf space was constructed as an aspiration, as this study does (see also Karinkurayil 2020).

It is noticeable how the foreignness of the Arabian Gulf is reflected in the sartorial choices made by the subjects of these photographs. While it is not rare to see images in which the subjects are wearing *lungi* (a wraparound worn on the lower body that is prevalent in Kerala) in indoor living spaces, the photographs depicting leisure show clothing choices that are aspirational in nature. This chapter is based on these sartorial choices, and to create a rounded story, I focus on photographs provided by just one of the participants of my project. Abdul Gafoor (name changed) was in his late sixties when I interviewed him. He first went to the Gulf in 1971, shortly before the formation of the United Arab Emirates. He spent a little more than thirty years there working as a migrant laborer, and he served some very important offices in that country as an office boy.

The Clothes and Their Codes

Abdul Gafoor was born in a village of south Malabar before the formation of the state of Kerala, in around 1950.[1] He belongs to the majority Muslim Mappila community of the region.[2] His parents came from landed and influential families from the same village, although they were a poor twig of a richer family tree. Gafoor's father worked as a supervisor of some contract works that were being undertaken by his cousin in the Nilgiris district (now in the neighboring state of Tamil Nadu) before he returned to the village and to a job in which he assisted with paperwork connected to real estate deals. This was possible because his education was better than many of his contemporaries (even though he was a school dropout) and because he had gained work experience outside the village. Gafoor's mother was the youngest of a family of four siblings, and she was orphaned at a very young age. Abdul Gafoor was the eldest child, and in 1971 became the first member of his family to migrate to the Gulf. In the village he was preceded by only two others, both from his father's generation. After spending a few years of his adolescence doing odd jobs in Madras (now Chennai), Gafoor decided to try his luck in the Gulf. He arranged for a place on a *dhow*, for which he paid Rs. 400 ("400 rupees then could have brought 40 crores today," he exclaims), and he was ferried across in a trip that took around sixteen days. He carried with him, as was instructed, a spare set of clothes, a small bag of flattened rice, a couple of lemons, some *nendran* banana, and glucose powder. He also took along a photo of himself wrapped in plastic—in case the worst occurred and the boat sank.

The first thing that emerges from viewing Abdul Gafoor's photo album is his fascination with suits. In one picture from 1988, Gafoor stands behind his boss's daughter and her husband, who is sharply turned out in a black suit and fiery leaf-patterned tie. Gafoor is wearing sky blue trousers and a maroon and grey striped shirt hanging loose. In another photograph, a highly placed bureaucrat is dressed in a cream suit and matching tie, with a suitcase in one hand and a pair of glasses in the other. He stands by the door as if on his way out. Gafoor was probably behind the camera. From the first photograph, as well as a few others taken in office spaces, it can be inferred that Gafoor's regular style at work was an untucked shirt. However, two studio photographs show him with his shirt tucked in and wearing a tie. One is with his wife, taken in a studio in Kozhikode, and another one, with his brother, was taken in Abu Dhabi in 1981 (see fig. 5.1).

The photo belongs to the genre of formal studio portraiture. The brothers look directly at the camera, their full profiles on view. The trousers are cut in bell-bottom style, the flares almost entirely covering their shoes. This style is ubiquitous in the photos I have collected from the period, mostly in studio photographs. Abdul Gafoor's trousers are striped while his younger brother's are plain. The tucked-in shirt and the tie (supplied by the studio) symbolize a life in which these clothes are worn as a matter of course. Neither suit nor tie was part of Abdul Gafoor's regular style, as evidenced by the other photographs, but here they suggest for the audience an association with the life of high rises and high offices, something that is offered as aspirational.

The first impulse for us here would be to read this image as an instance of the hegemony of the West, in the vein of John Berger (1991), who reads the misshapen and ridiculous peasant bodies in suits as evidence of the hegemony of the sedentary classes. However, in the context of this photograph, such an inference would be a mistake: we cannot assume a binary of modern/traditional and implication of dominant/subaltern. A concrete analysis of these binaries in terms of costume gives us a more complex picture, and the rest of this chapter is an attempt at properly contextualizing figure 5.1 in the light of other photographs.

The second photograph (fig. 5.2), from 1980, was taken near Abdul Gafoor's village and features two of his younger brothers (left and center; Abdul Gafoor is the eldest of nine siblings) and one of their friends (right). Those at each end are dressed in white shirts and *mundu*,[3] while the one in the center has matched his white shirt with white bell-bottom trousers. The one on the left seems to be wearing a white shirt with a print, and the oth-

122 ■ *Mohamed Shafeeq Karinkurayil*

Figure 5.1. Abdul Gafoor and his brother, Abu Dhabi, 1981. Reproduced with permission.

Figure 5.2. On top of the world, Kerala, 1980. Reproduced with permission.

ers are wearing plain white shirts. There is a distinct sense that their white clothes are new. One wonders if it was the day of Eid, or whether their elder brother, just back from the Gulf, has brought them new clothes from the nearest town. The young men, with the top buttons of their shirts unbuttoned, pack a swagger. Two wristwatches are conspicuous, as if consciously being turned to the camera. The man on the right does not have a watch to display. They are standing on high ground near the village, with paddy fields below and a winding country road framing it, while in the distance it is possible to distinguish verdant hills.

In order to read this photograph in its historical context and discover how this intertwines with the narrative of the suit, one has to look at the contestations around clothing in Kerala. Colonial Kerala was characterized by sumptuary laws that regulated the sartorial regime of different castes and communities. In his study of clothes and their value under colonialism,

Bernard S. Cohn (1996), citing earlier works, notes how caste had to be maintained through one's clothes. Different castes had to abide by defined sartorial codes. The rebellion against the caste system was fought across sartorial lines too. White was associated with the landlords and suggested privilege. The move from the previous state of (forced) undress of the lower castes to the purity of the white was seen as a civilizational process by the Christian missionaries. P. Sanal Mohan, documenting the work of the Christian missionaries among the former slave castes in the early twentieth century, notes: "missionary journals carried contrasting photographs of lower caste Christians in white clothes with neat oiled and combed hair standing proudly in front of newly-built brick huts with half-naked lower caste non-Christian men in loincloths with unkempt hair pictured against a background of thatch and coconut leaf dwellings, the latter usually captioned—lest the reader had any doubts—'Pulayahs or Out Castes in Travancore'" (Mohan 2005: 43).

In her work on community formation among Hindu fisherfolk (the Dheevara caste), Deepika Rose Alex notes the measures taken by the reformer K. P. Karuppan (1885-1938) thus: "promote 'hygienic practices' among the Dheevaras like bathing twice a day, wearing clean and preferably white clothes, and keeping their houses and premises clean" (Alex 2020: 203-4).

In the Muslim milieu of Kerala, the choice of sober white shirt and *mundu* was caught up in the discourse of modernity. It had associations with the nationalist mainstream, which identifies this dress code as part of the Keralan identity. Vaikom Muhammad Basheer, a luminary of Malayalam literature, wrote the novel *Ntuppuppakkoranandarnnu* (1951), which is set in a Muslim milieu of Kerala, publicized as a "story of Muslim Life in south India" in its English translation.[4] The story contrasts the old order of the Muslim patriarch with the rise of a new educated and reformed Muslim class, inter alia in sartorial terms. The old patriarch—the father of the female protagonist Kunjupathumma—wears "only a dhoti. Hanging carelessly over his shoulder he will have a long stole" (Basheer 2017: 14), the representative of the new generation of educated Muslims is admirably wearing "a white shirt and a white dhoti" (Basheer 2017: 50).

The white and white combination—white shirt and *mundu*—is still associated not only with politicians, but also elders of the household as well as the community. The choice of white in the Muslim community in Kerala belongs to a universe of values that do not linearly flow only from the nationalist tradition but are also informed by Islamic values that state white clothes are preferred by the Prophet, thus combining ideas of purity and piety. The ubiquitous uniform of *madrasah*s in Kerala, and of the *ustad*s and religious leaders, is a white shirt and wraparound. In the early 1980s, when the photograph under discussion was taken, white shirt and *mundu*, together with a white kerchief covering one's head, was the ubiquitous costume of bridegrooms during their wedding (this function of white and white is almost completely obsolete now). The choice of white is also to be mapped on to internal differentiation within the Muslim community. White was the color of *khadi*, Gandhi's preferred wear and his weapon against the British. *Khadi*, and white, became symbols of the Congress party, which led the independence movement of India in late colonial times. Pro-Congress nationalism in the Muslim community in Kerala was usually associated with the property-owning classes (Osella and Osella 2008), which had an uneasy relationship with those in the community who were perceived to be of lower status (Arafath 2016: 51). These internal differentiations continued even after the independence of India and served as markers of class distinction within the Mappilas themselves. Saidalavi (2017) observes that it was through the process of Islamization that—contrary to popular perceptions on caste being foreign to Islamic society—claims of hierarchy expressed through notions such as "purity, morality and piety" (Saidalavi 2017: 28) were sustained in the Muslim community of Malabar. Thus it is of note that unlike the loose white shirt associated with the Islamic religious establishment, the young men in the photograph are wearing slim-cut shirts with their top buttons undone. While the loose white shirt of the religious establishment stands for piety and is therefore uncool, that is not the case here.

To return to the photograph, the choice of white on white is a coded message about respectability that operates on two levels. On the one hand, it establishes a level of invisibility in the secular mainstream of Kerala, and thereby allows its wearers to shun a particular identity, because, as I have noted, white was aspirational across communities. On the other hand, as if in a cross-stitch, it creates a respectable upper order within the Mappila Muslims, thereby giving the white on white a particular identity.

The white bell-bottom trousers gesture to the stellar movies of Amitabh Bachchan from the second half of the 1970s, such as *Sholay* (1975, dir. Ramesh Sippy), *Deewar* (1975, dir. Yash Chopra), *Amar Akbar Anthony* (1977, dir. Manmohan Desai), and *Don* (1978, dir. Chandra Barot), to name just a few. These films mobilized the actor as the icon of stylish and rebellious Indian youth because, as one commentator notices, what made Bachchan's characters special was that he was at ease with the trappings of high life despite his characters' humble origins (Mazumdar 2000). An icon of mobility and aspiration, Bachchan was also, as Prasad (1997: 138–59) notes, emblematic of a mode of resistance to the establishment, and marked therefore as a receiver of subaltern energies. The bell-bottoms were in vogue in Malayalam cinema too, with the immediate association being with the actor Jayan, known for his stunts and now especially remembered for his forceful delivery of the dialogue from *Angadi* (1980, dir. I.V. Sasi): "Maybe we are poor, coolies, trolley pullers, but we are not beggars!" Bell-bottoms also feature prominently in the Malayalam cinema depictions of college life, a phase completely absent in the lives of school dropouts such as Abdul Gafoor.

One also cannot help but notice the prominence of the wristwatches in the photograph; as I mentioned earlier, it looks as if they have been purposefully turned toward the camera. As Ratheesh Radhakrishnan notes, in the mainstream Malayalam cinema of the time, wristwatches were one of the prominent markers of the Gulf, the illicit nature of Gulf money (smuggling), and the threat this money posed to the order of things back home (Radhakrishnan 2009: 220). Before the opening up of Indian markets in the early 1990s through the process referred to as LPG (Liberalization, Privatization, Globalization), strict regulation of the economy made electronic gadgets emblematic of the foreign. Their apparently easy availability to those village youth employed in the Gulf who couldn't boast of any inheritance gave them the connotation of ill-gotten wealth.

What the picture of the three young men taken outdoors in Kerala (fig. 5.2) suggests is that away from the Gulf, within the space of Kerala, one had to negotiate a world in which clothes continued to speak of a seemingly obsolete hierarchical social order. As Osella and Osella (2000: 119–22) show in the context of southern Kerala, newly acquired sartorial choices may ironically have reproduced many of the older divisions, and thereby undercut its potential for escaping the old order. The choice of white on white, as noted, was a bid to invisibility in the nationalist mainstream that was overlaid with Islamic injunctions. This choice also became the means to escape a lower rung while keeping the rung intact. The white on white combination at once denotes the dissolution of identity into a purported secularity and equality in which all communities cease to be, while at the same time maintaining fault lines within the religious community, which often mobilizes religious discourse to such social distinction. Importantly, the white on white combination, which would have stood for the austere purity of the feudal order, is now inflected with the wrist watches and the bell-bottoms, thus infusing the order with newer elements as if in a declaration of an insurgent modernity that refuses to bow to the old order. As noted by Osella and Osella (2000) and Sreekumar and Varman (2019), conspicuous consumption was a route to overcome premigration inferior social status. It has also been observed that by the 1980s, the advertising industry's discourse on consumption had shifted from the paradigm of development to that of shared modernity (Mazzarella 2003). As seen from the photograph, the insurgent modernity did not do away with order itself but was about reworking one's place in the hierarchy. Conspicuous consumption stopped short of a revolution because one's worth relied not on establishing a level field of equality but on a logic of stratification that would ensure one's worth with respect to others.

In sartorial terms, the Gulf existed as a double image: while one was that of the suit and resonated with what was Western and modern, the other was that of the *kandura* (Arabic tunic). In a study of the representation of Arabs in Malayalam cinema, Ratheesh Radhakrishnan illustrates how the presence of a foreign element, such as the *kandura*, in the self-assured universe of white *dhotis* (*mundu*) disrupts this self-assuredness and the normative orientations of these settings (Radhakrishnan 2021). A reading of figure 5.3, which I shall attempt presently to discuss, puts this disorientation experienced by the feudal space of Kerala in the face of *kandura* into greater relief. It not only disrupts the feudal order, but also forces Kerala, the Arabian Gulf, and the migrant body in between into a comedy of manners.

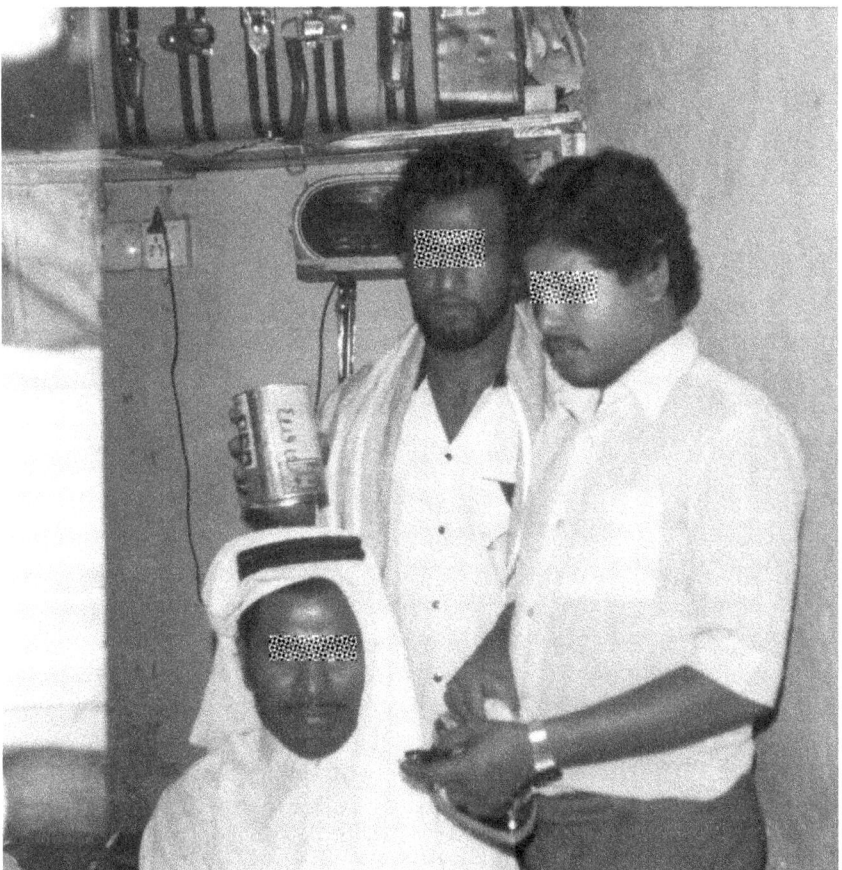

Figure 5.3. With friends, Abu Dhabi, 1979. Reproduced with permission.

Taken in 1979, figure 5.3 records a moment in which the *kandura* was transforming itself into the national dress of the UAE, a period characterized by the almost overnight revolution in the economy, the arrival of migrant laborers, the transformation of the local Emirati population into a minority, the erasure of traditional forms of living, and the new-found insistence on tradition, heritage, and religion. At this historical moment, the white *kandura* marked out ethnic purity and privilege. As Sulayman Khalaf notes: "Viewed within its broad multi-ethnic contexts the Emirati national dress is meant to convey a sense of cultural difference, social conservatism, moral decency, social poise and respect. Moreover, it has become a skin colour of the Emiratis as it advertises them immediately as a privileged and powerful national minority" (Khalaf 2005: 246).

The 1970s and 1980s, as James Onley suggests (2005: 77–78), were the time in which Gulf states adopted a common national dress, a measure that erased the other forms of clothing that were present until then in those societies, such as Kashmiri shawls and the Iranian turbans (on Arab national dress, see also Longva 1997: 120–23; Kanna 2011: 120). The purpose of implementing these measures was to differentiate the local citizens from the migrant others.

In figure 5.3, Abdul Gafoor wears the *kandura*, and his smile communicates that he finds himself out of place in foreign attire. He is in a playful mood and his friends around him have planted a Nido milk powder tin on his head, on which the word *thenga* (coconut) is written in green marker. A marker of the Gulf along with accessories such as watches, transistors, and camera, the Nido can is a legible sign for the audience at home of "close distance": the chimera of good life that is abstract and attributed to foreignness but can be partly experienced through consumption (Mazzarella 2003: 256). The facial expressions of Gafoor's friends suggests the solemnity of a judge, as if they have deemed the peculiar get-up fit for him despite or because of the fact that the latter is not really himself when he is wearing it. The Nido can has just had a return journey from Kerala: after having been carried there as a milk powder can, it has come back again, localized elsewhere and repurposed as a can with grated coconut, an essential ingredient to many Malayali dishes. The name of the state of Kerala (in some accounts) itself derives from the word for coconut (*kera*). The playfulness embodied by Abdul Gafoor is an effect of many things at the same time: a repurposed can that once carried a symbol of advanced modern machinery and now carries the most mundane product, which at the same time is an authentic marker of home; a reminder of home that is also a remainder of previous journeys, and the need for this endless cycle of journeys; a foreign body in local dress, which only accentuates the body's strangeness; and the confusion of the photograph's style, which is somewhere between the sobriety of a portrait and the playfulness of a candid shot. As Pinney (1997) notes with reference to colonial times, portraiture in India was caught between the demand to represent individuals and population types (castes, tribes, etc.). Gafoor's photograph in the *kandura*, through its playfulness, enacts the failure of the one to fit into the other: the individual doesn't fit comfortably into a national dress, while the latter fails to arrest the playfulness of the individual, which exceeds generic type.

The impossibility of citizenship in the Gulf, and the implicit impossibility of integration, suggests that wearing a *kandura* can only be an act of mimicry, that is, an act of imposture precisely because the original is defined as unattainable by any other (Bhabha 1984). Bhabha's observations about mimicry were made in the context of colonial rule, and stressed its subversive possibilities of underscoring the racial truth of colonialism as opposed to the colonizers' own justifications of being a civilizing mission. The unattainability of *kandura*, what makes it particular, was the racial nature of nation-building in the Gulf that was coded into the privilege of wearing the garment, as noted by Khalaf (2005). The idea of mimicry can also be inflected with a Keralan form of entertainment called "mimics parade," or simply "mimicry"; this became a popular mode of outdoor entertainment in the 1990s. In this, the artists imitate prominent personalities, especially film performers. Their imitations evoke laughter among the audience, not because the imitator can never be the star,[5] but because the artist accentuates the idiosyncrasies of the original. The imitation brings forth as comical excess what in the original is a sign of distinction—the passionate stutter in one, the guttural insanity of another, the nasal awkwardness of a third, and so on. The excess of the *kandura*, a native dress, on the migrant body and its ill-fitting nature go with and contradict the smugness of the smile. The *kandura*-migrant body-smile assemblage becomes an oddity in the evolving discourse of national purity both in the Gulf and at home.

Conclusion: A Photographic Reality

Let us imagine Abdul Gafoor's village in the early 1980s. It sits on a national highway with commercial establishments lined up on either side. Two roads, one going west and the other east, meet the highway in a junction at what can be considered the center of the village. These are much narrower roads, and they divide further into many more roads, connecting the majority of the inhabitants' houses to the highway. The most important commercial establishment in the village is a sawmill: the constant whirring of its blades is audible from the junction, even though the mill is a few hundred meters to the south. Right on the junction is a small restaurant, a solid structure with a tiled roof. This is appropriately named to suggest that it is meant for wayfarers: those who have come to catch a bus may have tea there and perhaps buy one of the three or four varieties of sweetmeat stacked in glass cases facing the bus stop. The other establishments are small shops of identical rectangular pattern selling groceries, stationery, magazines, and other knickknacks. The vegetable shop has its produce displayed outside under the shade of a cloth that is held aloft by poles. The preferred destination for local elders is a thatched tea shop close to the sawmill, which has a signboard hanging outside announcing that it serves tapioca dishes in addition to tea.

Most elders wear checkered *lungi*s and some wear white *mundu*. Those wearing a lungi also wear a broad belt around their waist, usually green in color, with a pouch that carries a small knife with a slight curve in the middle (known as a Malappuram knife), which is used to cut betel nuts: these are carried in the pouch, along with tobacco leaves and lime paste. Some of them don't wear a shirt; others wear white vests, and some wear white or light-colored long shirts shaped like a V-neck T-shirt (similar to *kurti*). Almost all have a white cloth, usually a towel, hanging from their shoulders; some of them occasionally wrap this around their head. A few youngsters wear shirts and trousers. No one tucks their shirt in here, let alone wears a tie. It would look out of place, even ridiculous, if someone were to wear a suit. In this village, which is fairly representative of others in the region, no one wears a *kandura*. They do not belong here—only in Gulf photographs. They live there and give rise to possibilities in this village.

It has been observed in the context of Kerala that photography was deployed to suggest an interior plenitude of the people photographed by an artful arrangement of props (Parayil 2014; also see Karinkurayil 2020). Gulf photographs activated an alternative world that nevertheless connected to the glamour of Bombay cinema and beyond. The material plenitude of this alternative world displayed for this village a vicariously lived "modern life" that would soon be realizable; the gadgets were already making their way in. However, villagers did not harbor any wish to wear the suit or the *kandura*; there was no point in wearing them in the village. Expressing dignity had to be in a code that others would recognize. The white on white combination did this, but without compromising on the flashiness of wristwatches or the high-waisted cut of the bell-bottoms. By being (just) one step away from the austere Kerala modernity, migrants and their families announced themselves to be "one step ahead of modernity" (Pandian 2002: 1,740). The Gulf was the theatre that afforded these dreams, the blank space on to which the claim to dignity and thereby citizenship could be projected and drawn from.

It is now that one can appraise figure 5.1 for its crosscurrents of signification. Being from a family of respectable social standing but poor material wealth, Abdul Gafoor is also caught between traditionally sanctified notions of respectability and the desire to register his newfound economic mobility. While in Berger's reading of the photographs by August Sander of German peasants the suit is a hegemonic upper-class attire that produced their own bodies as less than ideal (Berger 1991), the same cannot be said for suits in the context of Kerala. They were signs of a plenitude elsewhere that made a claim on the white-on-white culture of purported universality. The suits were a prop that would strengthen the claim of the community in its aspiration back home for universality by displaying transcendence from the stereotype.

The spectral nature of photographs is easy to overlook in the era of smartphones, but one should remember that these were the only visual access to another land when they were taken in the early 1980s. Even color television, which was boosted by the 1982 Asiad (or Asian Games), became popularly accessible only toward the end of that decade. The photograph was an expression of an "other scene"—the Gulf as a dream. The allure of the photograph lay in its teleporting abilities, to be here and there at the same time. This other scene could only be lived within the neighborhood in an inflected format, as it had to negotiate custom. What we see in the photograph is the representation of another space of strangeness and aspiration that makes sense when employed in a cultural milieu in which one is, paradoxically, trying to differentiate oneself but at the same time trying to be indistinguishable from the mainstream. On the other hand, there is the playful disdain of an impossibility, an empty gesture of refusal of what one was not offered in the first place—which is to feel at home in the Arab national dress.

The Gulf becomes the route through which high fashion, accessible only on the big screen, could itself be short-circuited away from its gatekeepers back home. But since these fashions would look out of place in the feudal bodily orientations of Kerala in the late 1970s and early 1980s, they can only exist in the reality of another place in which migrants can lay claim to escape the particular. This is not by their assuming to be agents of the universal but by showing that the universal, as expressed sartorially, fits them as well as others. The strength of the migrant was his or her own body, which could inhabit different costumes—and hence could be assumed to be a body independent of its costume.

Mohamed Shafeeq Karinkurayil is Assistant Professor at Manipal Centre for Humanities, a constituent unit of Manipal Academy of Higher Education (MAHE), Karnataka, India. His research focuses on literary and visual cultures of migration. He has been published in *BioScope: South Asian Screen Studies, South Asia: Journal of South Asian Studies,* and *Economic and Political Weekly,* among others. He is currently working on a monograph on migration and popular culture.

NOTES

1. The state of Kerala was formed in 1956 after parts of the Madras state were merged with the erstwhile princely states of Cochin and Travancore. South Malabar refers to the southern region of those parts of Malabar that eventually became part of Kerala, generally referring to the two former *taluk*s (a smaller administrative unit of a district) of Eranad and Walluvanad, a region that comprised mostly of Muslims.
2. For a classic account of the community, see Miller (1976).
3. A white, unstitched wrap-around for the lower half of the body.
4. The novel was translated into English in 1980 by R. E. Asher and Achamma Coilparambil Chandrasekharan as *Me Grandad 'ad an Elephant* and published by Edinburgh University Press–UNESCO Cultural Series.
5. Many of the reigning film stars of Kerala were mimicry artists. The entertainment form is also part of and at times the central element of many Malayalam films.

REFERENCES

Alex, Deepika Rose. 2020. "From Untouchables to Vyasa's Clan: Fishermen's Reform Movement in Kerala." *South Asia: Journal of South Asian Studies* 43, no. 2: 199–214.

Arafath, P. K. Yasser. 2016. "The Nadapuram Enigma: A History of Communalism and Violence in North Malabar (1957–2015)." *Economic and Political Weekly* 51, no. 15: 47–55.

Basheer, Vaikom Muhammad. 2017. *Me Grandad 'ad an Elephant!* Translated by R. E. Asher and Achamma Coilparambil Chandrasekharan. Kozhikode: Mathrubhumi Books.

Berger, John. 1991. "The Suit and the Photograph." In *Rethinking Popular Culture: Contemporary Perspectives in Cultural Studies,* edited by Chandra Mukherji and Michael Schadson, 424–31. Berkeley: University of California Press.

Bethke, Svenja. 2019. "How to Dress Up in Eretz Israel, 1880s–1948: A Visual Approach to Clothing, Fashion, and Nation-Building." *International Journal of Fashion Studies* 6, no. 2: 217–37.

Bhabha, Homi. 1984. "Of Mimicry and Man: The Ambivalence of Colonial Discourse." *October* 28: 125–33.

Chatterjee, Partha. 1986. *Nationalist Thought and the Colonial World: A Derivative Discourse.* London: Zed Books.

———. 2004. *The Politics of the Governed: Reflections on Popular Politics in Most of the World.* New York: Columbia University Press.

Cohn, Bernard S. 1996. *Colonialism and Its Forms of Knowledge: British in India*. Princeton: Princeton University Press.

Dhareshwar, Vivek, and Tejaswini Niranjana. 2000. "Kaadalan and the Politics of Resignification." In *Making Meaning in Indian Cinema*, edited by Ravi Vasudevan, 191–214. New Delhi: Oxford University Press.

Fargues, Philippe. 2011. "Immigration without Inclusion: Non-Nationals in Nation-Building in the Gulf States." *Asia and Pacific Migration Journal* 20, no. 3–4: 273–92.

Gardner, Andrew M. 2010. *City of Strangers: Gulf Migration and the Indian Community in Bahrain*. Ithaca, NY: Cornell University Press.

Ilias, M. H. 2018. "Memories of 'Nations' Past: Accounts of Early Migrants from Kerala in the Gulf in the Post-Oil Era." *Oxford Middle East Review* 2, no. 1: 69–88.

Kanna, Ahmed. 2011. *Dubai: The City as Corporation*. Minneapolis: University of Minnesota Press.

Karinkurayil, Mohamed Shafeeq. 2020. "Reading Aspiration in Kerala's Migrant Photography." *South Asia: A Journal of South Asian Studies* 43, no. 4: 598–612.

———. 2021. "The Days of Plenty: Images of First Generation Malayali Migrants in the Arabian Gulf." *South Asian Diaspora* 13, no. 1: 51–64.

Kaviraj, Sudipta. 2010. *The Imaginary Institution of India: Politics and Ideas*. New York: Columbia University Press.

Khalaf, Sulayman. 2005. "National Dress and Construction of Emirati Cultural Identity." *Journal of Human Sciences* 11: 230–67.

Kooria, Mahmood, and Michael Naylor Pearson. 2018. *Malabar in the Indian Ocean: Cosmopolitanism in a Maritime Historical Region*. New Delhi: Oxford University Press.

Koya, C. H. Muhammad. 2011. *Yatra*. Kozhikode: Olive Books.

Longva, Anh Nga. 1997. *Walls Built on Sand: Migration, Exclusion, and Society in Kuwait*. Boulder, CO: Westview Press.

Mazumdar, Ranjani. 2000. "From Subjectification to Schizophrenia: The 'Angry Young Man' and the 'Psychotic' Hero of Bombay Cinema." In *Making Meaning in Indian Cinema*, edited by Ravi Vasudevan, 238–64. New Delhi: Oxford University Press.

Mazzarella, William. 2003. *Shoveling Smoke: Advertising and Globalization in Contemporary India*. Delhi: Oxford University Press.

Mohan, P. Sanal. 2005. "Religion, Social Space and Identity: The Prathyaksha Raksha Daiva Sabha and the Making of Cultural Boundaries in Twentieth Century Kerala." *South Asia: Journal of South Asian Studies* 28, no. 1: 35–63.

Miller, Roland E. 1976. *Mappila Muslims of Kerala: A Study in Islamic Trends*. Bombay: Orient Longman.

Onley, James. 2005. "Transnational Merchants in the Nineteenth-Century Gulf: The Case of the Safar Family." In *Transnational Connections and the Arab Gulf*, edited by Madawi Al Rasheed, 59–89. New York: Routledge.

Osella, Filippo, and Caroline Osella. 2000. *Social Mobility in Kerala: Modernity and Identity in Conflict*. London: Pluto Press.

———. 2008. "Islamism and Social Reform in Kerala, South India." *Modern Asian Studies* 42, no. 2/3: 317–46.

Pandian, M. S. S. 2002. "One Step outside Modernity: Caste, Identity Politics and Public Sphere." *Economic and Political Weekly* 37, no. 18: 1,735–41.

Parayil, Sujith. 2014. "Family Photographs: Visual Mediation of the Social." *Critical Quarterly* 58, no. 3: 1–20.

Pinney, Christopher. 1997. *Camera Indica: The Social Life of Indian Photographs*. Chicago: University of Chicago Press.

Prange, Sebastian R. 2018. *Monsoon Islam: Trade and Faith on the Medieval Malabar Coast*. New Delhi: Cambridge University Press.

Prasad, M. Madhava. 1997. *Ideology of the Hindi Film: A Historical Construction*. New Delhi: Oxford University Press.

Radhakrishnan, Ratheesh. 2009. "The Gulf in Imagination: Migration, Malayalam Cinema, and Regional Identity." *Contributions to Indian Sociology* 23, no. 2: 217–45.

———. 2021. "Habits and Worlds: Malayalam Cinema's Travels with the Gulf." In *Industrial Networks and Cinemas of India: Shooting Stars, Shifting Geographies, and Multiplying Media*, edited by Monika Mehta and Madhuja Mukherjee, 167–80. London: Routledge.

Ricci, Ronit. 2011. *Islam Translated: Literature, Conversion and the Arabic Cosmopolis of South and Southeast Asia*. Chicago: University of Chicago Press.

Saidalavi, Palamadathi Chemban. 2017. "Muslim Social Organisation and Cultural Islamisation in Malabar." *South Asia Research* 37, no. 1: 19–36.

Sater, James. 2013. "Citizenship and Migration in Arab Gulf Monarchies." *Citizenship Studies* 18, no. 3–4: 92–302.

Shafeeq K., Mohamed. 2015. "Translating the Past: Minor Writing as Democratization." *Humanities Circle* 3, no. 1: 163–76.

Sreekumar, Hari, and Rohit Varman. 2019. "Vagabonds at the Margins: Acculturation, Subalterns, and Competing Worth." *Journal of Macromarketing* 39, no. 1: 37–52.

Vora, Neha. 2013. *Impossible Citizens: Dubai's Indian Diaspora*. Hyderabad: Orient Blackswan.

Zachariah, K. C., and S. Irudaya Rajan. 2012. *Kerala's Gulf Connection, 1998–2011: Economic and Social Impact of Migration*. Hyderabad: Orient Blackswan.

CONCLUSION

The Gulf Space in Words
In Dialogue with Author Deepak Unnikrishnan

Lorenzo Casini and Deepak Unnikrishnan

Lorenzo Casini (LC): *Temporary People* (2017) by Deepak Unnikrishnan is a novel-in-stories set mostly in Abu Dhabi. The collective heroes of the novel are people originally from Kerala who were born in the Emirates or who spent most of their lives there. In Malayalam, they are referred to as pravasis,[1] a term that remains untranslated in the book but whose multiple connotations the narrative struggles to reach and embrace. Winner of the Restless Book Prize for new immigrant writing in 2016 and of the prestigious Hindu Prize in 2017, the novel has come to be regarded as a classic of migration literature from the Gulf. The text constructs a fictional world that is strongly connected to the social and political reality of the Emirates, but which is granted an autonomous existence. In *Temporary People*, language is always figurative and its relationship with "the real" is never univocal. Although no story in the book can be read as a mere allegory of social and cultural relationships, each one emanates from the lived experience of the Gulf space. In the author's own words, his work dwells "on the consequences of migration to the Gulf, on what that movement of people does to both home and host countries, to languages, and to families" (Unnikrishnan 2020). These words also very clearly exemplify why the author's narrative world gives expression to many of the concerns that inform the rationale of this book and its theoretical approach. *Temporary People* is not a novel about migration, but a novel about what the movement of people does (i.e., how it participates in the construction of social space in the Gulf and elsewhere).

In the article "The Hidden Cost of Migration," published in *Foreign Affairs* in February 2020, Deepak Unnikrishnan refers to his participation in the academic meeting that took place at the Leibniz Zentrum Moderner Orient of Berlin on 17-18 December 2019 and describes his surprise when some of the European participants told him that they found themselves mirrored in the fictional world of his novel (Unnikrishnan 2020). Actually, that meeting was, in several respects, a transformative experience for many of us. It brought together several scholars from Kerala, the Gulf, the United States, and Europe whose life trajectories and family histories do not always conform to neoliberal narratives of globalization and make us, in one way or another, "temporary people." In turn, Deepak Unnirkishnan, after presenting his novel, was actively engaged in the discussion that revolved around this publication project. In this concluding dialogue, and similarly to what happened in Berlin, the fictional world of *Temporary People* interlaces with our discussion of the contents of the different chapters of this volume.

Deepak, I would like to begin this dialogue with you by focusing on the role of language in *Temporary People* and in the extratextual world that you represent therein. Language is the basic constituent of any social space; but, as Nadeen Dakkak shows in her chapter, in the Gulf space, the social function of language(s) becomes particularly apparent. Personal and collective subjectivities and hierarchic power relations are constantly forged, negotiated, and contested through the resort to specific languages and to different varieties of the same language. The language of the book is at one time the product of a particular space and the means to represent the complexity of this space. Your novel is written in English, but it is a unique and hybrid variety of English where many words from Arabic and several South Asian languages converge in a symphony of different influences. At times, while reading *Temporary People*, I felt that you were engaging in a battle with language in order to be able to represent the social space and individual experiences that resist normative grammars and national languages.

DEEPAK UNNIKRISHNAN (DU): Battle? You might be right. Is it the right word? Depends.

In my opinion, language, mother tongue or learned tongues, is currency. What you speak, English, French, Arabic, Malayalam, you name it, the language outs you, and opens and/or closes doors/borders. And if you are literally unable to speak, because you don't or are unable to hear, perhaps you sign—the language of the nonhearing. Language is then literally performative, where your body and lips and hands become words. Think of language as costume too, what you drape around your tongue to communicate and get things done. Therefore, how you speak (or even write) something matters. Language, to me, is also race, class; and in some families, certainly mine, spoken language flags caste and faith. Then there is the language of nationality and bureaucracy, prevalent at airports and visa centers. The language of government, capital, even sex. And in my current role, there is the language of academia and scholarship, which can be insular and sometimes difficult to parse. Finally, language, what you say, how you say it, is also about your passport—an indicator of where you are, or could be, from. And I've just gotten started.

Temporary People is primarily a book about languages (and the people who inhabit these languages) in a transient space like the Gulf. And it is no accident Malayalam, the language of my immediate family, seen through the lens of English, fuels the book, even though English is the only language I pick apart with ease, and have appropriated and made mine.

The book is also an attempt at producing new language to push back against presumed expectations of what a writer like me, honed in the Gulf, or people like me, are supposed to sound and write like. It is also unabashedly a book about people like my parents, men and women who weren't Arab or Khaleeji and took a chance on the Gulf. It is also a document for their children, those they raised or left behind, to remind everyone our history counts too.

And the impact of multilingualism in a Gulf space? Depends on whom you are asking. I first responded to Abu Dhabi as a child. I went to an Indian school, hung out with the kids of Indian families, and lived in a neighborhood predominantly populated by people who looked like me. In school, we were instructed in English, the vestige of Empire. On paper, on account of my father's job as an engineer, my family should have been okay, but my parents lost most of their money and fell into debt when we were little, so we never knew what it was like to have money in the Gulf. No money, no power. And we learned quickly that when you have no language either, and I'm talking about Arabic, that's a disadvantage too, even though we learned Arabic in school, but our teachers didn't care to teach us well. And some of us chose to dismiss Arabic because it wasn't ours. I suppose we were arrogant too, assuming we didn't need it. A big mistake.

As I began interacting with Abu Dhabi more, I quickly sensed language wielded immense power. I especially paid attention to places of commerce, where language got interesting, because the objective between the buyer and seller was pretty straightforward: try and communicate your respective needs. In these places, whether it was a department store or a restaurant, it felt as though concessions could be made, that you could get away with, not be embarrassed by, and even feel proud of speaking pidgin Arabic, some-some English and utilitarian Hindi or Urdu. And you didn't feel too bad about not knowing enough, perhaps a naïve assumption. But people being accepting of someone else not being fluent in Arabic, or English or Malayalam, did not guarantee individuals would not be or feel othered. I guess what I am saying is that it is important to be case-specific if we are to break down the deployment of power through language in Gulf spaces.

Do such linguistic soundscapes affect Arab residents too? I am sure they do. How? Again, I believe a lot depends on who they are (race), what they do (class), where they come from (nationality), perhaps even how long they are staying. When we were young, my buddies and I assumed all Arabs were the same. We didn't think about geography or politics or dialects. I suppose we categorized Arabic speakers, especially young males, as much as they categorized us. But we were also afraid, because we didn't enjoy being bullied, and we didn't know how to stand up to people who spoke to us in a language we couldn't communicate in. Yet, I was part of the problem too. As a young boy in the Gulf, I wish I had put more effort into learning more about the Arab world, or the region, and I regret that. Sometimes I wish I had been a different kind of kid. However, a particular set of circumstances made me obsequious and world-wary. As a result, I took out my frustrations on the other by assuming things about people I didn't know because I felt othered myself. The irony doesn't escape me. Still, I wonder sometimes whether things would have turned out differently if I met Arabic speakers who wanted to learn the language of my parents. That would have given them an in, too, into our world.

LC: The relationship between "tongue" and "flesh" remains undefined in the title of the novel's second part (Book 2), which displays these two nouns separated by a full stop. However, some of your stories convey the impression that the split between "language" and "being" constitutes a distinctive feature in the life of temporary people, namely, part of the social space that you represent. One of the aspects of your reflection on language concerns the complex relationship of temporary people with Arabic. In the prologue, we read of an English-speaking student from an Indian school who is unable to understand the meaning of words he can pronounce very well, while in the story "Glossary" we find Arabic words fighting with words of a different origin or taking possession of entities that do not correspond to what the words designate. Could you comment on this?

DU: I don't believe the relationship temporary people have with Arabic, especially if they don't speak it, is complex. I would argue the relationship, for the most part, is fairly straightforward. In the South Asian community, Arabic, I would argue, represents power. It is the language of those in charge; as young boys, we believed Arabic was the key to acquiring wasta. Arabic unlocked doors, we felt. An illusion perhaps, and not by much, but an incredibly effective one. The English-speaking teen you speak of in the book is me. And the part about words fighting each other to maim, dominate, and murder is my way of having some fun with the truth. If you take a walk around Abu Dhabi's old city center, where I grew up, pay attention to the signage. At some point you'll come across a name that doesn't make sense or is misspelled. For people interested in malapropisms, there is great fun to be had. But misspellings and the mangling of syntax and grammar is something I was raised on. As I said before, for the most part, the objective was communication. And to communicate, people would almost get desperate and inventive with the limited vocabulary they possessed. The book needed to represent that, as well as to represent words or phrases that couldn't have been made anywhere else. The noun Gulf Return registers differently in Kerala than any other state. Tata-Bye-Bye reminds me of aunts who don't speak English. To me, language is sound, an amalgamation of different sounds, taken from multiple roots and histories, with words battling or mating with each other to become new words. And language is also about the body, how your body moves when you sound stuff out. I needed my book to think about that too, because I think about these things all the time, inhabiting the body I do. Look at me. I am a brown man. I am not always in control of my visibility or invisibility in the societies I orbit. And remember, I am a writer of the Gulf. My writing reflects these vocabularies.

LC: Despite your appropriation of literary English as a language of the Gulf, you make an abundant use of words from other languages too. Two Malayali words, in particular, are used to identify key thematic concerns of the novel: pravasis and veed.

DU: In my family, veed is an important word, probably more important than air. It means "home" in Malayalam. Or place, *where* (emphasis intended) a person is from, the house they grew up in. Even when I write it out in English, I don't italicize it, because veed isn't foreign to me and the English word *home* isn't good enough. The echoes of veed marked my parents in the Gulf because, as I said before, veed also means house, something my parents hoped to return to and even build. After my parents left the Gulf for good in 2018, they returned to a house that they had laid a foundation for and began to build, and which my sister and I helped finish. By then, my mother's house, the one my grandfather built, was gone, sold for cash. My grandmother, who inhabited that house, was gone too. And my parents returned to a homeland emptied of the people who bid them goodbye when they left for the Gulf. Veed, in some families, is also loss, even though veed doesn't mean loss.

And pravasi? My parents were pravasis in the Gulf. Meaning they left Kerala behind to go elsewhere. If I were to call my father a migrant to his face, he would nod. But if I were to ask him what it meant to be a pravasi for most of his adult life, I can assure you the word registers differently in Malayalam. But why use it in an English text? Well, I am not only a writer who uses the English language, I am also a Malayalee boy. And since the book came out, almost everyone unfamiliar with the word wants to know: What is a pravasi? I would call that mission accomplished.

LC: Most of the stories in the first section ("Limbs") deal with the relationship between labor and subjectivity. Throughout several of these stories, bodies are objectified as mass-produced goods, they are dismembered as assemblies of organs or transform themselves through frequent metamorphoses. Despite the pervasive use in your writing of antirealist and dystopian elements, to me, your stories seem to constitute a deep narrative exploration of the process through which specific subjectivities are produced that pays particular attention to its material bases. Do you think it is correct, at least in some of the stories, to read the narrative dismemberment of the body as a metaphor of the dismemberment of the characters' subjectivity?

DU: The body is a kind of suitcase, isn't it? Skin sewn over bone and organ and nerves and cells and blood and brain and waste. I am not the first one to notice this. And our bodies evolve and deteriorate over time. Again, no surprise. It isn't accidental that characters in *Temporary People* are sometimes literally taken apart, disassembled like machines, or categorized as useful (or not) based on what they do, how they age. I suppose I am fascinated by labels, certainly how people are branded. Every nonlocal in the Gulf, to my knowledge, is supposed to be tagged and categorized, as is the case in most countries, I'd guess. But then, in a place where imported bodies are crucial, as in the UAE, what position do nonlocal children occupy? Does their class matter? Nationality? Skin?

Being a child in (or of) the Gulf is not a professional vocation. Yet, for a foreigner/nonlocal to bring their child over to the Gulf, or parent their child in the Gulf, certain conditions, related to pay and housing, need to be met. This means the child is then entered into the system as a dependent, under the protection of their sponsor, the parent. In documents filled out by the parent, to sponsor this child, the child is broken down by first name, family name, nationality, religion, date of birth, and so on. The process is invasive and intimate.

But being a child of the Gulf also outs your class, and often, based on where you go to school, shop, live, eat, and hang out, the position of your family. I am old enough to remember a time when the young children of the

Malayalee taxi driver hired by my parents to drive a few of us, girls in the morning, boys in the afternoon, to my gender-segregated high-school, rode with us. The salary cap hadn't come into effect yet, so this man, whom we called Uncle, made extra income taking us to school, then returned to his apartment and his wife. And once the cap came into effect, I never saw his children again. I don't know what happened to him either, but I've never forgotten him.

You could be right about my fascination with picking stuff apart. What do those moments represent? Well, think of the act of packing a suitcase. And pretend in this suitcase you are expected to pack key moments of your life. You could include the military jacket your mentor gave you to keep warm, as I would. And you may include photographs and other inanimate objects. But let's stretch this further. If you could pack items we aren't supposed to have, or devices that don't exist, like a machine that would permit you to revisit five minutes from your past, where would you go? Or if you could speak to some of your dead relatives and friends, people who lived and died in the Gulf, as soon as you opened the suitcase, wouldn't you hold onto this suitcase for as long as you could? This suitcase, in the process of being packed, then becomes a repository of your life, and perhaps your family's life. When my parents packed their stuff up before their final return home (to Kerala), some items felt more valuable than others. My grandpa's briefcase will mean nothing to future and present scholars of the Gulf, but in my family, we continue to hold on to this object that an old man who died in the Gulf went to work with. My sister and I continue to mourn the loss of the VHS tape of my parents' wedding, which was always present in our home in Abu Dhabi. And then one day, we couldn't find the tape anymore. My mother married a man who lived in the Gulf, and she followed him there. This lost tape documents the beginning of my parents' lives together in the Gulf. We didn't find the tape, but if we had, it would've gone into that suitcase.

So yes, metaphors and symbols and fables have a place in my work. What are their roles? Sometimes, I am not sure. I want to tell stories. This I understand. And when readers read me, I want them to pay attention and to not forget me. Or my people.

LC: Let's further explore the theme of the construction of the pravasi subjects. You have just referred to the experience of Malayalee children raised in the Gulf. The idea of subject formation as a process of "disassembling"—to use the verb of your previous answer—is the very reverse of the idea of *Bildung*, as it is portrait in realist/nationalist narratives in both the European and the postcolonial novelistic traditions. If Bildung narratives trace a trajectory that leads the young subject to merge with his/her social reality, your stories, on the contrary, hint at a subject who is torn apart by the social space in which he/she grows. Do these subjects have any agency within this space? Can they hope to have a transformative role within it?

DU: To assume that the people I write about in *Temporary People*, particularly the working class, do not possess agency, and need to be spoken for, is a dangerous road to take. It is also untrue. I write about the Gulf because the place interests me, besides the fact that I am from the Gulf. Not *based* in the place, but of the place, and the region is important to me, a realization that continues to surprise me, because if I didn't care, few would fault me.

In my youth, having had family members visit our little apartment, for tea or meals, who were employed as part of the working and/or lower to upper middle class provided me proximity to their bodies and minds, interactions that cannot be duplicated in a classroom or textbook. Most of my relatives in the Gulf were men, and I got to see them outside their respective professions. Many of them were family. I am not saying I was taking notes as a kid, yet as an adult, when I returned to those memories, or spoke to my parents about them, I learned things I had long suspected. Tales of men and women struggling with depression. Stories of birth and death. Gossip and infidelity. Unpaid debts. Imprisonment. Bits of joy too, as people remembered their youth, or why they came, and what they did, and what they accomplished. And as I sat with these memories, years later, they morphed into people I made up, with memories and fables of their own. *Temporary People*, without question, pays attention to individuals who have had to operate a certain way because of their appearance, the languages they speak and don't speak, or their positionality in Gulf society. I won't dispute that. It is a book about class, race, loss, ambition, pain, joy, and in-between realms. It is a book about the people who raised me, men and women who looked like me, whose histories I wanted to document, chart, and voice. To your question about whether the characters in the book were shaped by the Gulf, aren't most of us shaped (and for better or for worse) and defined by the places we inhabit?

And by agency, if you're asking me whether foreign bodies, like mine, have appropriated spaces in the Gulf, I'd say yes. Kids playing cricket in the parking lot, where the sport isn't permitted, is not rebellion, but it can be. But it is also one example of children trying to be children: impetuous, rowdy, wild, impressionable, and vulnerable. And signage in languages other than Arabic or English, to be found on lampposts, or alleys, or restaurant menus, is not disrespectful to Arabic or English, yet I am not sure how to respond when I run into people, recent arrivals, who sign up for Arabic classes in a heartbeat, yet barely think to learn Malayalam, Urdu, or Tagalog. Our languages count too, don't they? Shouldn't they? They are part of the city's ecosystem too. I am not sure what I'm disappointed by, but fiction offers solace and an opportunity to reflect.

And transformation comes in many forms. For example, my English with the boys I went to school with, Indian boys, sounds different to the accent I put on when I speak to my colleagues (or students) at university. The tone of my voice when I want attention in a shop, or the register it holds when I am at the airport. I sound different at JFK than I do when I'm speaking to an officer in Kochi.

LC: The narrative world of your stories contains several examples of interactions between Arab characters (who are citizens of the Emirates or migrants) and South Asian migrants. However, the reader gets the impression that they never really share a common space, that they belong to separate worlds, that they almost possess a different ontological status. Is it really difficult for a member of a Malayalam community to be integrated within the space of an Arab or Emirate community through personal relationships and friendship, and the other way around?

DU: The Abu Dhabi I knew, back in the eighties and nineties, certainly in their personal lives, people stayed with their flock. But that's what I thought everyone did. Remember, I was a kid. My parents were in charge. I grew up around and hung out with Indians and went to an Indian-community school. At school, and most places in the city, especially if you were raised to be Indian-like, it was easy to pretend you were surrounded by members of *your* community, because you were. It didn't register with most of us that we were different, children who belonged to in-between realms. I think my parents did what they thought was best for us. They also put us in a school system they could afford and felt familiar, something that wouldn't lead us astray. I'm speculating about much of this, you understand. If I had been in their place, I wonder if I would have chosen a different school. Truth is, I don't know. In my head, I like to think I would have favored a school where the mode of instruction was in Arabic and English. But I say that now because I know Arabic would have given my make-believe child a window into another world, a world my parents didn't understand, nor were a part of. You asked me whether the Malayalee could easily integrate into Arab or Khaleeji society? Well, what kind of Arab does this Malayalee want to be? The Arab world is not straightforward, is it? Does this Malayalee want to be Masri, or someone from the Levant? Or does this Malayalee want to stay in the Khaleej? Oman? Saudi? Would this Malayalee be interested in looking beyond the Middle East perhaps? Algeria or Morocco? And even if this Malayalee wanted to be Khaleeji, pick a tribe, an emirate. Or a terrain: sea, desert, mountain? I thought about none of these things in my youth because I didn't know enough and didn't feel I was good enough. I can't speak on behalf of all my friends, but I knew I struggled with confidence because of what I looked like. I was hyperaware of my place in Gulf society. I don't remember being asked to be anything other than the Indian I was supposed to be. But at some point, I normalized my skin and the notion of transience being part of my day-to-day. When did this happen? Once I shelved thinking about permanence to the side. Did anything trigger this position? It didn't occur overnight. I am certain of that.

And Kerala, by the way, is no stranger to the Arab world, especially the Gulf. There was contact pre-oil through trade and seafarers, vestiges of which can be spotted in Kerala to this day. Traces of Arabic can be found in the language too, embedded in dialects and accents, and marriages and intermarriages too, communities that can trace their histories back to the Gulf.

I suppose we could spend some time on whether the Malayalee could integrate into Gulf societies, a discussion that cannot be had without dipping into class, race, and rank via nationality, but shouldn't we talk about assimilation too? Is the Malayalee willing to assimilate into Gulf society, if that option was on the table? I am personally interested in what is accessible to different communities as well, via race, class, nationality, and professions. And where communities and people can bump into each other, and through persistent contact, inquire and reflect and perhaps learn more about one another—an ideal, maybe, but not a terrible one to yearn for. Yet would enough people prefer separate worlds in the Gulf? Less contact with strangers, the other. No harm, no foul. Sure. I can't fault my parents' generation for going with the familiar. My generation on the other hand: What do we want?

And if we are genuinely interested in talking about integration, we need to talk about language and the power some languages hold over others.

I am under no illusion that language, like nationality, is ranked in the Gulf, something I've accepted. At the same time, as a writer of fiction who writes in the language of Empire, I believe language vocalizes presence. In the world I occupied as a young man, I barely paid attention to Arabic, a combination of arrogance and self-preservation. Malayalam was the sound of home, my parents and grandparents, their homeland. Arabic was the stranger I paid my respects to and feared in secret. As a result, Arabs were strangers. Yet one of my fondest boyhood memories involves playing tennis-ball football in a parking lot with three Arab boys my age. Why? Because we were kind to each other, even though we knew nothing about one another, and all that mattered was the game, not our names or lands.

As an adult, I continue to endure a complex relationship with Arabic, as do some of the characters in my book. It is so familiar, Arabic, yet distant. I studied the language in school for many years. But not one language teacher, all native speakers, spoke to us in Arabic. Nor cared whether we learned the language or not. We reciprocated their indifference. I followed the herd, but I've wondered whether I would've thought about Arabic differently if our teachers took their time with us, to reflect on the power Arabic had over Brown people. To recognize that some of us feared the language, because we were wary of the people who spoke it, because we were asked by our parents to be wary of those who spoke it.

Every few years I return to the language to try and learn it, and then quietly give up. And I am not sure why I feel shame in not being able to speak Arabic. Like I said, no one would blame me. Sometimes I whisper in secret, it's my language too.

And there have been times when I've heard people, ranging from scholars to friends to strangers, claim the Arabic spoken by Brown people in the Gulf isn't Arabic, mostly pidgin. What's wrong with pidgin? To me, as I said before, language is the vocalization of presence. A person saying, I am here, do you see me? Can you hear me? Do you understand me? May we talk? But I am not naïve. I know accents matter. I grew up in a part of the city where so many languages collided with each other. What and how you spoke mattered.

LC: The question of memory receives much attention in our book. Elizabeth Derderian, for example, reflects on the relationship between the construction of a national identity by state sponsored projects and the way these projects simultaneously involve and exclude noncitizen artists. These artists are involved in the construction of collective memory and identity, but their own trajectory and personal memory is silenced (or rendered almost invisible) within these narratives. On the other hand, Shafeeq Karinkurayil reflects on the role of photography at the level of personal and collective memories/imaginaries that pravasis bring into the space of south Indian society.

These two different sides of memory are also present in your stories. On the one side, there are figurative references to institutionalizations of memory in museums and anniversaries; and on the other side—especially in the third part of the book—you explore the pervasive presence of Kerala.

DU: I wrote what I did to offer my generation a document to return to, as well as to push back against set narratives about what my people were supposed to be, or what they could write about, or how they could be written about. *Temporary People* isn't an Indian book. It is a book that emerged out of Abu Dhabi, a Gulf city, written by a writer of the space. It is also a book for my parents, or people like them, who took a chance on the Gulf, on behalf of others: notably immediate and extended family. And perhaps to fulfill their own adventurous pursuits because they had them at the time. And then, in the blink of an eye, these people aged overnight, while assuming the only narrative that counted was the narrative of the homeland. Or the return. That their native places were waiting to welcome them back. And then, eventually, many of them, like my parents, went back. As far as I know, their memories haven't been sought out and archived by the State, or the homelands they returned to. And perhaps this is why I write: to reflect and document.

My book, I'd like to think, is part of an archive that is gradually being built by a very different generation of writers and artists from the Gulf, people who have something to say, in multiple languages, working on books and/or monographs that have been published or are about to be, making work that may be shown and/or performed, content with breadth, depth, and heft. We are not all on the same page or interested in the same things, which is why this body of work, when taken as a collective, will hopefully prove to be relevant over time, because our interests vary. And because they do, our work wouldn't make sense to be lumped and labeled as Gulf Stuff, even though that's definitely going to happen.

LC: Shafeeq Karinkurayil and Jaafar Alloul explore two different sides of the notion "aspirational place." In his chapter, Shafeeq examines pictures taken by migrants from Kerala who moved to the Gulf during the first oil-boom period and argues that these pictures contributed to "creat[ing] a culture of migration to the Gulf." He examines in particular how specific forms of dress (*kandura, mundu,* and suits, but even particular objects like watches) were resignified in the space of Kerala, and how they were strategically deployed in the pictures, testifying to the personal trajectories of migration. According to Shafeeq, this imaginary exerted an important role in integrating the Gulf in the space of contemporary Kerala.

In Jaafar's chapter, we find EU Muslim citizens of Maghrebi origin who praise their life in Dubai. These citizens seem to share the official narrative of a cosmopolitan society that can accommodate people from different origins. Their aspirations of upward social mobility have been fulfilled in Dubai where their religious faith becomes an added value to their European passport. In this sense, their experience in Dubai is the reversal of the discriminations many of them suffered in Europe, especially for being Muslims "of foreign origin." Despite the different thematic focus of the two chapters, both emphasize the role of "representation" in creating an "aspirational place." An aspirational place becomes such because of particular narratives that are constructed about it.

I would like to know your opinion about the Gulf as an aspirational place in Kerala, but also about your experience as a person who grew up where many people in Kerala would aspire to live. When you travel to Kerala, how do you sense the legacy of the imaginaries that have been created about the Gulf during several decades? Like Shafeeq, you often stress the importance of photography. What, in your opinion, is the role of pictures in constructing a relationship between the two places?

DU: Among Kerala's youth, I am not sure if the Gulf is the stand-in for El Dorado anymore, as much as vestiges of the Gulf are prevalent throughout Kerala, in the language as well as pop culture. Why? One, the mystery is gone. Back in the day, especially during the seventies and eighties, without 24-hour cable or the internet, many yarns were spun, mostly by men, about prosperity on tap in the Gulf. And Kerala lapped it all up. The evidence, in the form of houses and scooters and cars and Japanese electronics and acquired land, couldn't be ignored. Then there was geographical proximity, offering the illusion that the Gulf was next door, hosting cultural and familial cues familiar enough for Keralites to wander over and feel safe. Importantly, the Gulf wasn't the West, like America, a country that felt too alien, depicted in Malayalam cinema as venal and dangerous, where families and children fell prey to the evils of capitalism, vice, and purported assimilation. The Gulf on the other hand was a reasonable transit point, where a few years were bartered for money, to help facilitate a better life back home. I suppose there was also the presumed safety and comfort in the assumption that anyone who worked in the Gulf would eventually head home.

And then, over the years, as different generations took turns living and working in the Gulf, as myths evolved, as cities and villages changed, reality got a lot more complex. Most of my uncles lost thirty years (if not more) to the Gulf. My father was instrumental in bringing them all over, because back then you could. Then there were the rare few who didn't take to the Gulf, who refused the money, who came and left. But it wasn't always about the money. As I grew older, I realized it was also about people not knowing how to transition back into the societies they left behind. Also, families like mine used their children as an excuse to stick around for a few more years. Why? Because the English-medium education was arguably better in the Gulf and there was more to look forward to. India on the other hand was perfect for college. The reasons also varied from family to family. Over the years, I've met Malayalees who've cited safety as their number one reason for sticking around in the Gulf, besides lifestyle.

In the seventies, eighties, and nineties, before air travel became so casual and normative, relatives in Kerala, especially my maternal grandmother, waited patiently for summer vacations. My family would try and make the trip once every two years. During those visits, my grandmother and mother had conversations about my mother's eventual return, but my grandmother didn't live long enough to savor that moment.

For my parents' generation, the Gulf gamble may have been part curiosity, as well as part aspiration, and/or part circumstance. But the Gulf also inspired many who came and seduced them considerably. To this day I meet people from Kerala, especially the old-timers, who envy the UAE's progress, and then turn wistful about Kerala, because people who looked like them, they are prone to say, were responsible for building and maintaining large swaths of the Gulf. Why couldn't Kerala be as modern, as safe? If Kerala had work, open commerce, we wouldn't come, is another refrain I've gotten used to hearing. But the fundamental difference between what I remember in my youth to what I'm observing now as an adult is how the Gulf's cool factor has ebbed.

My father did white-collar work for a government entity for forty-five years. With the advent of Emiratization, the emergence of a younger, more educated, and hungrier Emirati work force, I don't foresee many Gulf jobs offering the kind of stability (and benefits) my parents' generation enjoyed. I am particularly interested in the evolution of the Gulf's blue-collar workforce, where they'll keep coming from, because cites like Abu Dhabi and Dubai need foreign labor to function. Then keep in mind the policy changes, like the introduction of value added tax (VAT) in the UAE, and the dirham not going as far as it once used to do in India, especially in Kerala.

With Covid-19, the scare of foreigners returning in droves to their respective homelands, once speculative, almost came to be, so the governments in the region, whether they like it or not, will need to think about what they want, and the kind of people they wish to attract and keep. And whether policies encouraging social mobility should be introduced. For instance, could a woman who showed up as domestic help work a senior administrative job a few years down the line? Another possible game changer would be the introduction of taxes, or taxing remittances. If this occurs, who will come? Then there is the issue of those who grew up in the Gulf, whether their loyalties to the State are hedged between realms or simply nonexistent. Among the people I went to high school with, many of those who remain don't want to end up like their parents, coming of retirement age in a city they cannot fully claim. Interestingly enough, they want their children to grow up in an environment that feels less ephemeral or transient.

Finally, let me end my response with a word I spend much time with: *dignity*—three syllables that pack a mighty punch. I think about dignity a great deal. For me, dignity is directly proportional to visibility, to be in a position where you feel your mind and body and intellect count, irrespective of what you do, the color of your skin, the languages you know, or which country you come from. When I was a boy, my parents and high school saw to it that I respected the UAE and its leaders. I thought that expectation was fair and important. What I struggled to come to terms with was seeing my own father and other members of my extended family remain quiet and obsequious to insults they copped in the street from individuals who felt Brown people could be treated with disrespect, and I didn't know what to do. It was as though being Indian wasn't good enough or made you less than. So not only did I normalize transience; I normalized being picked on for what I looked like, the religion I was supposed to be, or what my people represented. So in Berlin, when I heard Jaafar's presentation about EU citizens of Maghrebi descent cashing in on the privileges of their faith and citizenship in a city like Dubai, it made me think about how nationality is often weaponized, particularly in Gulf spaces. And whether EU citizens of Maghrebi descent take into account their own positionality in Gulf cities? And when they come across people who look like me, or those holding passports that can't compete with EU passports, do they contemplate discrimination, race, and class with as much ferocity as they did in Europe? Or have they already moved on from what they believe they used to be?

But none of this fermenting angst I have about race and class is apparent in the family albums, where all of us, relatives, friends, and strangers, pose because we are meant to pose. Unless someone lets you in on a secret. For example, there is a picture of my mother and grandmother by the corniche. I am with them, eating ice cream, both women behind me, holding onto me. My father was the photographer, using my late grandfather's Nikon. To the casual observer, the photograph is nothing but an ordinary snapshot. Speak to me and I'll tell you this picture was taken months after my grandfather's passing in 1983. It is a photograph of personal significance because I remember my grandmother's visit, I remember telling her to be wary of the mice in our house. I was barely three.

Photographs have the ability to push back against presumed narratives. This is why Shafeeq's scholarship is significant. I have a black and white photograph of my father doing a handstand in Abu Dhabi. He is wearing only shorts. His curls, which I've inherited, are visible. I adore this picture because it's a nothing picture. When it was taken, my father did not know how his future was going to turn out. It would be hard for a stranger, especially a scholar or a reporter, to look at this picture of my father and transfer their presumptions about the Gulf onto him, simply based on what he looked like. My father grew old in the Gulf, but he had little moments of joy and fun too, precisely why this picture means a lot to me. His relatives would have seen this picture too, especially his mother, alongside the usual snapshots of him in pants, standing next to something significant enough for Malayalees to *ooh* and *aah* over. Pictures back then were as good as letters. Or supplements to letters. Nowadays the surprise has gone out of photographs, but my mother returns to her albums often. The albums return her to another time, where she continues to think about and can be in conversation with the living and the dead, people like her father, who died in Abu Dhabi.

LC: Several chapters in this volume show that the normative ordering of the bureaucracy of different Gulf states and dominant national imaginaries in the region do not prevent noncitizens from articulating feelings of belonging and attachment to a place that is "transient by law." In your answers to my previous questions on language, you clarify how the dynamics of power relations (class, race, passports) are reflected in the use (and mastery) of different languages, and in the relationship between body and language. Nadeen Dakkak's reading of *Samrawit* and *Temporary People* focuses on these aspects. On her part, Rana AlMutawa focuses on the experience of space by the privileged group of Emirati nationals and the contradictory feelings they share toward the presence of foreigners.

When you wrote *Temporary People*, you were in the United States and you did not know for sure if you would settle again in the Emirates. However, you did settle again in Abu Dhabi, and you took a position at New York University. I would appreciate if you could tell us something about your return to Abu Dhabi. How does your actual experience of the city differ from the one you represent in *Temporary People*? Did your new status as an academic and a writer change your relationship with the city?

DU: I wrote *Temporary People* in Jersey, New York City, and Chicago to negotiate my feelings about the Gulf, as well as to recall/remember/preserve and mythologize the people and languages I left behind. In the beginning, I didn't understand that as a writer and a son I desperately wanted to leave something behind for people like my parents, their friends, the kids I grew up with, strangers in the street, individuals who had normalized transience. At the risk of sounding dramatic, I wanted my parents to know, as an adult, I finally understood everything they had put on the line to care for us and their family members. That their lives, albeit ordinary, mattered to me. And I wanted to express all this on my own terms, as a writer from the Gulf, not someone based in, or who used to reside in, but as someone who identified as a child of the Gulf. But since I didn't major in literature in college, or take any writing classes, or didn't think writing was a permissible vocation; I needed time to process what I was doing. The presence of intuitive teachers, who left me alone when I needed to be left alone, and decent friends, not many, but enough, helped immensely. And distance from my immediate family triggered the need to write because I didn't see my family for long periods. I needed to find my own ways to cope. So I read widely to reflect and introspect. I wrote to remember. And while I was writing, I was under no illusion that I was writing the grand Gulf narrative. As early as the first draft, I chose to write about the Gulf that made sense to me, in the syntax and rhythm and the languages I had.

I wanted the reader, especially strangers who knew nothing about the Gulf, to read me and not forget me or the people I made up and wrote about. And I wanted those familiar with the Gulf to read my book and feel something visceral. That said, the book operates the way it does because I was convinced there was going to be no return. In fact, the return hadn't crossed my mind at all. I almost cracked in my fourth year in the States when I asked my father if I could head back, and he persuaded me to stay, because money was tight back home. I never raised the subject of the return again. So yeah, I was down with the rituals of departure, less comfortable in knowing what to do if I harbored hopes for the return.

Fast forward many years later and I am sitting at my desk in Abu Dhabi, typing all this out. What's changed? My social class and standing because of what I do. As an academic working for a respected foreign institution with reasonable clout, I am not my father. My father didn't have access to non-Indian establishments or the confidence to interact with the hoity-toity. In the eighties, British nationals snuck my uncle into the British Club, where he wasn't welcome. As a teen, I started paying more attention to wasta, as well as power; what people did in the British Club; or what expat life, which felt directly proportional to a person's nationality, might look like; what people with money did with their cash; where they shopped for groceries; what confidence looked like.

Since I've been back, I've had a taste of a very different life, finally having money to visit family twice a year (pre-Covid), not having to live paycheck to paycheck, being able to pay bills and put money away, keeping an eye on my parents, people smiling and nodding at you when they realize you're a professor, or that you've got a book out, a few interviews in the press, one or two prizes. Or running into people on campus, individuals who look like you, treating you differently because you're not them and thus deserve to be paid attention to, because you move like someone important, speak like someone fancy. And that's when you realize that you've got a chip on your shoulder, that it's hard to walk away from the reality that service labor in the Gulf is dominated by people from Asia, Africa, and the Arab world. That you're embarrassed by how fortunate you've been, that you don't wish to return to your previous life.

Then there are moments where you're quickly brought down to size, especially when you're not on campus anymore, by the very people who look like you, who relish in pushing back against you, asking you for ID, their eyes following you in the store, expecting you to do something. In these moments, if I'm itching for a fight, that's when I turn American. My r's are rolled, my speech is clipped. But if I want conversation and wish to cut the ice, my body language changes, and I turn to some of the other languages in my arsenal. Believe me, as much as Arabic and fancy English can open doors, Malayalam and Hindi can do the same in the neighborhood I grew up in. So yes, my relationship to the city has evolved, but that was expected because the city changed too during my absence.

As a writer, a personal concern of mine is whether I can continue to write about people like my parents and uncles and the young man I used to be, because my present vantage point is different. Perhaps that's why fiction is useful, why I turn to the medium constantly, because the words are mine, and in fiction, I can dare to introspect with impunity about class, race, and nationality. There's no question that the second book is going to be different. That said, what I have genuinely treasured in being back is having had multiple opportunities to work with different generations of students (even artists and writers), especially local kids, who wish to write and tell their own stories, or reflect on what their respective cities have become. No doubt I get to teach and interact with these young folks in privileged surroundings, at an elite institution that would have most certainly rejected my application if I had applied as a freshman with the credentials I had then. The irony doesn't escape me.

Lorenzo Casini is Associate Professor of Arabic Language and Literature at the University of Messina. He has been Jean Monnet Fellow of the European University Institute (2006-2007) and has taught at several Italian universities. He is coauthor of *Modernità arabe. Nazione, narrazione e nuovi soggetti nel romanzo egiziano* (*Arab Modernity: Nation, Narration and New Subjects in the Egyptian Novel*) (Mesogea 2012).

Deepak Unnikrishnan is a writer from Abu Dhabi. His book *Temporary People*, a work of fiction about Gulf narratives steeped in Malayalee and South Asian lingo, won the inaugural Restless Books Prize for New Immigrant Writing, the Hindu Prize, and the Moore Prize. His essays and fiction have appeared in *Foreign Affairs, The Guardian, Guernica, Drunken Boat, The State*, Vol. IV: *Dubai, Himal Southasian*, and *The Penguin Book of Migration Literature* (Penguin Classics), among others. His fiction was commissioned for the written publications of the National Pavilion of the UAE at the Venice Biennale (2017) and the Oslo Architecture Triennale (2019) and his voice and work can be heard on musician Sarathy Korwar's album *More Arriving*. He teaches at New York University Abu Dhabi.

NOTE

1. The Arabic and Malayalam terms employed in this concluding chapter—such as "pravasis," "wasta," and "veed"—are not italicized because they are regarded as an integral part of the English language spoken in the Gulf.

REFERENCES

Unnikrishnan, Deepak. 2017. *Temporary People*. New York: Restless Books.

———. 2020. "The Hidden Cost of Migrant Labor: What It Means to Be a Temporary Person in the Gulf." *Foreign Affairs*, 7 February 2020. Accessed 6 October 2020. https://www.foreignaffairs.com/articles/india/2020-02-07/hidden-cost-migrant-labor.

Index

A

Abu Dhabi
  art scene of, 25, 29
    Arts and Cultural Heritage Authority
      (ADACH), 25, 26
    Guggenheim, 25, 27, 30, 38n5
    Louvre, 25, 27, 30, 38n5
    NYU Abu Dhabi Art Gallery, 5
    Saadiyat Island, 25, 27, 29-30, 37
    Salama Foundation, 30, 32-33, 35
    Zayed National Museum, 25, 38
  belonging to, 43, 45-46, 50, 53, 55-57,
    60-61, 74, 135, 137, 139, 141,
    143, 145, 149-51 (*see also*
    belonging)
Addleton, Jonathan, 3
affect, 90, 92-93, 95, 108-109
  affective geography, 116
  affective power of representation, 36
  affective relations with place, 45, 48,
    50
Algeria, 95-97, 143
Al Owais, Abdul Rahman Bin Mohammed,
  28
Arab Spring, 4, 9, 90
Arabia, 115-16.
aspiration, 7, 12, 14-15, 71, 87, 89-90,
  94-95, 97-100, 106-9, 120-21,
  125, 131, 146-47
assimilation, 33, 34, 46, 48, 53, 58-61,
  64n11, 144, 147

B

Bahrein, 5, 10
Belgium, 89, 92, 95, 96-97, 102, 105
belonging, 3-5, 8, 13-14, 22, 33, 43-62,
  63n3, 68-69, 73, 82-83, 90, 92, 93,
  107-8, 117, 119, 150
bidun, 6
Bourdieu, Pierre, 97

C

citizen
  contingent, 6, 7, 10, 13, 23, 31, 33, 36,
    106, 109
  noncitizen(s), 1, 3, 6, 10, 13, 14, 22-24,
    26, 31, 33, 37, 37n2, 43, 52, 56,
    59, 63n7, 69, 74, 75, 93, 108, 150
citizenship, 3, 5-7, 9-10, 12, 14-15, 21-23,
  26, 31-33, 37n1, 38n4, 44-46, 49,
  53-55, 59-60, 62-64, 89, 93, 96,
  100, 116-19, 129-30, 149
  Belgian, 96
  Emirati, 23, 26, 33, 93
  Jus sanguinis, 64n8
  jus soli, 64n8
  Western, 93, 100
class, 7, 10, 35-36, 46, 56, 69-71
  managerial, 70
  merchant, 11-12
  middle, 68-70, 73, 77
  upper-middle, 5, 12, 14, 47, 68-69
  working, 89, 92, 95-97, 102, 142
clothing, 118-120, 123, 128
cosmopolitanism, 4, 7, 10, 13-14, 23-24,
  28, 33, 35, 37, 44, 68-69, 72-77,
  82-83, 89, 91, 108
  concept of, 4, 13, 91, 108
  as Gulf, 4-5, 7, 13, 14, 33
  Indian Ocean, 35
  tolerance and, 14, 24, 28, 37
  Western forms of, 68-69, 72-77, 82

D

diaspora
  diasporic communities, 48, 50, 61
  diasporic subjects, 13, 44, 46-49, 55, 62,
    63n1
dress
  abaya, 67, 74, 76-78, 80-81
  ghutra, 60

hijab, 72, 75, 115
jallabiyya, 75
kandura, 127, 128-129, 130
khadi, 125
lungi, 120, 130
mundu, 121, 124, 127, 130, 146
Dubai
   art scene, 25, 28
      Dubai International Financial Centre (DIFC), 67, 68, 71, 74
      Dubai Ladies Club (DLC), 72
      Dubai Mall, 74, 77-79, 99
      Jumeirah, 67, 70, 74, 78, 102
      Tashkeel Art Center, 25, 35
   belonging to, 33, 35, 59, 70, 73, 93, 107-8 (*see also* belonging)
   city spaces of, 27-28, 38n6, 68, 70-71, 75, 77, 79, 82-83, 91-92, 102, 104, 106
   Muslim cultural symbolism in, 90, 94-95, 97-98, 102-3, 105
   neocolonial ambiance, 107-9
   upward mobility in, 90, 97, 99, 104-5, 109, 146, 149

E
Emiratization, 23, 26, 148
Eritreans, 44, 46, 48, 50-52, 58, 60, 62, 63n3
European(s) (of Maghrebi background), 12-13, 91-93, 96-99
expatriate (expats), 3, 89-90, 103, 106-7, 109, 151

F
Foucault, Michel, 91, 93, 106, 108
France, 22, 36, 44, 92, 96, 98-99, 103-4

G
Gafoor, Abdul, 120-122, 126, 128-29, 131
Gargash, Lamya, 26-27
ghurba, 50
governmentality, 23
guest worker, 2
Gulf cities, 3-5, 7, 11, 45, 50, 54, 56, 63n6, 64n7, 68, 102, 149
Gulf Cooperation Council (GCC), 92-93, 99, 100
Gulf Labor, 30

H
heterotopia, 89, 91, 93-94, 102, 106, 108-9
home, 7, 9, 14, 33, 35, 43-47, 50-55, 58, 61-63, 73, 93, 95, 99, 106-8, 128, 131, 139, 144, 146

I
India, 45, 117-19, 124, 125, 129, 147-48
Indian Ocean, 10, 35, 91, 116

J
Jaber, Haji, 14, 43-45, 49-50, 52-55, 61-62. *See also* Samrawit
Jeddah, 5, 14, 43, 44-46, 48, 50-53, 58-59, 61-62, 63n6
   al-Nuzlah (neighborhood), 50, 51-53

K
kafala, 3, 36, 38n4
Kerala, 1, 10, 15, 43, 115-20, 123-132, 35-36, 139-41, 144-48
   Kozhikode, 116, 121
   Malappuram, 116, 119, 130
khulasat qaid, 23
Kuwait, 3, 5-10, 12, 26, 64n10, 79

L
language
   Arabic, 8, 45, 56-58, 62, 63, 63n1, 71, 97-99, 136-38, 142-45, 152
   English, 45, 63, 136-40, 142, 147, 152, 153n1
   Hindi, 137, 152
   Malayalam, 119, 124-127, 135-139, 140-144, 147, 152, 153n1
   Tagalog, 142
   Urdu, 7, 137, 142
Lefebvre, Henri, 3, 7
literature, 13, 44, 63, 63n1, 135
lived experience(s), 13-14, 45-46, 51-53, 59, 61-62
Longva, Anh Nga, 3, 12

M
Madinah, 116
Makkah, 115-16
Mecca, 115. *See also* Makkah
Middle East, 91, 143
mobility
   geographical, 3, 7-12, 92

social, 13, 89, 94, 96-97, 100, 106, 108-9, 125, 131, 146
modernization, 2, 8, 50, 55
Morocco, 42
multiculturalism, 24, 32, 34
museum, 5-6, 13, 22, 25, 27, 37-38, 145

N
Nasar, Hammad, 33, 35
national imaginaries, 14, 44, 52, 150
Netherlands, 92-97
al-Nuzlah. *See under* Jeddah

O
Oman, 5, 143
Orientalism, 115

P
Pakistan, 3, 5, 7-9, 11, 15-16, 75, 99
Paris, 115-16
passport, 12-13, 22-23, 33, 38, 44, 95-96, 99-101, 137, 146, 149-50
  of privilege (as whiteness), 100, 107
Philippines, 38n7, 101
photography, 27, 116, 119, 130
pravasi, 135, 139-40, 145, 153

Q
al Qasimi, Shaikha Hoor, 24, 30
al Qasimi, Sheikh Sultan, 24
Qatar, 5-6, 10, 13, 109

R
racialization, 101, 103-7
religion, 46-47, 53, 75, 90, 98, 118, 128, 140, 149

S
Samrawit, 5, 14, 43-46, 50-52, 55-56, 58-64, 150
sartorial, 1, 15, 118-20, 123-124, 127, 131
sartoriality, 119
Saudi Arabia, 5, 43-45, 51-53, 60, 64
second-generation (migrants), 8, 43-47, 50-51, 54-55-62, 64n13, 93, 100

Sharjah, 24-25, 27, 29-30, 32, 35, 39
Sharjah Art Foundation, 29-30, 35
Sialkot, 7-8
South Asia, 35, 38n4, 38n7
suit, 121, 123, 127, 130-31

T
temporariness, 45-46, 49, 54, 56, 120
Temporary People, 14-15, 43-45, 50, 53, 62, 135-38, 140, 142, 145, 150, 152
  "Moonseepalty," 45-46, 50, 53, 55-56, 58-59, 61-62, 65
tolerance, 14, 22-24, 28, 31-32, 35, 37-38, 70
topophilia, 46, 51
transnationalism, 10-13, 37, 47

U
United Arab Emirates (UAE), 1, 13, 21, 24
  National Tolerance Programme, 31
  Pavilion, 14, 21, 23-35, 152 (*see also* Venice Biennale)
Unnikrishnan, Deepak, 6, 14, 35, 43-46, 49-50, 53-55, 59-62, 135-53. *See also Temporary People*

V
veed, 139, 153. *See also* home
Venice Biennale, 21-25, 27-30, 34, 36, 152

W
Walls Built on Sand, 3
Westerners, 67, 69-71, 73-74, 76, 78-82, 98
whiteness, 36, 95, 100
worker
  blue-collar, 10, 13, 95, 148
  guest, 2
  migrant, 31, 45, 48, 16-17, 90, 103
  white-collar, 12-13, 148

Z
Zolghadr, Tirdad, 25-28

www.ingramcontent.com/pod-product-compliance
Lightning Source LLC
Chambersburg PA
CBHW071711020426
42333CB00017B/2223